THE LIBERAL CONSCIENCE

THE LIBERAL CONSCIENCE

POLITICS AND PRINCIPLE IN A WORLD OF RELIGIOUS PLURALISM

Lucas Swaine

COLUMBIA UNIVERSITY PRESS   NEW YORK

Columbia University Press
Publishers Since 1893
New York   Chichester, West Sussex
Copyright © 2006 Columbia University Press
All rights reserved

Library of Congress Cataloging-in-Publication Data
Swaine, Lucas, 1969–
The liberal conscience : politics and principles in a world of religious
pluralism / Lucas Swaine.
p. cm.
Includes bibliographical references and index.
ISBN 0–231–13604–8 (cloth : alk. paper) — ISBN 0–231–50981–2
(electronic)
1. Religion and politics. 2. Liberalism—Religious aspects. 3.
Democracy—Religious aspects. 4. Theocracy. I. Title.

BL65.P7S93 2006
322—dc22   2005050741

Columbia University Press books are printed on permanent and durable
acid-free paper.
Printed in the United States of America

c 10 9 8 7 6 5 4 3 2 1

Quae tibi laeta videntur dum loqueris, fieri tristia posse puta.

[Consider that those things that seem to you to be joys have power, while you speak, to change to sorrows.]

—Ovid, *Ex Ponto*, 4.3.57–58

Contents

Acknowledgments

THIS BOOK STANDS AS THE RESULT of sustained research and reflection on a primordial political problem: the conflict between religion and politics in free societies. It emerges thanks to the assistance of others, and here I would like to acknowledge a number of debts. First, my colleagues at Dartmouth College fostered and maintained an excellent environment in which to write this book. James Bernard Murphy offered luminous, exacting commentaries on the manuscript, improving it significantly. Walter Sinnott-Armstrong provided searching philosophical criticisms and proposed deeply helpful ideas for improvement. Allan Stam read and remarked on each of the chapters, giving trenchant theoretical analysis and sound suggestions on the organization of the text. I thank them, and I am grateful also to all my colleagues in the Department of Government for their respectful assistance. Especially helpful in discussing themes in this book were Deborah Jordan Brooks, Stephen Brooks, David Kang, Richard Ned Lebow, Michael Mastanduno, Roger Masters, Daryl Press, Anne Sa'adah, Benjamin Valentino, Dirk Vandewalle, Richard Winters, and William Wohlforth.

I profited greatly from a manuscript review sponsored by the John Sloan Dickey Center for International Understanding at Dartmouth. Charles Larmore and Kenneth Wald traveled to Hanover for that occasion, each taking time to articulate penetrating commentaries on the arguments and strategies embodied in the text. I am grateful to them for their assistance, and I thank Christianne Hardy Wohlforth, Douglas Edlin, and Dale Turner for their helpful contributions and for making the manuscript review as successful as it was.

This book also benefited significantly from funding through the Faculty Scholars Program in the Nelson A. Rockefeller Center for the Social Sciences at Dartmouth. In their capacities as directors of the Rockefeller Center, Linda Fowler and Andrew Samwick each provided thoughtful suggestions and research support to assist this project. I thank them both for their generosity, and I thank the Committee Advisory to the

President at Dartmouth for awarding me a Junior Faculty Fellowship in 2004–2005, granting release time to complete this book. Dartmouth's institutional commitment to research and scholarship has helped me a great deal.

I delivered in Scotland a series of six lectures entitled "Theocracy: Conscience, Conflict, and the Promise of Liberalism," as the Gifford Research Fellow at the University of St. Andrews, in October and November of 2000. My thinking on the prospects of a liberalism of conscience took wing with those lectures, and I am indebted to the Special Lectureships Committee at the University of St. Andrews for its generous support. I thank also the faculty of the departments of Moral Philosophy and Logic and Metaphysics at St. Andrews, and members of the School of Divinity, for the fine and fruitful intellectual gardens they provided for me as the Gifford Fellow. John Haldane furnished outstanding commentary and suggestions on the ideas and arguments developed during the St. Andrews lectures. David Archard, John Broome, and John Skorupski were ever helpful in discussing the finer points of autonomy, value conflict, and the nature of reasons. Richard Bauckham, Philip Esler, Trevor Hart, Esther Reed, Christopher Seitz, and Alan Torrance drew on their theological expertise to impart valuable remarks, and Nick Rengger and Ian Hall offered spirited, amicable discussions on a variety of issues in political theory and the history of political thought. I thank also Andrea Baumeister, John Gray, Dudley Knowles, Paul Markwick, Andrew Moore, Derek Parfit, and Richard Swinburne for incisive commentaries and criticisms during my time at St. Andrews. I owe a debt of gratitude to each.

I have discussed the ideas in these pages with many people and at a wide variety of venues in recent years. For their comments, criticism, and encouragement, I thank Veit Bader, Michael Blake, James Bohman, Corey Brettschneider, Julia Driver, Avigail Eisenberg, Christopher Eisgruber, João Carlos Espada, Robert Faulkner, Andrew Flescher, Antony Flew, Jeffrey Friedman, William Galston, John Gardner, Gerald Gaus, Robert Goodin, Kent Greenawalt, John Kekes, Sharon Krause, Chandran Kukathas, Jacob Levy, Steven Lukes, Stephen Macedo, Michael McConnell, Susan Moller Okin, Nicholas Onuf, Clifford Orwin, Davide Panagia, Alan Patten, David Peritz, Rob Reich, Oonagh Reitman, Pierre Rosanvallon, Kay Lehman Schlozman, Susan Shell, Jeff Spinner-Halev, Jeremy Waldron, Melissa Williams, John Witte Jr., and Alan Wolfe. Each of these people has made a mark on this book.

Wendy Lochner, senior executive editor at Columbia University Press, showed enthusiasm for the prospects of this book from the outset. She offered excellent ideas for cuts and changes to the manuscript. I thank her and the other press editors for their expert work. Sarah St. Onge brought her masterful editing skills to bear on the manuscript and infused some elegance in the text, for which I am indebted. And I thank my family for cajoling me to keep clear of philosophical, stylistic, and other gaucheries; I am very grateful to them.

Finally, I wish to acknowledge my gratitude to my professors at Brown University, who started me thinking about issues of theocracy and freedom of conscience. John Tomasi helped to foment my ideas and arguments at a critical, early stage. His impact has been tremendous. Dan Brock, David Estlund, Martha Nussbaum, and Alan Zuckerman assisted variously in forming my capacities to provide the arguments offered in this book. I thank them all for that. My greatest debt, however, is to Nancy Rosenblum. She provided formative assistance and exceptional guidance from the inception of this project to its completion. Her erudition, astuteness, and brilliance have made all the difference.

Chapter 1 is a revised version of "A Liberalism of Conscience," published in *Journal of Political Philosophy* 11 (2003): 369–91. Chapter 2 draws on sections from "Institutions of Conscience: Politics and Principle in a World of Religious Pluralism," *Ethical Theory and Moral Practice* 6 (2003): 93–118, copyright Kluwer Academic Publishers and used with the kind permission of Springer Science and Business Media. Chapter 2 also incorporates material from "Religious Pluralism and the Liberty of Conscience," my contribution to the forthcoming book *Pluralism Without Relativism: Remembering Sir Isaiah Berlin*, ed. João Carlos Espada, Marc F. Plattner, and Adam Wolfson, copyright Lexington Books. Chapter 3 is a revised and expanded version of "How Ought Liberal Democracies to Treat Theocratic Communities?" *Ethics* 111 (2001): 302–43, published by the University of Chicago Press and copyright 2001 by the University of Chicago. All rights reserved.

Introduction

FREE SOCIETIES FOUGHT AND WON decisive wars against communism and fascism in the twentieth century. Combat between political ideologies has waned away. Now the seas have changed, with religious challenges rising to the surface around the globe. Throngs of religious groups and movements worldwide reject liberal rights and freedoms, flatly claiming they are anathema to sacred doctrine. Domestically, liberal democracies continue to struggle with weighty and unwieldy religious problems on a wide range of divisive topics. American society is at odds with itself, marked by fractious and troublesome debates over religion and politics. Affiliates of America's religious Right complain that few liberals respect them, that they remain on the outside of a fallen and ungodly American life. Their adversaries are secular and religious liberals who see precious rights and freedoms under attack. To many liberals, members of the religious Right appear intensely unreasonable, given the social and political measures they promote, the ways in which they advance their positions, and the religious grounds on which they make their claims.

At the outset of the new millennium, the main adversaries of liberalism are theocrats, people who have strict, religious ideas of the good. Theocrats come into conflict with liberalism because their beliefs and practices fit uneasily with liberal principles and norms. They variously reject freedom of expression, separation of church and state, freedom of association, and women's equality. Some theocrats are outright violent, savagely attacking liberal citizens and government. Other theocrats, like the Christian Right, push domestic political institutions to recognize and promote their particular religious values. More reclusive theocrats, such as the Amish, try desperately to withdraw from society and to retreat into their own communities, away from public life, where they can practice their uncommon religion unmolested. Most religious practitioners are not theocrats, but then again most of the faithful are not especially difficult for liberalism to handle. Theocrats are the toughest:

they are the least likely to affirm free institutions; they are among the most likely to lash out when they believe they are under siege; and they sit at the center of serious domestic and international conflict as a result.

Three centuries of confrontation have not quelled the discord between liberals and theocrats. Basic toleration of religion within liberal societies has not swept theocracy into the dustbin of history, as many liberals hoped and expected it would. Nor has violence or confrontation succeeded in stamping out the appeal of theocracy and theocratic communities. The world remains deeply split over problems of religion and politics, and now liberalism itself is under fire, accused of being disrespectful of religiosity, incorrigibly invasive of religious communities, irremediably ungodly, and nakedly partisan. America joined other burgeoning free societies in extending toleration to religious minorities, and yet critics contend that liberal governments don't really care about religion and religious practice. This is puzzling, since liberal democracies are supposed to be welcoming and open to the faithful. Liberal democracies hold important, historically meaningful commitments to religious freedom, liberty of conscience, and freedom of association. But many theocrats have discounted and even dismissed free societies, and the countries standing at the forefront of rights and liberties are now literally under attack from theocrats. What can be done about this grim state of affairs?

Some people observing the situation conclude that there is no reason for theocrats to affirm principles of free government, no cause ever to expect theocrats to develop a more amicable relationship with liberal citizens and society. Here, liberals throw up their hands, exasperated. They say that they have given theocrats good reasons to support liberalism, but theocrats just won't accept them. They call theocrats irrational, claiming that one just can't reason with them. Liberals gripe that they don't owe theocrats anything more. But if liberals are honest, they will admit to being nonplussed, that they truly do not know what to do. For the arguments liberals have given to theocrats on crucial points of political and legal justification remain philosophically unsatisfactory. This is not only a serious failing on liberalism's own terms; the absence of an adequate, well-articulated justification for liberal institutions has also contributed to theocrats' continued resistance to liberal government, where they believe that true religion does not countenance liberalism and the free governing institutions it supports.

To those who reckon that one cannot and need not try to reason with theocrats, here is a word of warning: attempts to beat back theocratic adversaries have earned free societies no lasting moral or political victories. For theocrats spring up daily in countries and regions across the globe, growing quickly and thickly in opposition to illiberal secular regimes, a variety of local and international policies, and the very idea of a free society itself. It is a deeply misguided view that liberal polities must simply repel and retaliate against theocrats; the stance is kindling for combat, fuel for zealots' inflammatory plans. The outlook fits neatly with a simplistic "us against them" mentality: domestically, secular and religious liberals versus the religious Right; internationally, the friends of freedom pitted against the world's antiliberal religious mass. That attitude offers no plan for reconciliation, instead perpetuating nasty adversarial relationships that just make the world's problems worse. For a confrontational mindset leaves one overlooking an immense strength of liberalism: that it has resources to provide a philosophical solution for the problems of theocracy, as well as the capacity to better manage conflict with religious extremists, both of which can be employed finally to bring theocratic religious practitioners into greater harmony with liberalism.

Liberals and liberal government are by no means exclusively to blame for the conflict with theocrats. For theocrats have subscribed to a variety of untenable antiliberal political views and should modify their attitudes and behavior accordingly. A central problem driving this infelicitous state of affairs is one of perception: it *looks* to the eyes of many as though theocrats must by their nature be at odds with liberal principles. It *appears* that theocratic commitments and liberal values cannot be reconciled in any principled and politically auspicious way. But each of those appearances is false. For many aspects of the conflict between liberals and theocrats need not exist, and liberals can make a positive impact to mollify the problems. Some look askance at this very suggestion, responding disdainfully that it is not the task of liberal theory to try to solve such profound and lasting political dilemmas. They are incorrect. There are real prospects for liberals here, chances to make good on fundamental commitments to liberty of conscience, to the justification of a liberal order, and to the liberal's rightful aim to demonstrate respect and concern for persons.

Now is the time to renew the liberal project, to expand its legitimacy across the globe. Now is the moment to begin reducing the sense of disenfranchisement and disillusionment on both sides of the liberal/theocratic divide. Ready for the taking are opportunities to mitigate the sense of maltreatment found in theocratic corners, to diminish violent activity from local and foreign extremist groups, and to increase stability and comity between theocrats and liberals. Liberals must now fend off the rising sense of the illegitimacy of liberal government by providing theocrats with a principled, well-reasoned, and conscientious political settlement that liberals and theocrats can jointly affirm. This is the charge of liberalism.

Two things must be done. First, liberal political theory must demonstrate that reasons for theocrats to affirm liberal principles do exist. To date, liberals have failed to accomplish this important goal. Second, liberals should lead efforts to recuperate matters on the ground. Here, liberals can assist both as citizens of their own countries and as conscientious people of the world. They can give new, powerful reasons to support free institutions. They can support parallel social and political efforts, domestically and abroad. Liberals can also engage more respectfully and fruitfully with religious objectors; they can militate for a better legal framework for treating theocratic communities in liberal democracies; and they can demonstrate their affirmation of the crucial liberal commitment to liberty of conscience in so doing. Liberalism holds the promise of a new moral ground for governance of theocrats, a renewed and revitalized basis for liberal governing institutions. With innovation and fresh thinking, liberals can offer better ways to treat religious objectors and communities of faith.

In this book, I aim to demonstrate that there is reason for theocrats to affirm liberalism of a special, particular kind. It is not the overarching, comprehensive liberalism of John Stuart Mill or Immanuel Kant, one that relies on a controversial ideal of individuality. Instead, I develop a new case in favor of a political liberalism focused on institutions, a liberalism of free and limited governance that better harmonizes with the fundamental and reasonable goals and commitments of theocrats. The plan of this book is simple. In chapter 1, I explain the historical importance of theocratic governance, returning to the roots of theocracy and providing a definition of the term. I then identify and classify two main forms of theocratic allegiance in free societies, since I shall focus chiefly on the dilemmas that theocrats raise for liberal democracies. I distinguish a troubling series of prudential and moral problems that theocrats present for liberal government and clarify exactly why the problems of theocracy are both philosophically and politically serious. While liberal societies have done well to achieve basic toleration, I propose, the achievements of liberal political philosophy have amounted to disappointment with regard to the legacy of theocracy. In particular, I contend that liberals have not yet properly provided reasons for theocrats to affirm liberal institutions, have failed to identify grounds on which to govern theocrats, and have neglected to formulate a suitable schema for treating theocrats ensconced in liberal democracies. These problems risk the very legitimacy of liberal government and institutions, both at home and abroad.

In chapter 2, I work to make plain the reasons for theocrats to endorse liberal institutions, whether or not they live within liberal democracies. I begin by considering the limited appeal that liberal institutions currently hold for theocrats: many theocrats believe those institutions are inferior to the illiberal religious forms of governance they presently favor. Accepting theocrats' more reasonable values as a point of departure, I explain why secular arguments designed to identify reasons to affirm liberalism and its institutions simply will not reach theocrats. To address this shortcoming, I provide a new argument that proceeds on grounds familiar to theocrats and that there is reason for them to accept. I introduce three novel, cardinal principles of liberty of conscience and demonstrate that theocrats are rationally committed to them. The three principles are:

Conscience must be free to reject lesser religious doctrines and conceptions of the good (the principle of rejection)

Conscience must be free to accept the good (the principle of affirmation)

Conscience must be free to distinguish between good and bad doctrines and conceptions of the good (the principle of distinction)

I clarify the nature of these three principles and explain why there is good reason for theocrats to accept them, reasons generated from theocrats' own reasonable commitments to otherworldly values. In the process, I provide a groundwork for arguments that defeat antiliberal theocrats' most challenging claims and objections. Theocrats may not yet understand that they are rationally committed to these principles of liberty of conscience or that they should accept and affirm the institutions those principles require, but they can come to understand those facts. I maintain that liberalism could be made more appealing to theocrats, if the liberal commitment to freedom of conscience is clarified and modified and if liberals take a fresh approach to conceptualizing and promulgating liberal principles, institutions, and law.

In chapter 3, I argue that existing legal standards, including the popular legal standard of religious accommodation, cannot provide a legal framework for theocratic communities that adequately respects the theocrat's moral right to religious free exercise. But I propose that the free exercise problems pertaining to theocratic communities appear to be amenable to a distinctive solution. I contend that perhaps the only legal structure able to handle theocratic communities appropriately that could also be adapted to fit with the overarching legal structure of modern liberal democracies would be one that allowed those communities to gain quasi sovereignty. I then introduce a new legal standard of quasi sovereignty for theocratic communities, describing its main elements and listing its improvements over competing legal frameworks. Quasi sovereignty would require theocrats to own a distinguishable territory, delegating educational and human rights responsibilities to theocratic communities while superintending those responsibilities carefully. Theocratic communities would be enjoined to honor members' wishes to exit from their communities and would have to protect the interests of more vulnerable members such as women and children. I suggest that quasi sovereignty offers a liberal way out of conflicts that threaten the domestic tranquillity of many polities and the international security of states around the world. Where theocrats aim to withdraw from society, quasi sovereignty can help to provide a workable, ethically sound standard for them, one that demonstrates the liberal commitment to religious liberty.

I begin chapter 4 by considering how the arguments and findings I have made bear upon public reason and the role of religious argumentation in public discourse. I then focus on issues raised by religious extremists and other ambitious theocrats, advancing suggestions as to how liberals and liberal government might better interact with them. Drawing on empirical research in the social sciences, I consider how liberals might prompt theocrats to internalize principles of liberty of conscience and motivate them to behave in less violent and more amicable ways. I argue that liberals should enter directly into theocrats' social networks to engage in dialogue with them, and I provide strategies liberals can employ to make their interactions with theocrats vigorous, appropriate, and effective. I examine how liberals might inculcate respect for liberty of conscience in the minds of theocrats, concentrating on the prospects of shifting theocrats' sense of their own identities so that they adopt a less adversarial disposition to liberal institutions while retaining their central theocratic commitments. In the course of this argument, I consider the grounds liberals can provide for interfering with theocratic practices as well as the kinds of explanations for interference that liberals and liberal government might provide in that regard. I then reflect on strategies for increasing domestic and international comity between liberal institutions and theocratic communities and polities. I close by addressing and forestalling objections to the argument presented in this work in its entirety.

Liberalism need not be just another partisan theory of how to live. A new liberal theory awaits, one that properly acknowledges the fundamental values and commitments of theocrats and liberals alike. It is time for a more moral, optimistic, and constructive approach to religious conflict. The world needs a liberalism that better depends on ideas and healthy social and political engagement, taking fundamental theocratic commitments respectfully and seriously. We need a theory that does not rely on arbitrary violence or domination in its attempts to advance toward lasting comity and peace. A more solid basis on which to build institutions and law holds the promise of peace, of a chance for liberals and theocrats to lay down their swords, finally to live together under government they can both affirm. It is time for a liberalism of conscience.

THE LIBERAL CONSCIENCE

1. A Liberalism of Conscience

DESPITE THEIR STEPS FORWARD with respect to toleration, stability, and legitimacy, the liberal democracies of the new millennium have inherited unresolved and what appear to be ultimately irresolvable religious differences. The world's great democracies contain within them a wide variety of comprehensive doctrines, religious and otherwise. Not all these doctrines derive from a Christian fount: democracies are increasingly multicultural places, featuring wide racial and ethnic diversity and legions of religious communities representing every major religious tradition. The condition of permanence attached to this array of comprehensive doctrines prompts some writers to suggest, quite rightly, that there is a "fact of pluralism as such," in the sense that pluralism of this kind exists at present and is not likely to disappear at any time in the foreseeable future.[1] As John Rawls remarks, notwithstanding the efforts of those who have toiled in vain to unite, coalesce, or eradicate religious doctrines, "the fact of religious division remains."[2]

Religious divisions in contemporary liberal societies are not only permanent and profound; they also exist between liberal and non- or antiliberal religious devotees. For among the people who support the array of doctrines that simple pluralism implies are theocrats, those persons who affirm theocratic conceptions of the good. In this chapter, I describe the legacy of theocracy in modern constitutional democracies by identifying and classifying two main forms of theocratic allegiance in free societies. To begin, I outline the historical importance of theocracy, returning to its roots and providing a definition of the term. I then distinguish a particularly troubling series of prudential and moral problems that theocrats raise for liberal government. I explain exactly why the problems of theocracy are both philosophically and politically serious and clarify how those problems put the legitimacy of liberal government and institutions at risk.

I shall argue that despite the important gains won by liberal societies, the achievements of liberal political philosophy have amounted to disappointment with regard to the legacy of theocracy. In particular, I contend that liberals have failed properly to provide reasons for theocrats to affirm liberal institutions, faltered in identifying grounds on which to govern theocrats, where appropriate, and neglected to devise a well-formed schema for treating theocrats ensconced in liberal democracies. While these failures are serious, they do not ring the changes for liberalism. I close by providing suggestions on how liberals can speak to the challenges of theocrats and theocratic minorities, combat the legacy of religious discord, and revivify the liberal project for the future.

ELEMENTS OF THEOCRACY

"Theocracy" derives from the ancient Greek word *theokratia*, a term coined by the Jewish historian Josephus Flavius around A.D. 100. In *Against Apion*, the work in which the term first appears, Josephus argues that the best government is a theocracy, the government under which Jews were meant to live. Theocracy "[places] all sovereignty and authority in the hands of God," rather than in multiple gods, the populace, or elsewhere. Instead of sanctioning popular rule, Josephus contends, the theocrat embraces a Mosaic code enveloping "the whole conduct . . . of life" since nothing ought to be left "to the discretion and caprice of the individual." For the Jews, Josephus suggests, there could hardly be a finer or more equitable polity than one that "sets God at the head of the universe" and assigns the administration of affairs to "a whole body of priests," with one high priest presiding over the others.[3]

While the term originates in the first century, the way of governing to which "theocracy" refers dates back thousands of years. Jean-Jacques Rousseau claims that theocracy was in fact the first government known to people. In *On the Social Contract*, he states that men at first "had no other kings than the Gods, nor any other government than theocracy." Rousseau avers that under paganism gods were "placed at the head of every political society," suggesting that this produced as many notions of gods as there were peoples to be ruled. Paganism had few wars of religion, according to Rousseau, since each polity, having "its own cult as well as its government," drew no distinction between its laws and the gods that it worshipped.[4]

Consider the breadth and depth of importance of theocracy to political history. Theocracy frequently recurs in polities both ancient and modern, in religious communities outside the Western tradition, and in preindustrial societies. In Asia Minor, great theocratic cities such as Zela and Pessinus arose in the tenth century B.C., each one populated by sacred slaves and ruled by pontiffs wielding both temporal and spiritual authority. Ancient kings and queens often boasted priestly identities, standing as "intercessors between man and god," as James George Frazer puts it. People imputed to those rulers magical powers beyond the abilities of mere mortals, as was the case with the Mesopotamian kings, occupying intercessory roles between people and the gods, or the Egyptian pharaohs, thought to be gods in their own right.[5] According to Max Weber's analysis, Confucian Chinese bureaucracy in ancient Asia was theocratic, too, as was the rule of the Hindu Brahmins. Weber notes that early Islam also incorporated prescriptions for theocratic rule in the "ideal social stratification" that it identified.[6] Early Islamic theocrats may have envisioned an egalitarian holy life, but followers of Islam stood united under divine rule with regulations that embraced and strictly ordered their lives.

The history of theocracy within the Western tradition is also richly filigreed. Before the institution of kingship in Israel, Jews believed that Yahweh was their supreme ruler, accepting the demanding religious and civil obligations of his laws. Josephus's notion of strict government under a Mosaic code testifies to the presence of the idea in later Judaic thought. Theocracy was reborn in the medieval missives of Pope Gregory VII, during the twilight hours of the Holy Roman Empire. In the *Dictatus Papae* of 1075, Gregory VII declared that all nations should be subject to the pontiff and to Catholicism, that the pope may depose emperors, and that he himself may be judged by no one. The Reformation hardly did away with theocratic aspirations: Martin Luther's theology instead provided a new basis for strict religious governance. Following Luther, Reformation theorists strove to incorporate theocratic rule in various parts of Europe. Theocratic ideals were sought by such Protestant reformers as Johannes Calvin during his tenure in Geneva, in Ulrich Zwingli's theocratic work in Zurich,[7] and in less famous experiments such as John of Leiden's Anabaptist polity in Münster, in 1534–35. Calvinist political thought anchored a number of theocratic views in sixteenth- and seventeenth-century Europe, and the English Puritans, on their arrival in America, promptly set up a theocratic order in the New World.[8]

Latter-day writers display a curious tendency simply to view theocracy as an outdated political form with no current relevance to democratic life. The enterprise of political science succumbs to this temptation, having failed to study theocracy except where writers briefly broach the topic in examining ancient forms of government,[9] developing political forms,[10] or the historical relation between church and state. Witness Herbert Hoover's remarks in *The Challenge to Liberty*, dismissing theocracy as one of the "old systems of rule." Theocracy is a way of governing from the past, according to Hoover. As he puts it, theocratic polities "still linger in places in the world, but they have no present importance to us except as laboratory records of human experience."[11]

Hoover's assessment is deadly inaccurate, however. Theocratic religious traditions continue to establish regimes in countries around the world. A number of progressive, transitional countries quake with inner conflict propelled by theocratic energies, where religious zealots vie for political power. Theocratic forces remain powerful in the Middle East, where strong contingents of theocrats fight with governments and light firestorms of conflict. The recent historical record of theocracy in that area is inglorious. In Afghanistan, the theocratic Taliban relentlessly tormented women, killed homosexuals, and destroyed religious icons sacred to other faiths. Iran's supreme leader, Ayatollah Ali Khamenei, has forced the resignations of reformist, elected officials as part of an ongoing effort to maintain theocratic rule. Theocratic Islamic forces attacked the governments of Kyrgyzstan and Uzbekistan both in 1999 and 2000. Turkmenistan's government has limited religious freedom to followers of Sunni Islam and the Russian Orthodox Church, while destroying other Christian places of worship and beating and torturing members of other faiths. The recent terrorist attacks, launched by new generations of domestic and international Islamic theocrats, show how seriously theocratic ideals are held and how problematic theocrats can be for the stability of liberal polities.

I aim to provide a working definition of "theocracy" adequate to cover the phenomena described here, one that captures the defining elements of theocracy and does not include mere incidental or accompanying traits. From the definition that Josephus implicitly provides, one can abstract four components of theocracy: (1) it is a strict way of governing; (2) there is a religious understanding of the good in theocracy; (3) religious authorities direct daily affairs in a community, and (4) all sovereignty is in God.[12] I shall call this fourth property *Josephus's fourth criterion*.

Josephus's introduction of *theokratia* did not permanently fix reference to his favored form of government. For others converted the meaning of "theocracy" in subsequent centuries. In contemporary English usage, "theocracy" no longer implies reference to a way of governing in which God is sovereign, although it allows as theocratic some forms of government that do. The gradual shift in ordinary usage of "theocracy" and the imprecision of the word in common usage should not be surprising. As Herbert Hart notices, the terms of language have an open texture: the cost of "general classifying terms" is a lack of certainty on whether the terms apply to some specific particulars.[13] This limited guidance is "inherent in the nature of language."[14]

The vagueness of ordinary language usage of "theocracy" may be its vice, but its abandonment of Josephus's fourth criterion—that all sovereignty is in God—is its virtue. This is so for four reasons. First of all, were one to follow Josephus's conception of theocracy to the letter, only a certain kind of Judaic government would qualify as theocratic. It seems unreasonable to limit theocratic government only to Jewish polities: other polities ruled under different religious doctrines from Judaism, such as Catholicism, Protestantism, or Islam, surely could be theocratic as well. People speaking of theocracy frequently refer to examples from within the Christian and Islamic traditions, but following Josephus too closely would discount those examples out of hand.

Second, since some of the world's major religions do not propose that all sovereignty lies in God, Josephus's fourth criterion cramps an adequate understanding of the political phenomenon of theocracy by artificially rendering theocracy impossible for many peoples of the world. The fourth criterion would exclude Confucian and Hindu political forms as candidates for theocracy, because according to those religious doctrines sovereignty does not entirely rest in God. Consider Confucian government as Weber describes it: Confucian bureaucracy was theocratic due to the religious strictness of its rule but Weber recognizes that no gods are postulated under that religious form.[15] Similarly, ancient Hinduism constituted a highly consistent religious expression of an "organic view of society," in Weber's view, justifying the existing order of the world based on the merits and shortcomings of adherents' previous lives. Hindu Brahmins regulated politics and society by fortifying caste obligations with powerful religious sanctions, producing what Weber called "theocratic strata."[16] G. W. F. Hegel provides another example in *The Philosophy of History*, where he identifies a theocratic constitution of the Eastern world before the emergence of states.[17] Hegel suggests that a "realm of theocratic despotism" began with the Chinese and the Mongols even though their religious traditions neither located all sovereignty in God nor consistently posited God's existence.

So, not all religions locate all sovereignty in God; not only that, some religious doctrines posit the inferiority of God to a higher order, while others postulate several gods or none at all. Here, there is a third problem for Josephus's fourth criterion: it arbitrarily disqualifies nontheistic and polytheistic religions as possibly theocratic. As the Confucian example shows, speakers do refer to some religious polities as theocratic even when the respective religious doctrine postulates no god at all. And polytheistic religious doctrines also could be theocratic, it seems. Native North American tribes such as the Pueblo Indians postulate the existence of several gods, and theorists such as Will Kymlicka refer at points to the theocratic structure of Pueblo Indian government and society,[18] even though the polytheistic cosmology of the Pueblos violates Josephus's fourth criterion.

This brings to light a fourth problem with Josephus's fourth criterion, one that alone decisively disqualifies it as a defining trait of theocracy. The problem is this: the very idea of God would have to be clarified dramatically before it could do any definitional work with respect to theocracy, for there are broadly conflicting and contrary conceptions of God found in the discourse of the world's religious adherents. Some hold views of God that are anthropomorphic, while others do not; some propose that God is immanent in earthly affairs, while others construe God's existence as being almost entirely metaphysically removed; some conceive of the Almighty as having the capacity, even the tendency, to intervene in human affairs, but others deny the possibility outright. Simply to stipulate without further elaboration that all sovereignty is in God, therefore, is to require almost nothing at all. Consider an analogy from the problem of obedience to the Almighty: Michael Walzer notices that the idea of obedience to God itself "offers neither clear-cut definitions nor a program for action."[19] Obedience to God could entail submission to a wide variety of authorities claiming to speak in the name of God, Walzer suggests, just as it might permit or enjoin the heroic actions of those who challenge existing authority figures.

Josephus's fourth criterion cannot qualify as a definitive element of theocracy since it arbitrarily excludes phenomena known to be theocratic to scholars and to speakers, and it provides little guidance with respect to what would count as an acceptable conception of God. And so, following the limited guidance that ordinary language provides and considering carefully the properties that Josephus identified, *I define "theoc-*

racy" as "a mode of governance prioritizing a religious conception of the good that is strict and comprehensive in its range of teachings."

To elaborate this definition, I provide three clarifying remarks. First, the definition requires that theocracy is a strict way of governing. Governments that prioritize permissive religious conceptions of the good should not to be considered theocratic, for three reasons. In the first place, such conceptions do not fit with the spirit of Josephus's initial notion of theocracy. Conceptions of the good allowing people to worship as they may please or permitting people to seek their own paths without direction or supervision of religious authorities would sanction the very discretion and caprice feared by Josephus. Second, the idea of permissive government does not harmonize with common usage of the word "theocracy." Speakers normally understand theocracy to be a form of governance in which a strict, religious conception of the good takes priority over the right.[20] Theocratic polities and communities are generally nonliberal or illiberal, not because they all reject liberal values in the same ways but because they work to maintain their ways of life by discouraging or prohibiting liberal values and practices. Third, including open societies under the rubric of theocracy does not help to make the idea of theocracy distinct or useful. If theocracy could be either permissive or strict, then any government could plausibly be said to be theocratic if only one were to demonstrate that the authorities were sanctioned by a religious doctrine. Nor is it a theocracy where one finds strict rule by government but where authorities do not act in the name of any religion or promote any religious doctrine. Those governments acting in the name of no religious doctrine are simply authoritarian, to the extent to which they deny civil liberties.[21]

Second, this definition of "theocracy" allows, but does not require, rule by religious authorities. Here, one must be especially careful and clear. In the context of theocracy, ruling religious authorities will be those who hold political offices and positions of power consistent with the teachings of the doctrine they mean to represent. Religious authorities may be kings, clergy, or aristocrats; they are whoever is sanctioned by doctrine to exercise political control over the religious community in question. This distinguishes theocracy from government under which one finds strong religious establishment but where the ruling authorities are not legitimated by doctrine. Rule by religious authorities cannot, however, be a necessary trait of theocracy, lest one discount pacifistic and apolitical communities and ways of life as possibly theocratic. The Old Order Amish would be excluded by such a criterion, as might be Confucian systems, and so politically empowered religious authorities, while consistent with theocracy, must not be implied by it. To those objecting to this proposition, one notes the flexibility accorded to "democracy" and "democratic": people commonly refer to the democratic character of organizations and societies where the groups' officials enjoy no political power. I do not mean radically to reconstruct "theocracy" here; I wish simply to submit that "theocracy" and "theocratic" should have a modicum of flexibility in this regard, in accordance with a reasonable understanding of the term.

Third, the definition suggests that theocracy involves a comprehensive conception of the good. What does that mean? If a conception of the good is a set of worthwhile values, practices, aims, and ideals, so conceived, its comprehensiveness pertains to the range of life practices to which the conception applies. Theocratic doctrines are widely or fully comprehensive in the sense that they extend to cover "all recognized values and virtues within one rather precisely articulated scheme of thought," as John Rawls puts it.[22] Theocratic conceptions of the good range across nearly all life practices, covering personal associations, familial structures, institutional arrangements, practices of ritual and worship, and ideals of character.[23] A theocratic conception of the good is therefore other-regarding in its strictness and its thoroughness, looking to regulate the lives of a community of persons and not only focusing on the life plans of him who holds such a conception.[24] A theocratic conception of the good might aim at a small assemblage of devout believers, but the whole of humanity may lie within the regulative vision of the theocrat's conception, if, for instance, the doctrine strongly favors proselytizing.

By observation, one can readily detect that theocrats tend to reject a series of liberal values, such as freedom of religion, freedom of association, equality of the sexes, free choice of occupation, and free speech and dissent. This one observes in theocratic movements and polities internationally, as well as in theocratic communities within liberal-democratic countries, such as the Old Order Amish, the Satmar Hasidim of Kiryas Joel in New York State, or the Pueblo Indians of New Mexico. Nevertheless, it would be incorrect to include illiberality as a definitive trait of theocracy. There are two reasons for this. First, there is reason for theocrats to affirm liberty of conscience and the liberal institutions that best protect that value. Second, theocrats can and should uphold cardinal principles of liberty of conscience, while retaining their theocratic color and commitments, so an illiberal texture is not in the grain of theocracy. I aim to establish these points in the coming chapters.

THEOCRATIC MINORITIES IN LIBERAL DEMOCRACIES

Theocrats in modern liberal democracies divide naturally into two different kinds. I focus here on the American example, but this classification and the argument I provide have a wider application. The first kind of theocrat I shall call *ambitious*. Ambitious theocrats are enthusiastic participants in public life, engaging in public discourse and political affairs with a view to supplanting liberal institutions with stricter laws and regulations drawn from their religious conceptions of the good. Religious extremists and elements of the religious Right in America are exponents of ambitious religious conceptions of the good, as are members of the Nation of Islam and other Muslims who, in the words of Martin Luther King Jr., "have lost faith in America . . . [and] absolutely repudiated Christianity."[25] Ambitious theocrats are *politically* ambitious, promoting their doctrines fervently and in earnest and using a variety of means to try to topple the liberal establishment and the debased values that they believe its institutions enshrine. It is no secret that Western democracies have a healthy contingent of ambitious theocrats, since those religious adherents regularly are active and vocal across a broad spectrum of public matters.[26] They are a symptom of democracy's discontent, one could say, concerned with the loss of self-government, the collapse of public morality, and the erosion of community.[27]

The second kind of theocrat may properly be called *retiring*. Unlike their ambitious counterparts, these theocrats withdraw from everyday affairs; they are reluctant to participate in political or other public matters, working to live instead in small communities where they may practice their religion in seclusion. In America, examples of such communities include Old Order Amish settlements, the Satmar Hasidim of the Village of Kiryas Joel, Native Indians from the western pueblos of New Mexico, extant polygamous Mormon communities, and the former city of Rajneeshpuram in Oregon. Each of these groups strives or has striven to form and maintain its communities in seclusion from outside life, withdrawn into their own villages, settlements, or territories, for the purposes of religious practice.[28]

Theocratic communities are generally nonliberal, not inasmuch as they all reject liberty, equality, or religious neutrality in the same fashion, or equally, but in the sense that they undertake strictly to maintain the tenor of their religious communities by discouraging or forbidding outright such practices as individual free expression and freedom of association. Both retiring and ambitious theocrats are theocratic by degree: some are more hostile to liberal values than others, and not all theocrats are dedicated to replacing governing liberal institutions with strict religious laws and authorities. For instance, some retiring theocrats, such as the Amish, have neither the desire to wield the sword of secular authority nor the will to use corporal or more extreme forms of punishment against their members; others are not so tame. Furthermore, leaders of theocratic communities within liberal democracies are legally forbidden from coercing dissenters severely, they are unable to stop those who wish to exit their communities from so doing, and their authority over outsiders is very limited. Yet despite these restrictions, theocratic communities continue to manifest themselves in liberal democracies, representing religious traditions and ways of life stemming from each of a variety of religious doctrines.

DISCORD IN THE PUBLIC REALM

With this brief characterization of theocracy in hand and with the distinction between ambitious and retiring theocrats in place, consider two notable species of problems that ambitious theocrats cause for liberal government. First, ambitious theocrats create a problem of *political discordance* with the controversial and at times incendiary policy proposals they advance in public. By "political discordance," I mean to identify strife or variance produced in public arenas, respecting views on policy issues and other matters of debate and public concern. Ambitious theocrats variously demand a strong fusion of church and state; the reintroduction, vigorous promotion, and strict enforcement of religious values in public life; censorship of irreligious speech;[29] legal sanctions against minority faiths;[30] the legal prohibition of abortion;[31] and the penalization or criminalization of homosexuality.[32] The last two demands in this list are not made exclusively by theocrats, since less extreme religious devotees join the chorus of disapproval on abortion and homosexuality, as do some secular parties. Nor are all these demands common to theocrats, strictly speaking: the particular content of the theocrat's appeals depends on the doctrine to which he adheres. Some theocrats do not make serious objection to the practice of abortion, for instance, while others do. In any case, strong proposals of these kinds are often incorporated in theocrats' belief systems, and I identify them here so as to help to distinguish the landscape of theocratic views.

A second species of problems that ambitious theocrats create for liberal government is what I shall call *participatory discordance*, respecting the *way* theocrats participate in public affairs. Ambitious theocrats make demands based on religious reasons that they offer in support of some particular course of public action. The ambitious theocrat's demands often threaten and anger various sectors of the populace, with his proposals grating strongly against liberal values, public opinion, and accepted or received views. Further, ambitious theocrats at times ignore the concerns of their secular cohort, or contend that their religious reasons trump secular interests, or flatly propose that secular concerns are not worth considering at all. This is a well-known political problem, but it is not only a political issue. For beneath the participatory discordance, there lurks a knotty philosophical puzzle. Whether religious reasons should count as admissible in public debate is a hotly disputed matter philosophically, and it is an issue itself associated with political discord, since theocrats complain frequently about their disenfranchisement and disillusionment with liberal government and politics, where their reasons are said to be politically inadmissible or their political proposals are defeated.[33]

Do retiring theocrats cause problems for liberal government? Although they live withdrawn from participatory society, retiring theocrats' uncommon practices and convictions spark firestorms of controversy, igniting disagreement over the validity of their lifestyles and the extent to which government ought to tolerate their ways of life. For retiring theocrats do not fit well with the liberal-democratic frameworks that surround them, and their communities prove to be very difficult to handle under existing political and legal structures. This is an important way in which retiring theocrats differ from their ambitious counterparts: the retiring theocrat dwells in a community that is itself a source of political discordance. Four of the five retiring American theocratic communities mentioned above have been prodded to defend their practices all the way up to the United States Supreme Court. The Amish were forced to defend themselves against numerous challenges to their educational practices;[34] the Pueblo Indians were taken to task over their criteria for tribal membership;[35] Mormon polygamists were forbidden from living in un-common family units;[36] and members of Kiryas Joel found that the Supreme Court deemed state law to be unconstitutional where that law had created a special school district corresponding to the territory of their religious village.[37] The city of Rajneeshpuram disintegrated before any case could be made to the Supreme Court, but there was no shortage of controversy over that community's incorporation as a city. The state of Oregon successfully attacked the legality of the incorporation of the city of Rajneeshpuram on the grounds that the action violated the establish-ment clause of the United States Constitution, as well as article 1 of the Oregon Constitution.[38]

Now, it should be plain that the mere fact that theocrats cause politi-cal or participatory discordance does not suffice to show that there is any cause for alarm. That is to say, the kinds of controversy that theocrats cre-ate do not obviously give liberals or other citizens reason to take theo-cratic issues especially seriously. For a number of participatory groups and individuals make extreme demands in the public realm, or they par-ticipate in public debate in what one might call unreasonable ways, and those individuals and groups could be said to merit equal or greater con-cern. Furthermore, communities other than theocratic ones cause seri-ous controversy, too: private or residential associations are good exam-ples here, as they have excited debate and litigation in recent years; Nancy Rosenblum's work in this area is especially illuminating.[39] Theocrats seem to be just one problematic category of citizens among many others; what, if anything, is special or exigent about them and their concerns?

FOUR PRUDENTIAL PROBLEMS OF THEOCRACY

Here, I shall identify four prudential problems raised by theocrats, as well as the accompanying reasons for liberals and other citizens to take special notice of them. First, both ambitious and retiring theocrats clearly have a sense of deep disaffection with the governments of free so-cieties, cultivated in their belief that liberal institutions do not respect them, their concerns, or their ways of life. Ambitious theocrats fre-quently propose that secular government disenfranchises them, and for retiring theocratic communities the sentiment is similar.[40] Unlike other groups with a sense of disenfranchisement, however, theocrats oppose not simply particular policies or laws or the actions of particular arms or offices of government; nor do they complain merely about existing exclusion with respect to policy making or legal procedure. Rather, the theocrat's disaffection runs much deeper, reaching down to the very sea floor of liberalism and liberal governance itself. For the theocrat's dissent is not localized within a consensus on liberal principles and tends to be based instead on the very rejection of liberal values. This fact helps to illuminate a prudential reason for taking theocrats seriously. Since their objections to liberalism and its standing institutions are often fundamental, and since theocrats remain motivated to struggle to foster and maintain their religious practices, theocrats are a persistent source of public grief in liberal polities.

Second, the modern liberal state is strong, but some theocrats have shown a willingness to fight openly against it and its citizens nonetheless. The example of Rajneeshpuram in Oregon is a case in point: thirty-four of the group's leaders were charged with a variety of state and federal crimes, including attempted murder, assault, arson, burglary, racketeering, electronic eavesdropping, and criminal conspiracy.[41] The Sons of Freedom, a branch of Doukhobors in western Canada, are another case in point. Beginning in the early twentieth century, homestead laws, census takings, and public schooling for Doukhobor children enraged the Sons of Freedom. They bombed schoolhouses and burned or otherwise wrecked power plants, bridges, and rail lines.[42] The Sons of Freedom protested legal interference by destroying all their own property as well, forsaking even their clothing, and showed their loathing of liberal laws, values, and institutions by walking through the countryside, solemnly and en masse, completely naked. Not all theocrats are prepared to act in illegal or violent ways, of course: the Amish are resolute and unyielding pacifists, refusing under any circumstances to use force even to protect themselves physically. But theocrats are marked by a preparedness to defend their religion against attack, and in cases of perceived interference, they have a propensity to strike out violently; and while not only theocrats stand prepared to use violence to fight for their communities and their ways of life, this propensity distinguishes theocrats generally as posing a greater prudential risk than most dissenting parties in liberal democracies. Here, there is a second prudential reason to take theocrats seriously: a failure to do so can result in illegal activities or attacks from theocratic quarters, in cases where religious devotees have some quarrel with liberal institutions and where they believe that violence or other criminal activity is justified.

Third, where government's severe actions against retiring theocrats enjoy no sound, publicly accessible justification, its conduct may excite militant responses from extremist groups sympathetic to the theocrats' plight. The events consequent to the siege and assault on the reclusive Branch Davidians at Waco, Texas, in 1993 are a good example of how such phenomena can and have occurred in the recent past. Militant groups in the United States were outraged by the federal government's handling of the Waco affair. It was government's unprincipled and ham-handed treatment of the Branch Davidians that catalyzed strikes from militant groups, assaults that included the dreadful Oklahoma City bombing of April 19, 1995. The imminent danger of attack from militia groups was not unforeseen, either: six months before the Oklahoma City bombing, a report published by the Anti-Defamation League of B'nai B'rith warned that extremist American militia groups were dangerous and looking for suitable provocation for combat.[43] And the peril remains, for militant and other extremist groups continue to view the maltreatment of theocrats as indicative of the moral bankruptcy of liberal government, reacting where government is seen to ride roughshod over retiring theocratic communities.[44] In this, there is a third prudential reason to take theocrats especially seriously: where government mishandles theocrats, it risks attacks from extremist third parties within the body politic, against its own citizens and institutions. This is a grave concern that will remain as long as government has no principled, morally sound policy by which to treat theocrats. John Locke showed prescience in this regard, where he foretold, in *A Letter Concerning Toleration*, that there will be no peace so long as perceptions of religious persecution are found.[45]

Fourth, and finally, with government activity of the sort displayed at Waco, liberal polities may unwittingly cultivate a broad sense of the illegitimacy of liberal government, one expanding well beyond theocratic and extremist spheres. For people in democracies such as the United States have not taken well to recent terrorist attacks against their own institutions and fellow citizens. They naturally wonder why those assaults occurred, even questioning what value there is in a regime that does not effectively prevent such grave dangers from taking form. It is true that the terrible violence of September 2001 seems to have galvanized citizen support for U.S. government and institutions, contrary to the intended effects of the zealous assaults. Further attacks, however, could critically damage citizens' sense of the legitimacy of liberal government and affect their behavior in turn.

Is there any empirical evidence to support such a dark contention? Despite the weak connection between feelings of trust in government and voter turnout,[46] there is evidence to suggest that the most cynical are more politically engaged than are average citizens.[47] There is also reason to believe, as the study from *Voice and Equality* seems to show, that the decline in voting in the United States has not meant a decrease in political activism.[48] It seems therefore plausible to suppose that a strong sense of alienation or a widespread perception of illegitimacy could mobilize citizens at least to throw out officeholders and seek institutional redress, if not to take more extreme political action.[49] To this, one could add an auxiliary point on the obverse: Pippa Norris has argued that data from the 1995–97 World Values Study indicate that the perception of legitimacy in government contributes to voluntary compliance with the law, although strengthening civil liberties may be even more important in securing such compliance, at least in burgeoning democracies.[50]

So the fourth prudential concern is that an absence of a sense of legitimacy could contribute significantly to an undesirable form of citizen mobilization. Under a more dire scenario, one might witness disaffection moving from theocratic and militant pockets into the body politic, plaguing common citizen and tame religious believer alike. One must be chary here, since it is important not to overestimate the extent to which the continuing maltreatment of theocrats, coupled with attacks from extremist groups, could fuel a disastrous legitimation crisis. There is some reason to think, however, that a serious crisis in confidence in liberal government could ignite, sparked by perceptions of its lack of legitimacy, if the problems of theocracy are left to grow unchecked.

FOUR MORAL FAILURES OF LIBERALISM

The prudential problems pertaining to theocrats are serious enough to warrant careful and direct attention on the part of liberals and liberal government. But how will these problems auspiciously be addressed? The best effort to assuage the combativeness and public grief that theocrats bring to bear, and the prospects of a legitimation crisis, cannot simply amount to an exercise of public management on the part of liberal government. For liberal theory and liberal government each bear some responsibility for the prudential problems that I have outlined, and it will only be through a sustained treatment of a series of *moral* shortcomings in liberalism that these prudential problems will be stabilized and resolved. It is not my purpose to lay blame here, and certainly I shall not suggest that liberal government is blameworthy for the recent terrorist attacks against its citizens and institutions. However, four moral shortcomings of liberalism have contributed to the prudential dangers that I have distinguished here, as well as being serious failures in their own right.

The first moral failure of liberalism is this: liberal government lacks a well-devised and justifiable schema for treating theocrats dwelling in liberal democracies, one that is able to handle theocrats' contributions to public debate and is capable of treating theocratic communities properly under law. The lack of a standard of that kind places government in the awkward position of being at times unable to justify its laws and its procedures to its citizens. Furthermore, the missing standard permits government to commit injustices against religious devotees in cases where, for instance, government excludes ambitious theocrats' concerns from public debate without cause,[51] or where government violates people's moral right to religious free exercise by inflicting excessive entanglements on religious communities and making their religious practice very nearly impossible. I address this issue at some length in chapter 3, but it bears mention here since liberal government's current practice of handling theocratic communities is a clear case of moral failure on its part.

The second moral problem is that liberal government should, but does not, have proper and identifiable grounds in hand for governing theocrats. This issue is distinct from the question of whether liberals have devised a schema by which to handle theocrats in an appropriate manner; in fact, it is analytically prior. Here, the concern applies not merely to how government treats theocrats but, more fundamentally, to whether liberal government has any right to govern them at all.

I should like to expand on this concern briefly here, for the thought needs some elaboration. Why would one entertain the idea that liberal government might *not* have a right to govern its theocratic citizens? Consider first the kind of value conflict that obtains between theocrats and liberals. Like other religious practitioners, the theocrat holds firm to his belief in otherworldly powers and ends, such that disabusing him of the notion that such ends exist and are valuable would be very difficult indeed. But more pointedly, theocrats' conceptions of the good seem as though they may be fundamentally different and discordant with respect to those of other citizens, bringing forth a conflict of commitments and values for which no rational solution is available.[52] It could be the case that liberal and theocratic values are incommensurable, in the sense that they are not equal values but neither is one set of values superior to the other.[53] Why is this important? To some philosophers, this situation of deep value conflict has decided implications for political theory and for the prospects of resolving actual political conflict. Given the fundamental and rationally irresolvable conflict between liberal and theocratic conceptions of the good, they argue, government should aim for a modus vivendi between people. John Gray has proposed as much in recent years.[54] The arguments in this regard are not just that there is no way to show people like theocrats the appeal in any Enlightenment or universalist version of liberalism and liberal institutions but also that there simply is no reason for theocrats to accept liberal values.

That liberal government rules over theocrats dwelling in liberal democracies is quite clear. Government continually enacts laws that affect theocrats and their religious practices in numerous ways, regulating and interfering with the affairs of theocratic communities and sometimes coercing theocrats outright. However, the fact that liberals have brought theocratic forces partially or even largely under control says nothing of whether they have done so by right. Nor does it indicate that the continuing domination is morally acceptable. The mere fact that some combatant has won a victory over his opponent does not, and never could, justify the triumph in a moral sense. Here, one must take note of the fact that theocrats object strenuously and profoundly to liberal values and the impositions of liberal government, proposing that they have good religious reasons for departing from liberal standards. Their reasons, they argue, outweigh the claims and concerns of liberal government. Where liberals provide secular arguments in favor of liberal values and institutions and in defense of liberal government's right to govern theocrats within liberal polities, theocrats respond that those arguments belie their conclusions. The theocrat contends that his particular religious dictates override liberal concerns, justify the illiberal treatment of refractory members within his theocratic community, or undercut the supposed right of liberal institutions to govern theocrats. Liberals must think that the grounds on which to govern theocrats have been uncovered at some point, but the problems involved simply with locating grounds with which to justify liberal government's treatment of theocrats are serious indeed. Insofar as liberals have struggled to identify those grounds in a satisfactory way, they have failed to shore up a serious moral shortcoming of liberalism.

Here is a third moral inadequacy. Since liberal government is in the habit of coercing theocrats where they break the law, it would seem that government owes them an explanation for why it does so. Not just any explanation will do, either. The United States Supreme Court's decision outlawing polygamy, in *Reynolds v. United States*, is a good example of an inadequate explanation for a specific legal restriction on theocrats.[55] In that case, the Mormon George Reynolds was charged with bigamy for having married more than one woman. Reynolds claimed that it was his religious duty to practice polygamy, contending that the practice was enjoined by God and the Bible, circumstances permitting, with his failure or refusal to practice polygamy resulting in damnation.[56] In the Court's decision, Chief Justice Waite remarked that polygamy "has always been odious" to the northern and western nations of Europe; the English, he noted, have for ages treated polygamy as an "offence against society."[57] To this *argumentum ad antiquitam* he added that marriage is a "most important feature" of social life: marriage is a "sacred obligation" as well as a "civil contract," and so it can rightly be regulated by law.[58] Polygamy, on the other hand, edifies and enlivens "the patriarchal principle," fettering members of large polygamous communities in "stationary despotism"; Waite admonished Americans not to neglect the "pure-minded women and . . . innocent children" who suffer under polygamous arrangements.[59] Whether God might require such suffering among the faithful, Waite did not consider; instead, he moved to *petitio principii*, proposing that there "cannot be a doubt" that, in the absence of constitutional restrictions forbidding it, civil government may legitimately determine whether to allow polygamous or monogamous marriages.[60] As to whether Mormon polygamists might be granted an exception to bigamy law, the Court determined that taking such a course of action would be unacceptable: allowing exceptions simply because of religious belief would make religious doctrines superior to the laws of the land and make each citizen a law unto himself.[61]

The point here is not that polygamous arrangements should ultimately be considered desirable, morally unproblematic, or harmless to women and children. Rather, it is that arguments such as those expressed in *Reynolds* simply do not yield an adequate explanation for disallowing polygamy, certainly not in the face of the competing claim that God commands that practice among true believers on pain of damnation. The arms of liberal government should hand down explanations for policies, procedures, and laws that are powerful and well reasoned and that go a long way toward justifying the laws liberal institutions use to regulate theocrats and theocratic communities. And one expects that any liberal will agree that such explanations should be forthcoming as well.[62] After all, liberals are supposed to be united against excessive or unlimited government, lawless rule, state oppression, and unwarranted interference by state institutions in quotidian affairs. So there is a matter of principle at stake for the liberal, as well as a question of consistency. But there is even more on the block than this: for if no good explanation can be provided as to why liberal government may rightly govern theocrats or coerce them where they break the law, then probably liberal government should refrain from so doing. In cases where no compelling reasons to interfere in the lives of citizens can be provided, it is the liberal's contention that government should stand down from its threat of interference, allowing persons to behave as they will and in the manner in which they are inclined.[63]

Finally, here is the fourth moral failure of liberalism that I shall identify. I have suggested that liberal government owes theocrats an explanation, based on good reasons, for why government may apply its laws to them, given the deep disagreement that theocrats have with liberal values and government. Those reasons should at the very least be reasons that theocrats should accept, reasons that hold for theocrats given their basic otherworldly concerns and commitments. At best, the explanations liberals provide to justify the application of liberal laws to theocrats will be grounded in reasons or principles that theocrats *must* accept, going beyond even T. M. Scanlon's threshold of principles that persons cannot reasonably reject.[64] This is another point with which one would expect liberals broadly to agree, inasmuch as they concur with Rawls that liberal principles of justification must win their support by "addressing each citizen's reason."[65] But here is the problem: not all reasons hold equally well for all people. In stating this claim, I do not mean to dispute the thesis of the universality of reasons; indeed, it seems quite plausible that if something is a reason for one person to act, feel, or believe in a certain way, then that reason must hold for another person who is similarly situated.[66] Rather, I wish to point out that theocrats and liberals take quite different positions on the nature of otherworldly values and ends, on the content of religious dictates, and on the respective priority of secular and religious values in public life, such that it looks as though theocrats and liberals simply are not similarly situated parties. A series of good secular reasons for accepting liberal government might hold for other secularists, but for those who flatly deny the importance of temporal life or who give priority to salvation over toleration, secular reasons may not have much bearing. I do not suggest that theocrats are strangers to Reason, reasons, or reasoning; quite to the contrary: theocrats begin from different premises from secular liberals, but they are still receptive to reasons. I am instead proposing that no adequate explanation, based on good reasons, has yet been given to justify liberal government's right to govern theocrats dwelling within liberal polities, despite the liberal's rightful philosophical commitment to the principle that such reasons ought to be supplied as required.

THE CHARGE OF LIBERALISM: MEETING THE CHALLENGES OF THEOCRACY

Each of the four moral failures distinguished above is serious in its own right, and none is offset by liberalism's success in fostering and maintaining societies free from outright religious persecution. For while the toleration of liberal societies is a wonderful development, it does not excuse or balance out the moral shortcomings that liberal theory has displayed. For this reason, it seems fair to say that liberals bear some responsibility for the prudential problems mentioned above. Naturally, the extent of an actor's responsibility for a problem is logically independent of that party's ability to address and repair the matter. But in this case, a serious, sustained effort to address and fix the moral shortcomings of liberalism, on the part of liberals and liberal institutions, apart from being an effort worth undertaking for its own sake, could also lead to an improvement in the prudential dangers I have outlined in this chapter.

At this point, one might object to the idea that liberals need to do more to give ambitious or retiring theocrats an adequate explanation for why liberal government may apply its laws to them. The objector may contend that liberal theorists have already given justifications and guidelines for various forms and degrees of interference in the affairs of theocrats. One might admit that reasons for interference declared in various wings of government have been at times inadequate but insist the offerings of liberal political philosophers are surely better grounded and articulated. That theocrats have not accepted the reasons or justifications that liberals have presented hardly means those reasons and justifications are not powerful or compelling. Indeed, this objection might go, there is only so much that liberal theory can be expected to accomplish with regard to theocrats.

The problem here is that liberals have been notorious in their failure to address the most challenging claims of theocrats. There is no short-age of liberals who advocate some kind of interference in the lives of theocrats, but practically none has faced the prior question of the right of liberal institutions to intervene. For instance, Amy Gutmann, Meira Levinson, Stephen Macedo, and Rob Reich all advocate interference in the affairs of theocratic communities for the sake of education.[67] Levin-son and Reich plead in favor of interventions and restrictions for the sake of protecting minors within minorities; children are especially vul-nerable, they notice, and must be protected from illiberal practices by lib-eral institutions.[68] Susan Moller Okin has similarly admonished liberal multiculturalists and advocates of group rights for failing to take gender inequality sufficiently seriously.[69] Defenders of group rights or exemp-tions for cultural or religious groups "are often relatively insensitive to is-sues of gender," Okin charges.[70] She notes that liberal theorists agree on the centrality of the right of exit for members of minority groups in lib-eral polities. But when it comes to patriarchal religious communities that "discriminate against or oppress women," Okin maintains, mere formal rights of exit would repeatedly leave women in the "impossible position" of choosing between "total submission [or] total alienation" from their communities.[71]

Okin's reprimand is inadvertently ironic: she rebukes liberals for not having properly considered how women will fare under various schemes for minority rights and exemptions, but her own work omits any serious, scholarly consideration of religious arguments marshaled to defeat claims she advances on the proper treatment of women. That liberal po-litical philosophers should rethink the ways in which their theories might differentially and inequitably impact women I shall not dispute. But there are prior questions here about the acceptability of liberal gov-ernment interfering in the affairs of theocrats for the sake of women, for educational designs, or for other liberal purposes such as that of equal citizenship.[72] One needs to have an argument about the appropriateness of intervention in these areas, given theocrats' claims that they have God-given, *ultima facie* reasons to depart from liberal standards. Indeed, the theocrat who stands on those reasons may contend not only that he should be exempted from various liberal policies and laws but also that his religious conception of the good must be imposed on liberal society broadly, with a severe punishment for failure awaiting in the afterlife. Contemporary liberal arguments such as Okin's provide merely *pro tanto* and insufficient reasons to justify interference in theocratic affairs,[73] and they give little subjective reason for theocrats to affirm liberalism since they speak hardly at all to theocrats' most central and pressing concerns. Liberals must give reasons and explanations that can withstand theocratic challenges if the liberal project is actually to make headway on the prudential and moral problems of theocracy that I have identified. Otherwise, liberal theory will tumble to the floor of philosophy, rolling like a lopped and leering *caput mortuum*.

Nor will one find philosophical solace in liberal constitutional arguments such as those offered by Ronald Dworkin. In *Life's Dominion*, Dworkin argues that an appropriate constitutional understanding of religion, in the context of the free exercise clause of the First Amendment, illuminates a ground for abortion rights.[74] Theocrats could agree that the United States Constitution allows, perhaps even enjoins, laws protecting "procreative autonomy."[75] But to this they may add that God's commands overrule the Constitution and thus abortion simply must not be permitted. The same problem holds for Christopher Eisgruber's work on the constitutional value of assimilation: theocrats might grant that the Constitution endorses a series of substantive values that, when fostered appropriately, would dispense with the effective segregation of theocratic communities and assimilate theocrats into a stronger political unity.[76] But theocrats can claim that God's commands trump those constitutional values, and in the absence of further argumentation to demonstrate the implausibility of such a position, the assimilationist argument sputters and grinds to a halt.

Not even Rawls's promising work on liberal legitimacy and reasonableness suffices to ward off such strikes from theocratic challengers. The Rawlsian liberal does not count persons as unreasonable simply for being religious or for merely disagreeing on a political conception of justice. Instead, the Rawlsian contends that for persons to be counted as reasonable, they must accept a liberal principle of legitimacy.[77] But why *should* theocrats affirm a Rawlsian, liberal principle of legitimacy? Indeed, theocrats may not simply refuse to accept such a principle; they can also claim to have good reason to reject fair terms of cooperation or the burdens of judgment, as Rawls delineates them,[78] based on what they understand to be God-given commands on how to speak to others about such crucial issues as abortion, education, protecting rituals of worship, or tolerating heretics. Furthermore, with respect to Rawls's list of primary goods, theocrats can and do reject the idea that basic rights and liberties, freedom of movement, free choice of occupation, and income and wealth should count as "basic all-purpose means" to pursue a permissible conception of the good.[79] Theocrats do not make these maneuvers merely to suit some immediate selfish interest; to the contrary, they do so in the larger purposes of trying to save souls, avoiding eternal damnation, or achieving some other otherworldly value, so conceived. For these difficult theocratic challenges, political liberalism requires a more complete and powerful response.

Still, the argument to this point leaves unanswered the question of just what liberals can do to address liberalism's moral shortcomings. One might object that it is quixotic to hold that the conflict between liberal government and theocratic religious devotees could ever be settled. What real hope is there that any solution for this conflict could ever be achieved?

First of all, to assuage the conflict between liberals and theocrats, liberals would do well to scrutinize the values and commitments that theocrats hold in common. For a careful examination of the theocrat's commitments to otherworldly values and to strict, religious life holds the potential of bringing to light the reasons for theocrats to affirm a liberal order. I propose that such reasons do indeed exist and that theocrats should in fact accept them. That is to say, pace the complaints of John Gray, Stuart Hampshire,[80] and others who have proclaimed such value conflict to be insuperable by reason, I contend that the value conflict between theocrats and liberals *is a rationally soluble problem*. For theocrats seem to be committed rationally to normative principles of liberty of conscience, given their common purpose to accept the good, to reject the bad, and to distinguish between the two. This rational commitment has institutional implications for protecting liberty of conscience, implications that could be articulated to speak to theocrats in new and better ways. I provide a comprehensive treatment of this matter in the coming chapters. The point here is that if theocrats are indeed rationally committed to normative principles of liberty of conscience, that commitment could serve to build reasons for them to affirm liberal institutions. It might even illuminate a path liberals can take to justify the right of liberal institutions to govern theocrats in liberal democracies.

Second, liberals could marshal a complex of related reasons for theocrats to affirm liberalism as part of a larger effort to better relations with theocrats and to demonstrate the appeal that liberal institutions could hold for them. Those reasons will have three central components.

First, the reasons must have a *prudential* component, involving an account of the variety of threats and dangers countries face when ruled under unmitigated theocracy, such as the strong propensity for such polities to pervert the religiosity they mean to promote. This prudential element could also include an articulation of benefits of cooperating with liberal regimes and disadvantages for noncompliance.[81] Second, reasons for theocrats to affirm liberalism will have to have a *theological* element, speaking to such matters as what one rightly can believe God commands of his followers. This component will be crucial, since without it theocrats will have recourse to the claim that neither secular argumentation nor a Rawlsian understanding of public reason overrides the religious dictates that God has given them.[82] Third, the reasons must have a *conciliatory* component, according to which liberal government will need to show its willingness and its ability to develop a friendlier disposition even to theocratic religiosity and religious forms. One way to demonstrate this flexibility would be to grant semisovereignty to theocratic communities in liberal democracies, provided that those communities meet some general criteria such as respecting basic human rights, sound educational criteria, and rights of exit. Another way would be to behave more carefully and respectfully when it comes to religious practice and polities internationally. For it will be important for liberalism authentically to affirm religiosity, not just to tolerate religion, if there is to be any real advance on the moral and prudential problems I have identified.

Third, along with a careful consideration of theocratic commitments and the reasons there may be for theocrats to affirm a liberal order, a solution to the challenges of theocracy will involve institutional innovation. As a first step here, it will be important to consider a broad range of possible structures of governance for ambitious and retiring theocrats. Without a broad consideration of this kind, it remains premature to conclude, for example, that only a modus vivendi between theocrats and liberals is possible, or that liberal government can never rightfully govern theocrats, or that liberal government has no right to apply its laws to theocrats other than that given by the sword. I have suggested above that one piece in this institutional puzzle will be a well-formed schema for handling retiring theocratic communities, as a way of addressing the moral and political problems that those theocrats raise. The option of semisovereignty for theocratic communities could free retiring theocrats from a range of injustices to which they are currently subject, properly respecting their moral right to religious free exercise and enlivening the liberal commitment to religious freedom as well. A second step toward solving the institutional components of this puzzle will be to fill in the missing standard for admissible discourse in public reason and, in particular, to clarify the kinds of religious reasons admissible in public debate. This latter problem has not been handled well, unfortunately, and its presence does liberals and liberal government no favors. The lack of an adequate, well-reasoned, and publicly accessible standard by which to handle religious contributions to public debate has alienated growing numbers of ambitious theocrats from liberalism and its trademark values and institutions, threatening the very stability and legitimacy of the liberal order.

Current liberal theory has made little effort to try to show the appeal of liberalism to theocrats, perhaps because of the relatively recent belief that liberalism must not only be neutral toward reasonable conceptions of the good but also justified in terms of secular reasoning alone. This was not the approach of primogenitors of liberalism, such as Thomas Hobbes and John Locke; those theorists were keen to try to provide a religious ground for their political theories, one that could appeal to a broad range of religious devotees.[83] The extent to which Hobbes and Locke were themselves Christians or authentic believers in the religious arguments they advanced is an independent question. The point is that both understood that religious devotees might well only be reached with arguments that speak to their deeply held religious values, and so they engaged religiosity at that level, considering problems in the interpretation of scripture, arguing that apparent religious differences between Christians are not as great as they may seem and working to provide a religious justification for the political institutions and frameworks they advocated. Indeed, theological efforts such as these were once perennial, blooming colorfully in the liberal gardens of John Stuart Mill, Lord Acton, Bernard Bosanquet, and Thomas Hill Green.

Liberals, however, have largely abandoned the attempt to provide reasons for problematic religious devotees to affirm a liberal order. What accounts for liberalism's movement away from Hobbes and Locke in this regard? While this, too, is a complex and difficult question, one notices that liberal theory currently is marked by the refusal even to engage with philosophical or theological political visions advanced under religious conceptions of the good, especially those visions of the nonliberal or illiberal variety. A number of liberal theorists now assume, or argue explicitly, that no engagement with theological matters is required for a full-flowered liberal theory sufficiently broad to handle the range of persons and conceptions of the good to which it is meant to apply. Jeff Spinner-Halev reflects that liberals and multiculturalists may simply "have little sympathy for the reasons why people are religious," insofar as many of those theorists assume that religion is in the end just another obstacle to human progress.[84] Along with Spinner-Halev, Robert Audi and William Galston stand among the handful of liberals who have considered the value of arguments for more extreme religious devotees to affirm liberal institutions; their sensitive efforts count among only a few exceptions to the rule.[85]

CONCLUSION

Contemporary liberal theorists have done well to build on the secular elements of early liberal and protoliberal arguments, and liberals have as a result produced some powerful political theories for modern constitutional democracies. However, liberalism's response to one of the most serious challenges of simple pluralism amounts to a qualified failure. Here, one must give some credit to those critics of liberalism who have voiced concern that the laws of liberal polities are based on fiat rather than on consensus or sound moral and political principles.[86] Some such critics maintain that liberalism proves in the end to be just another partisan doctrine, one giving priority to more autonomous conceptions of the good and disadvantaging others, including those conceptions that may not even be inimical to liberalism and liberal institutions. Other critics have gone so far as to prophesy gloom and doom for liberal polities, suggesting that liberalism's partisan nature will be its downfall. I fear that the critics are correct, to the extent that they have noticed that the actual practices of liberal governments often are not morally justified and insofar as critics have realized that citizens of liberal polities could come to see that the ideals of liberty and equality have not been promoted fairly within their countries. The good news is that none of it suffices to show that theocrats are in fact correct to deny politically liberal values. For that matter, the shortcomings do not indicate that no version of liberalism could properly meet the challenge of handling its theocratic citizens in an appropriate way, and neither is it obvious that liberalism could hold no appeal for theocrats.

A sustained treatment of the moral failures of liberalism is worth pursuing for moral reasons, but such a treatment also holds the promise of attenuating the significant prudential and political problems that I have outlined in this chapter. If in fact there are reasons for theocrats to affirm a liberal order, the communication of those reasons, articulated and voiced in suitable ways,[87] should help to mitigate the prudential problems caused by insurgent theocrats and extremist third parties. After all, theocrats have been inflamed by what they take to be the dearth of reasons for them to affirm liberal institutions and laws and for a liberal order to apply its laws to them. Steps forward of the sort I have proposed in this chapter could be of some help, and they could serve to head off the most extreme prudential problem I have identified here, namely, the widespread perception of the illegitimacy of liberal institutions, fostered by the perception of the mistreatment of theocrats and promoted by the ongoing conflict between theocrats and liberal government.

Of course, shoring up the failures of liberalism by providing adequate, accessible, and acceptable reasons for theocrats to affirm a liberal order will not solve all the problems associated with zealotry in the world, nor would it easily harmonize the values and practices of reclusive theocrats with those of other citizens in a well-formed liberal order. It would be unrealistic to hold that the provision of such reasons will suffice to quell all religious discord, if only because new theocratic groups continually burgeon forth in democratic societies as new flora in the simple pluralistic array. Nor do I wish to suggest that it would be desirable or reasonable to expect theocrats and liberals ultimately to converge on a shared conception of the good; conflict and disagreement are important conditions of politics itself, and free societies will never do away entirely with political and participatory discordance. Rather, the point is that theocrats' objections to liberalism appear to be serious and profound but the conundrum is not rationally irresolvable. It is still too early to suggest that the attempt to provide reasons for theocrats to affirm a liberal order can only fail to mitigate the prudential problems associated with the legacy of theocracy in democratic polities.

It is the liberal's charge to face the challenges of theocracy in the spirit of his primogenitors in order to renew the liberal project. Perhaps now more than ever, liberal theory needs a sound argument as to why theocratic religious practitioners have good reason to affirm liberalism and liberal institutions, based on arguments *for them*, run on premises that theocrats should accept and that they might even find appealing. To make this argument, liberals will do well to treat the problems of theocracy with public reasons, respectful dialogue, and institutional innovation. This shall form the heart of a liberalism of conscience. The renewal of the liberal project will require such work, despite the aversion to such endeavors in contemporary liberalism. The promise of such efforts is a new dawn for liberalism; the failure to respond shall mean not just persistent moral disappointment but, one fears, possible political disaster.

2. Liberalism and the Liberty of Conscience

IN CHAPTER 1, I OUTLINED AND DESCRIBED four special moral problems pertaining to ambitious and retiring theocrats dwelling within liberal democracies. I suggested that, first, no appropriate legal standard has yet been devised for dealing with theocratic communities and, second, the grounds on which liberal government may govern theocrats have not yet been properly articulated. The third moral problem I identified was that theocrats are still owed an explanation as to why liberal government has a right to regulate their behavior. The fourth, I proposed, is that an explanation to this effect, and for a particular standard under which to treat theocrats and theocratic communities, should be provided in terms that theocrats should accept. I defer treatment of the first three questions to chapters 3 and 4. In this chapter, I focus on the question with which I concluded chapter 1: is there reason for theocrats living within modern constitutional democracies to affirm liberal institutions?

I aim to answer this difficult question affirmatively by demonstrating that there are reasons for theocrats to endorse liberal institutions whether or not they live within liberal democracies. I begin by considering the way in which theocrats view liberal institutions: those institutions do not appeal to theocrats, I suggest, insofar as theocrats do not believe them to be as valuable as particular nonliberal or illiberal religious forms of governance. If one accepts some of the theocrat's more reasonable values as a starting point, I argue, secular arguments designed to identify reasons for persons to affirm liberalism and its institutions simply will not reach theocrats. To address this problem, I provide a novel theological argument that proceeds on grounds familiar to theocrats and that there is reason for them to accept. I plan to demonstrate that theocrats are committed rationally to three principles of liberty of conscience and that the commitment makes it rational for them to support and affirm liberal institutions. Further, I argue that liberalism could be made more appealing to theocrats as well, with the liberal commitment to freedom of conscience clarified and modified and if liberals take a fresh approach to conceptualizing and promulgating liberal principles, institutions, and law.

ELEMENTS OF REASONS

I wish to flag at the outset the classic divide between reason and appeal, which many writers ignore, since it is important to distinguish the two for a discussion of the compatibility of theocrats, their values, and liberal institutions. I mean to point out the following difference: some things that a person finds appealing have that appeal for no good reason, and sometimes a person has good reason to find something appealing but simply does not. This distinction, which ought not to strike anyone as remarkable, holds with respect to actions, desires, aims, choices, and endorsements, among other things.

There exist happy occasions where reason and appeal do not grate against each other: the prospects of that which there is most reason for one to do, one also finds appealing. Yet it is not always the case that reason and appeal harmonize well. A man may have good reason to stop drinking alcohol entirely, but that does not imply that the idea appeals to him or that he would willingly change his ways without a struggle. In the same way, a charismatic figure may appeal greatly to a voter, so that the voter finds him attractive, charming, and worth supporting, but where that candidate's policies are half-baked or confused or where another candidate would better serve the voter's interests, the voter may struggle with reasons she has to support that politician over another. Here, I do not mean to highlight the distinction between that which motivates action and reasons that in fact ground actions.[1] That distinction is important, but it is not the one that I wish to emphasize here. For I am concerned not only to discuss the reasons for theocrats to affirm liberal institutions but also to consider the actual prospects of making liberalism more appealing to theocrats, which I shall not take to be implied by the fact that reasons exist for theocrats to endorse liberal institutions.[2] To avoid confusion, I shall bring into sharp relief reasons for theocrats to affirm liberal institutions and the appeal that liberalism presently has for them. I aim not only to depict the differences between the two but also to show the bearing they may have on each other.

THE THEOCRAT'S ASSESSMENT OF LIBERALISM

Theocrats believe deeply in otherworldly powers and ends, such that disabusing them of the notion that such powers exist and are valuable would be very difficult indeed. But theocratic conceptions of the good also seem to be fundamentally at odds with those of liberals and other "reasonable" persons,[3] bringing forth a conflict of commitments and values for which there is no rational solution. In chapter 1, I argued that liberal political theorists and government alike have failed to provide adequate explanations justifying interference in theocrats' ways of life. I proposed furthermore that liberal political philosophers have failed to provide reasons for theocrats to affirm liberal institutions, inasmuch as liberals have not yet provided arguments that speak to theocrats' most central and pressing concerns. I noted that various theorists propose that government should seek a mere modus vivendi with uncommon and problematic religious devotees, given the seemingly fundamental and irreconcilable conflict between theocratic and liberal conceptions of the good. Proponents of modus vivendi maintain that not only is there no way to show people like theocrats the appeal in liberalism and liberal institutions but also there simply is no reason for theocrats to accept liberalism, if one takes their values and commitments seriously.

I also distinguished between ambitious and retiring theocrats in chapter 1 and emphasized the fact that theocrats are found across quite dissimilar religious traditions. Theocrats such as the Satmar Hasidim, the Amish, and the Pueblo Indians all exist in contemporary America, and theocratic communities exist as well in many other countries where government allows at least a modicum of freedom of association and does not attempt to stamp out liberty of conscience. Nor is there any shortage of ambitious theocrats in the modern world: ambitious theocrats continually spring up in liberal democracies and in other polities and regions around the globe. Some ambitious theocrats have made their presence known in recent years by attacking liberal institutions using violent means; they stand sharply in contrast to the pacifistic Amish and their peaceful theocratic communities. Given this broad diversity across theocrats, what is it that allows one to classify these various groups, communities, and movements together? How are they suitably similar, given that their differences are so immediately apparent? Is the category of "theocrat" merely a poorly defined, arbitrary catchall for phenomena that are more importantly different than they are the same?

Despite their theological, cultural, organizational, and historical differences, theocrats are alike inasmuch as they believe deeply in otherworldly powers and endeavor to achieve otherworldly ends. Their ends vary, since some theocrats seek salvation while others hope for a particular afterlife or a noble rebirth but all hold in common a belief in the existence and extreme importance of ends of this kind. For my purposes here, I shall take the theocrat's commitment to otherworldly values as given. I proceed this way for two reasons: first, to disavow the reasonableness of the theocrat's belief in otherworldly values, one may have to show cause against God's existence or the existence of otherworldly powers more generally. It is not at all obvious that one could accomplish such a task, and I simply will not attempt it here.[4] Second, to deny that it is reasonable to place value in otherworldly powers and ends would be to deny the fact of reasonable pluralism.[5] Many citizens of modern democratic polities, not only theocrats, believe in some manner of otherworldly powers and wish to practice their religion as a corollary to their convictions. I do not intend to attack their beliefs here, for it seems to be reasonable to believe in such things, in the sense that one can affirm religious beliefs and practices as part of a reasonable comprehensive doctrine.[6] I reserve the right, however, to examine the extent to which theocrats may properly subscribe to strict, religious governance, given their belief in otherworldly powers and other basic commitments they may hold. From this point, therefore, I shall begin, taking no quarrel with the value of putative otherworldly powers and ends, assuming that it is reasonable for one to believe in such things, and understanding that separating the theocrat from his commitment to those values would be very difficult indeed.

WHAT REASON IS THERE FOR THEOCRATS TO AFFIRM LIBERAL INSTITUTIONS?

Is there reason for theocrats to affirm liberal institutions?[7] The answer to this question might seem as though it will have to disappoint. It may be the sort of question that, as Isaiah Berlin said, not only do we not know the answer but also we have no clue even as to how to address. For theocrats certainly appear to hold values fundamentally at odds with those of almost any liberal. Nor does liberal government treat theocrats all that well: existing legal standards used to handle theocrats are ill conceived, and government's tendency is either to ignore theocrats or to abrade their religious practices. A close examination of the treatment of American theocratic communities testifies to this fact. Liberal government is an unhappy fact of life for theocrats living in contemporary Western democracies, a rocky *pis aller* for zealous religious devotees, and little seems to bind the theocrat to liberal governance and institutions other than weak instrumental and prudential reasons to abide the law.

To uncover the reasons that exist for theocrats to affirm liberal institutions, one needs first to examine the benefits liberal government can provide to theocrats. I shall identify three such benefits here. Liberal government, first of all, protects theocrats from the physical harms of religious persecution. In this, liberalism delivers on one of its most cherished promises: as a theory of government stepping forward out of the Reformation's religious wars and revolutions, liberalism cultivates religious toleration and holds it dear. Liberal government prohibits hateful groups and individuals from persecuting members of religious communities because of a commitment to protecting religious liberty, as well as an understanding that persons ought not to be harmed by other citizens simply because of religious differences. One would think that this basic protection surely gives some reason for theocrats to endorse liberal institutions: after all, theocrats are often unpopular with others, thought of as strange, ungodly, or deeply misguided, even threatening. One might thus expect that theocrats could agree that protection from persecution is an important good furnished by liberal government. Here, the actions of religious practitioners are telling: since the Puritans departed for America, many uncommon religious communities have fled to burgeoning liberal democracies in search of a place to practice religion without molestation.

Beyond protecting religious practitioners from straightforward persecution, liberal government gives its citizens building blocks of religious free exercise. Liberal governments refrain from invading or impeding religious practices to the extent that is characteristic of other kinds of government. This is a second benefit that liberalism provides to theocrats. Liberal government also protects theocratic communities from proselytizing religious groups bent on invading and converting particular theocrats to a different way of life. This is a third benefit. Neither of these last two provisions by government amounts simply to protecting theocrats from physical harm, but the absence of such measures must surely count as deleterious to the theocrat's religious practices. Government has not perfectly provided these protections, it is true: the world's constitutional democracies have a tarnished record in this respect, being at times overzealous in their legal invasion of minority religious practices and at others insufficiently attentive to the harms caused to uncommon religious practitioners by citizens at large.[8] Nonetheless, liberal government holds a commitment to protecting religious practice even though it has gone astray at times and despite the fact that the commitment to fostering and protecting religious liberty could be better realized than it is at present.

Could the tolerance that liberal government brings to bloom provide reason for ambitious or retiring theocrats to affirm liberal institutions? This is a difficult question indeed. Consider first whether theocrats value toleration for its own sake, or whether it is merely an instrumental value in their eyes, and what is at stake in that regard. If theocrats were to value toleration for its own sake, one expects that it would be deeply appealing to them and so, perhaps, would be liberal institutions. Theocrats such as the Amish might be thought to hold a general principle of toleration close to heart, but the appeal of such a principle even for them is limited, since there exists no wish on any theocrat's part to see the principle universalized.[9] For theocrats do not believe in tolerating religious difference within their communities, whatever else they believe. If they did, they would not be theocrats in the way that I have characterized the term above and as common usage of the term implies.

Basic toleration is important to theocrats because it provides them with the opportunity to pursue their strict and uncommon religious ways of life and it gives them the ability to honor otherworldly powers and to try to achieve valued otherworldly ends by so doing. Toleration is necessary for the Christian theocrat's attempt to achieve salvation: without it he may not be able to perform any of his important religious practices and rituals at all. But just because religious toleration may be necessary for achieving otherworldly ends does not mean that there is reason for theocrats to conceive of it as deeply valuable. Nor does it imply that there is reason for theocrats to value toleration as itself part of the good life for persons. Institutions fostering toleration may be necessary for the achievement of the theocrat's higher ends, but it is unclear whether the value of those institutions extends any further, at least as far as the theocrat is concerned. In this the theocrat makes no mistake: it is plausible to think that some things understood to be necessary for the good life are not themselves part of it. Aristotle famously placed slaves in this category, contending that whereas slaves are necessary for the best polity to exist, they are not part of that polity per se. "The truth of the matter," writes Aristotle, "is that we cannot consider all who are necessary conditions of the state's existence as citizens."[10] Slavery may not be an institution of which the modern sensibility is very fond, but Aristotle's suggestion makes the point well: the mere fact that something may be necessary for the good life does not go to show that it is part of it. The fact that liberal government promotes and enforces toleration in its body politic does not ipso facto give the theocrat reason to affirm liberal institutions.

One way to try to demonstrate the reasons there are for theocrats to affirm liberal institutions would be to point out that liberal government is proficient at providing protection to theocratic communities. But a better way to illuminate the reasons for theocrats to affirm liberal institutions would be to point out how superior liberal government happens to be when it comes to ensuring toleration of religious practices. This is a weighty point: other forms of government, such as communism or fascism, or authoritarian regimes generally, or polities that incorporate a strong religious establishment, value religious toleration insufficiently at best. After all, the flight of religious practitioners to the American colonies, to Canada, and to other liberal democracies surely is no accident. In addition, one notes that many religious devotees continue to live in liberal democratic countries instead of heading elsewhere, as many theocrats have declared themselves prepared to do.[11] Communist countries work to exterminate religion; polities with strong religious establishments or civic religion often try to dissolve theocratic groups; and strongly authoritarian governments provide an unstable basis for toleration, since theocrats can appear unable or unwilling to acknowledge the superiority of the state or officials may view theocrats as a threat to established authority for other reasons.[12] None of these forms of government is committed to the value of religious free exercise; indeed, each embodies values that do not look favorably on religious pluralism. Of the wide variety of theories of government on which polities are based, only those countries that adopt liberal values and build liberal institutions seem able to protect religious diversity consistently and well.

Now, the theocrat might easily agree that liberal government better provides protections for religious practice than do communist or authoritarian regimes. The theocrat also may not take issue with the value of the three protections as I have described them, whether or not he accepts that existing liberal structures provide each of the protections especially well. Granting these two points for the sake of argument, the problem remains that reason for theocrats to place value in liberal institutions is still wanting. For theocrats might deny that there is any good reason to settle for life in a polity where a variety of comprehensive doctrines and conceptions of the good life are found. Particularly zealous theocrats can and do claim as much. Those theocrats propose that even if liberal government and institutions are best under conditions of pluralism, such government nevertheless stands as a solution for an inferior social construct, one that is fallen and ungodly, simply the best sort of government available in very nonideal conditions. For *theocracy* can properly provide each of the protections required, these theocrats aver, and that way of governing by its very nature is not tolerant of religious diversity. Theocracy and theocratic institutions provide a much preferable alternative to liberalism, since: (a) that mode of governance is consistent with that which the theocrat believes his religious doctrine requires; (b) religious authorities are empowered in accordance with the dictates of religious doctrine; (c) theocracy allows or requires that particular institutions of government are to be constructed according to the theocrat's doctrine, instead of stipulating that the institutions of government should be disestablished or secular; and (d) government is more godly as a result of its impermissiveness, enforcing and maintaining rule as religious doctrine commands. And so to the especially zealous theocrat's mind, even if liberal government were the best kind to have under conditions of irremediable pluralism, its institutions would not therefore be the best to employ.

If theocratic polities were effective at providing the protections necessary for the pursuit of the theocrat's conception of the good, reasons for him to value liberal institutions could prove to be very limited indeed. But theocracy is not effective in that endeavor: theocratic governance fails to protect devout religious practitioners from persecution, instead putting them in jeopardy of that very fate. First of all, the risk of persecution certainly exists for members of theocratic polities who dissent from established doctrine and religious authority. Consider what occurs where theocrats change their beliefs about the instructions of their religious doctrine, while religious authorities remain fixed and consistent in their understanding of religious teachings. Those dissenting from the religious conception of the good that government enforces, however sincerely they may do so, will be forced to comply with the authorities' understanding of their doctrine, or they will face punishment or correction. Historical cases from a variety of religious traditions show how punishments for heresy or apostasy under theocracy are often harsh.[13] Theocratic authorities punish dissenters in a variety of ways, depending on the particular religious doctrine they exalt: theocratic Islamic regimes such as the Taliban in Afghanistan stoned, shot, flogged, and dismembered dissenters and unbelievers, whereas earlier Christian theocrats burned heretics at the stake. The very logic of theocracy is such that its institutions endeavor to promote strict observance, and this has serious practical consequences for those who do not agree with the authoritative vision.

There is a second way in which theocratic polities prove ineffective at providing necessary protections for their members' pursuit of the good. It is evidenced in the propensity for a defect in government to lead to the ascension of wayward and illegitimate authorities.[14] In such cases it is theocratic subjects who remain constant in their beliefs while the conceptions of governmental authorities change in some way. Alterations on the part of religious authorities may occur sincerely, where authorities authentically believe that they must amend the existing conception of the good promoted in their community, or changes may be motivated by no sincere wish to ameliorate spiritual conditions in the polity, as where theocratic authority becomes corrupt or where an empowered despot makes subjects "victims of his suspicions."[15] In either of these two situations, theocratic subjects risk persecution at the hands of authorities since they end up at odds with new practices or beliefs strictly enforced. As these occurrences are hardly without lengthy historical precedent, there is further reason for theocrats to hold that theocracy puts them at serious risk of oppression.

Pointing out the ways in which theocracy places theocrats at risk of persecution may go some distance to providing a strong prudential reason for the theocrat to accept and affirm liberal institutions. For it appears not only that liberal institutions may be the best ones to shield religious free exercise in pluralistic societies but also that theocracy does not provide the protections from persecution that its members need. But this argument does not take one very far, since the theocrat is able to contend that the problem of corruption is overstated and that those who depart from religious doctrine, in thought or in action, *should* be silenced, corrected, or punished otherwise. On corruption, theocrats can easily suggest that even though such depravity would be undesirable, a failed attempt to live under godly theocratic governance is better than survival under the regulation of a liberal polity. Seyyid Qutb lays groundwork for a proposal of this sort where he contends that only Islamic and *jahili* (i.e., ignorant) societies exist and claims that all the latter are "unIslamic and unlawful."[16] On the matter of punishment, the theocrat may readily admit that, regrettably, some stray from the path to salvation. But the theocrat can add that those persons ought to have their actions curtailed, on the grounds that the faithful require protection both from outsiders who would rob theocrats of their religion as well as from those who hold dissenting or heretical views within theocratic communities. Here the theocrat provides a strong response to T. M. Scanlon, who maintains that while there will be disagreements in "any society, no matter how homogeneous," those who disagree "must somehow live together."[17] Quite to the contrary, the theocrat may retort, those who dissent from the dictates of established religious authorities will need to be brought into line, rightly facing a range of possible punishments ranging from separation or excommunication to capital punishment, as religious doctrine requires.

One might try to respond here by insisting that there is a fact of pluralism as such, which is to say, with John Rawls, that a simple plurality of conceptions of the good is "a permanent feature of the public culture of democracy."[18] If simple pluralism is a permanent and inescapable condition, does that not provide a strong reason for theocrats to affirm liberal institutions? And could it not also be a source of appeal for them? Unfortunately, the permanence of pluralism is unhelpful in this regard. First of all, the fact of simple pluralism does not speak to the issue of a theocratic polity in which very little pluralism exists; theocrats may just wish to eradicate pluralism as far as possible within their theocratic polity. Islamic theocrats have worked toward this end in Iran, Malaysia, Turkmenistan, and Afghanistan under the Taliban. Second, the fact that numerous comprehensive doctrines exist in democratic polities in which ambitious and retiring theocrats are ensconced does not furnish any reason for theocrats to affirm liberal institutions, even were liberal institutions the only ones able to provide the protections necessary for theocrats to practice their religion under such conditions. For the theocrat still may hold a deep dislike for pluralism even where he realizes that it is inescapable, viewing the political order that protects religious liberty in pluralistic polities as a very distant second-best solution to the question of how to live on earth. Furthermore, he may see no reason to accept the full legitimacy of liberal governance if he believes the protections of its institutions to provide only a modus vivendi.[19] Where theocrats lack reasons other than prudential ones to affirm liberal institutions, governing structures that allow them to practice their religion without fear of outright persecution simply will not yield reason enough to value those institutions deeply. The mere fact that simple pluralism is inescapable can hardly inspire the theocrat to exalt liberal institutions or to enjoy his religious freedom on his own terms; instead, existence in such circumstances will be construed as a prison term in a liberal penitentiary, and one that the theocrat will not suffer gladly.

With this, the hopes of providing theocrats with reason to affirm liberal institutions flicker; for it looks as though the arguments are exhausted. In each case, the theocrat has a response showing how the ratiocination fails with respect to the existing commitments that he holds, at best acknowledging only weak prudential reasons to endorse liberal institutions. In his rejection of the arguments proffered to him, it is not obvious that the theocrat is irrational, even if one were to slight him by calling him unreasonable. For the theocrat's religious conception of the good identifies values and ends quite different from those the liberal upholds; their dismissals of the arguments made above reflect theocrats' differing commitments and the high priority they give to the otherworldly powers and ends they aim to achieve.

The failed case I have discussed thus far consists of secular arguments aimed to deliver reasons for theocrats to affirm liberal institutions. I certainly have not here cataloged or articulated all the secular arguments that could be given. I have described, however, perhaps the best cases that secular argumentation provides, and one fears that its arguments may not be able to reach the goal sought here. I have suggested that the value of toleration ought to be considered important for theocrats because government committed to that value is the sort that best protects theocrats and their communities from infiltration or outright persecution, even if one accepts that the historical record is tarnished in that regard. But the argument does not suffice to show that there is reason for the theocrat to affirm liberal institutions or that such institutions should hold appeal for him, since the theocrat maintains that theocratic institutions can achieve the same goals as government committed to liberal values in a more godly and pious manner. I have also proposed that theocracy does not effectively prevent the persecution of theocrats within religious communities because it allows for the punishment of such crimes as heresy or apostasy, but to such procedures the theocrat takes no objection, so long as those punishments are consistent with the demands of faith. Further, I have argued that theocracy falters in its aim to prevent political corruption or to check its political institutions. This latter point may go some distance toward providing the theocrat with reason to affirm liberal institutions, but alone it is not sufficiently robust to reach that destination. The theocrat has a response for each of the secular concerns raised here, from within his religious commitments. Without some furtherance or complement for the secular case, the hope of providing theocrats with reasons to affirm liberal institutions seems slight.

THE THEOLOGICAL ARGUMENT

I aim to provide reasons for theocrats to affirm liberal institutions on grounds they should accept, without circumscribing or casting aside their most basic otherworldly aspirations and assumptions. Here, I wish to provide a new and different argument for theocrats, one that proceeds more properly on theological grounds. I distinguish the following argument as theological since it proceeds from each theocrat's most basic otherworldly assumptions rather than progressing from secular premises that conflict with theocrats' religious suppositions regarding the nature of otherworldly powers and their deep value.[20] Instead of eliding, attacking, or ignoring the religious values that theocrats hold dear, I shall provide an argument that grants from the outset their importance, to show how, on the theocrat's own terms, there exist good reasons for him to affirm liberal institutions.

A claim of this nature will be met with immediate resistance. Surely, it will be said, one cannot provide a theological argument that rests on grounds acceptable to all theocrats, since no such grounds exist. The fact of pluralism as such implies that the religious doctrines of different theocrats are neither reducible to one particular reasonable comprehensive doctrine nor able to be boiled down to a common set of unreasonable beliefs, religious or otherwise.[21] The wide variety of ambitious and retiring theocrats testifies to the fact of simple pluralism since the different groups are organized around what appear to be fundamentally different and irreducible religious doctrines that confirm, in places, what other religious doctrines deny. The Pueblo Indians just do not adhere to the same religious doctrine as the Satmar Hasidim, evangelical Protestants, or the Nation of Islam, one might remark. Members of those various communities do not share the same conception of the good: they vary on most aspects of their religion, from their beliefs about the nature of God and otherworldly powers to the practices and prohibitions that they observe. With this in view, how could one construct an argument giving reasons for all theocrats to affirm liberal institutions, when there is such a broad spectrum of theocratic allegiances across the citizens of modern democracies and peoples of the world?

The key to making such an argument lies in what is common and peculiar to all theocrats, namely, their advocacy of a theocratic conception of the good. Theocrats certainly vary in the religious doctrines they exalt, and their practices and beliefs differ widely, but they converge on this point at least: theocrats all support governance in which a strict, comprehensive, and religious conception of the good is prioritized.

Now, it is clear that theocrats adhere strongly to another belief as well, one that is quite reasonable: that otherworldly powers and ends are deeply valuable. I identified and articulated the common importance of this belief for theocrats in the second section of this chapter. But this does not exhaust the common beliefs and commitments of theocrats. Here, I shall pick out two assumptions to which theocrats are committed, in addition to the various beliefs they affirm, regarding the ways in which life can be led. Theocrats assume, first, that people can live wayward, irreligious lives; second, they hold that such paths will not advance people toward valuable otherworldly ends, such as salvation, an afterlife, or a noble rebirth.

These two assumptions require some elaboration. What reason is there to think that every theocrat holds either one? First of all, the possibility of a wayward life must be presupposed in the theocrat's conception of the good because without it there would be no reason for creating institutions designed to cultivate and maintain a strict, religious way of life in some collection of persons. The strictness the theocrat requires has implications: in his view, neither all adherents of the best doctrine necessarily will observe its teachings voluntarily; nor will adherence to doctrine be guaranteed at birth. In this, the theocrat reveals agreement with John Locke's suggestion that: "No Body is born a member of any Church; otherwise the Religion of Parents would descend unto Children, by the same right of Inheritance as their Temporal Estates, and every one would hold his Faith by the same Tenure he does his Lands; than which nothing can be imagined more absurd."[22] The theocrat may not agree with Locke that membership in his religious community is "free and voluntary," but he must be sympathetic to the view that faithful allegiance and adherence to doctrine are not transferred at birth. The theocrat must also hold that people can lose their strength of conviction as well; if unwavering adherence were provided at birth, strict institutions would not be required to keep people on the right religious path. Certainly, not all theocrats must suppose that all people can live wayward lives (for instance, some may wish to make exceptions for rulers, priests, or kings), but the assumption that people could take deficient paths generally must hold for the theocrat with respect to the body of religious practitioners he has in focus.[23]

The theocrat's second assumption is evident in the very purpose of theocratic institutions: theocrats value those institutions because of the higher, otherworldly values toward which they aim. If observance of any number of religious doctrines were able properly to advance otherworldly values and at the correct pace, then any of those doctrines and the institutions they may sanction could be acceptable to any theocrat. But theocrats are strict and exclusive, each demanding adherence to his doctrine rather than another. The theocrat holds that it is important to be intolerant of religious diversity, at least within his theocratic community, because a failure to do so will put salvation at risk or otherwise jeopardize otherworldly values. It is therefore clear that theocrats take as a basic assumption the notion that there is something deficient in the lives of those who depart from the chosen religious path. The theocrat may identify waywardness in atheists and agnostics, in those who are faithful to ungodly or paganistic religious practices, or in people who are not sufficiently religious even though they have the right religious doctrine in view.

Now the theocrat may point out that just because it is possible to live a spiritually deficient life, irreligious or otherwise, that does not mean that he will live in such a way. For example, while the Christian theocrat reconciles himself to the notion that many shall not gain salvation, nevertheless he maintains that such a fate will not necessarily befall him. Lives of sin lead to damnation for the fallen, the theocrat may say, but surely that in no way implies that such a fate awaits him.

This matter requires more careful consideration, however. Could the theocrat not come to be devoted to a deficient doctrine that dishonors otherworldly powers and stultifies his progress toward otherworldly ends? Other things being equal, the answer is unequivocal and in the affirmative. On the theocrat's account, just as many people are moderate in their religious observances and are by that fact inadequate in their religiosity, so many theocrats are devoted to deficient doctrines. A great number of theocrats must be committed to the wrong doctrine altogether: some are devotees of Hinduism, others are Mormons, Satmar Hasidim, or Roman Catholics. People with those religious attachments cannot all be on the right path, in the theocrat's reckoning. And it could be that another religious doctrine entirely is the one that will yield valued otherworldly ends. That the theocrat is strict and not moderate in his observance notably heightens the tension here: if he follows the wrong doctrine to an extreme, he may veer off the spiritual rails and crash more sensationally than if he followed more moderately the same, lacking doctrine. And yet this must be the fate to which so many people around the world are resigned, if theocrats are correct in their assumptions. For the wide variety of plural and irreducible religious doctrines implies not only that not all theocrats do well by otherworldly powers but also that most of them do not. The fact of simple pluralism implies this fate for most theocrats within liberal democracies when only ambitious theocrats and members of reclusive theocratic communities from those countries are considered. When the focus is widened to include the millions of religious practitioners in the world, one sees how practically all theocrats are relegated to this fate. All other things being equal, with the range and diversity of actual and possible religious doctrines available to persons, any particular theocrat has a very low likelihood of being committed to the right one.

The problem of holding an errant religious doctrine is not the only one that the theocrat faces. For it is not just that the theocrat has to have the right doctrine in view; his community must also prioritize the appropriate conception of the good as well. Even if one were to assume that some particular religious doctrine were the one that leads the faithful to Heaven, the details of the particular theocratic conception of the good under that doctrine would still be wanting. For instance, Christian theocracy naturally implies practices and institutions based on some conception of what Christian religious doctrine sanctions or commands. Under Christian doctrine, there is, of course, a fissure between Roman Catholic and Protestant understandings of scriptural teachings, on what institutions a Christian polity requires or allows, and on what Christianity demands of adherents otherwise. For any Roman Catholic or Protestant theocrat, there can and does exist a great variety of claims as to what particular elements Christian conceptions of the good should include.

Consider, for instance, how different theocrats within the Protestant tradition make varying claims on the question of whom to empower politically in a Christian commonwealth. One finds conflicting views across the works of Johannes Calvin, Johannes Althusis, George Buchanan, Richard Baxter, George Lawson, François Hotman, Increase and Cotton Mather, and John Davenport. These are but a few Protestant theocrats who differently detailed how to construct and organize churches, how to pick out spiritual leaders and what role those people should have, how to distinguish between spiritual and secular authority, what laws, in particular, ought to be enforced and what punishments should be given to those who violate them, what professions or employments may be acceptable in quotidian life, what vision of God should be taught to the faithful, what otherworldly ends, exactly, people should try to advance, what practices of prayer and worship ought to be promoted, and so on. Divisions and distinctions on these matters have hardly disappeared. To the contrary, they have changed and proliferated throughout the world, with new theocratic Protestant groups continually popping up in distinction from others. And so even where one could rightly say that two theocratic groups have the same general doctrine in hand, it would be quite another thing to confirm that both communities give priority to the same conception of the good, since there are so many places at which their conceptions of institutions, practices, and ends can vary.

Strict adherence to a wayward religious doctrine or a deficient conception of the good would count among the worst things for the theocrat, given his two assumptions. With the wrong doctrine or conception of the good, the theocrat will find that he has empowered authorities and institutions promoting deficient religious principles and ends. With a flawed doctrine prioritized in a theocratic polity, its teachings pressed and enforced by theocratic authority, the theocrat will have no escape from the chains of depraved institutions and oppressive regulations. In the theocrat's conception, a spiritual disaster of this sort would be the worst thing that could befall him. After all, the theocrat means to dedicate his life to the pursuit of those religious ends that he believes to be most valuable. But where government does not help in that pursuit, theocrats may be led toward disaster, forced to practice a religion that, in their view, God does not favor.

To what extent could the theocrat avoid, mitigate, or resolve these problems? Even if the theocrat were to have assurance that he holds the correct religious conception of the good, he would nevertheless need to ensure that his polity's conception will not become perverted through the corruption of officials, the ascension of a tyrant, or the dereliction of subjects' duties. The theocrat cannot contend that his community could never fall away from grace because of his advocacy of the ongoing strictness that he means to enforce on his fellow subjects. But what is more, there is good reason for him to think that theocratic institutions will not easily fend off corruption: authorities in theocratic polities reprove dissent and try to inculcate an attitude of reverence for authorities and offices, making the practical matter of identifying and thwarting corruption problematic. Here, the examples of contemporary Islamic theocratic polities such as Iran are instructive. Even assuming that theocratic institutions were proficient at preventing or ferreting out corruption, those checks could not provide any assurance that the community would give priority to the appropriate religious conception of the good life. For that issue is temporally prior to the concern about ensuring that corruption does not take hold. If a deficient conception of the good life were given priority and rigorously enforced, then effectively checking authorities, offices, and institutions would ensure strict observance of the wrong practices. A similar problem would exist if a community were to have the wrong doctrine in view. In that case, the specific elements of religious practices, prohibitions, and institutional arrangements would be deficient, and yet no institutional mechanism designed to guarantee the integrity of existing religious practice could be of any assistance. Where religious communities prioritize errant conceptions of the good life, whether or not those conceptions are derived from the right religious doctrine, institutional checks would only ensure that everyone followed that conception.

LIBERTY OF CONSCIENCE: THREE PRINCIPLES

Theocrats clearly seek to avoid at all costs a spiritual disaster, but the institutions of theocracy are of little assistance. Contrary to what one might expect, it appears that theocratic institutions cannot resolve the issue of looming spiritual disaster to the theocrat's satisfaction since they neither provide assurance that the theocrat actually has the correct doctrine or conception of the good life nor effectively check corruption of the religious order within the theocrat's community. And given the fact of pluralism as such, if theocrats are correct in thinking that the path to salvation is narrow, then they will have to concede that members of most theocratic communities are led astray from the outset, forced from youth to observe the religious dictates of an errant tradition, habituated to pursuing practices and observing prohibitions, even to accepting values, that are decidedly ungodly. But how could the theocrat elude or resolve this terrible dilemma? Might there be some way to solve the theocrat's problems on grounds he should accept, drawing on resources from within his commitments? To answer these questions, one must delve down to the understanding of conscience to which the theocrat is committed, that is, to theocrats' presuppositions respecting the nature of conscience and its freedom. The theocrat's drive to avoid spiritual waywardness implies that he is committed rationally to the view that conscience ought to be free to reject false doctrines. The theocrat is committed rationally to the principle that conscience must be free to reject pretenders to the doctrinal throne, and this leads toward a solution to the spiritual dilemma with which he and his community are faced.

Liberty of conscience is an important touchstone for liberals. Concern for freedom of worship and political stability, its concomitant, played an important role in the formation of early liberal views,[24] and an expanded understanding of liberty of conscience remains central for contemporary liberal theory. In *A Theory of Justice*, John Rawls suggests interestingly that the question whether there should be equal liberty of conscience is "settled."[25] In the original position, Rawls proposes, persons could only acknowledge a principle of equal liberty of conscience; that is to say, "[they] cannot take chances with their liberty by permitting the dominant religious or moral doctrine to persecute or suppress others if it wishes."[26] For there would be grave risks attached to denying equal liberty of conscience and wagering that one would be part of a religious majority, Rawls reflects. As he puts it, "to gamble . . . would show that one did not take one's religious or moral convictions seriously."[27]

In *Political Liberalism*, Rawls refers to this point as a "first ground" for liberty of conscience but notes that it does not provide an argument for liberty of conscience per se.[28] He reaffirms the importance of liberty of conscience, however: reasonable people endorse "some form of liberty of conscience," Rawls writes, since those people understand that the burdens of judgment place limitations on what can reasonably be expected to be justified to others.[29] Rawls also adduces a second ground for liberty of conscience in *Political Liberalism*, relating to a person's capacity for a conception of the good. He proposes that if "the liberty to fall into error and to make mistakes" is one of the social conditions necessary for the proper development of a capacity to form, revise, and rationally pursue a conception of the good, then another ground exists for persons to affirm liberty of conscience.[30] The third and final ground Rawls offers for liberty of conscience springs from the relation between deliberative reason and one's way of life. This very relation can become part of a person's determinate conception of the good, Rawls notes, where it is rationally affirmed. Here, the capacity for a conception of the good actually becomes an essential part of a determinate conception, not simply a means to it.[31] In such cases, we may make our individual conceptions of the good "our own," Rawls suggests, and this can hold true even for those who come from conservative or communitarian religious backgrounds and traditions.[32]

Could an argument from the principle of liberty of conscience help to provide the rudiments of reasons for extreme and uncommon religious devotees to affirm liberal institutions? I shall give reason to think that it could, but to detail the special importance of liberty of conscience, it will be useful to provide some basic understanding of the idea of conscience as I refer to it here. An adequate conception of conscience, in the sense relevant to this discussion, must be able to take account of what Roger Williams calls its "Christian . . . Paganish, Jewish, Turkish, or Antichristian" varieties.[33] Conscience could be considered variously as a negative judge of one's actions, as it was with the Greeks;[34] or as a habit or property of the mind, soul, or will; or as a distinct element within the mind or soul, with its own capacities and properties; or as an amalgam of cognition and emotions; or as something else altogether. Thomas Aquinas suggests that conscience is a particular kind of judgment, the sort that one reaches in endeavoring to apply practical principles to specific situations.[35] In that account, conscience differs in most instances where one deliberates, acts, or reflects on one's actions, since it just consists of the judgment at which one arrives in each respective case. I shall employ a broader understanding of conscience than Aquinas's here, instead considering it to be a distinct capacity to identify and bond to notions of what is right and good. I shall remain agnostic as to whether conscience is itself an element of the mind or soul or whether it is an independent faculty otherwise. This formulation allows that conscience could have both cognitive and affective dimensions, but it takes no particular side in that dispute. Furthermore, the formula provides that conscience may be used in judging but also allows for the strong attachments that conscience normally is thought to have the capacity to cultivate. Conscience can be informed and persuaded in this view,[36] and it is within its capacities to bond strongly with a religious or moral doctrine. One can act against conscience, as I understand it, but serious emotional and cognitive obstacles may make such actions difficult.[37] I abbreviate this explanation of the idea of conscience for the sake of the larger argument, but one expects that it neither runs afoul of modern understandings of conscience nor is remarkably contentious otherwise.

I shall not merely suggest here that there is some reason, independent of their various commitments, for theocrats to value freedom of conscience. I propose instead that the theocrat ought to understand that he has a powerful rational commitment to the notion that conscience must be free, given his values and the ends he aims to achieve. But how could it be that theocrats hold such a commitment, when the very notion may strike them as outrageous? Theocrats are strict in their observance, after all, enjoining others in their communities to observe religious practices as well. The theocrat's strictness is evidenced in his condemnation of heresy, apostasy, and other such religious infractions and likewise in is his willingness to use shunning, excommunication or more extreme forms of punishment against refractory community members. Understanding this, why would one expect freedom of conscience to be a value to which theocrats have a commitment of any sort, beyond the weak instrumental value that liberty of conscience may provide for repressive practices?

To demonstrate that the theocrat is committed rationally to the view that conscience must be free, it serves to notice, first of all, that he presupposes that conscience has a *capacity* to be free. The theocrat assumes that conscience has this capacity, inasmuch as he holds that conscience is able to exist apart from the grips of false doctrine. Theocrats realize that other doctrines than their own lay claim to conscience, understanding very well that rival claims to faith or defective interpretations of doctrine could be attractive to fellow adherents. This one infers from the fact that theocrats disallow religious free exercise within their communities, reproving those who may wish to depart from the accepted religious conception of the good. But the theocrat does not appear to hold that conscience inevitably gravitates toward true or false doctrine or that conscience necessarily adheres firmly and permanently to a conception of the good once it arrives. Instead, he holds that conscience could be free to follow that path leading toward valued otherworldly ends. Evidence of this is given in the theocrat's effort to attract potential or burgeoning adherents and in the way that he and his fellow theocrats work to keep members from departing. Had conscience no capacity to be free, that task would be pointless, and the theocrat would not be concerned with it. Theocrats assume that rival claims to faith can for a variety of reasons be rejected by conscience, just as they realize that their own doctrine could be repudiated by fellow devotees. This implies that conscience has the capacity to be free, in the theocrat's view, since no theocrat's conscience would be able to decline the false doctrines and errant conceptions of the good life or reject the best religious doctrine if it were not.

The theocrat presupposes that conscience could be free, therefore, but this has no obvious implication whatsoever for the matter of whether he holds that conscience *should* be free. The fact that one holds that some capacity exists does not mean that one is committed to the view that it should be actualized. One could consistently hold that conscience is free but also maintain that liberty of conscience is something to be suppressed or overcome wherever possible, for instance. In addition to supposing that conscience has the capacity to be free, however, the theocrat also is committed rationally to the normative view that conscience *must* be free. This commitment takes form in three normative principles of liberty of conscience:

Conscience must be free to reject lesser religious doctrines and conceptions of the good (the principle of rejection)

Conscience must be free to accept the good (the principle of affirmation)

Conscience must be free to distinguish between good and bad doctrines and conceptions of the good (the principle of distinction)

These three principles require some elaboration. Consider the first. Conscience must be free to reject false and lesser religious doctrines, just as it must be free to reject inferior conceptions of the good. I call this *the principle of rejection*. A rational commitment binds the theocrat to this principle, for he supposes that conscience ought to be free to reject the full range of wayward and ungodly doctrines that may lay claim to conscience, as well as the many other fallen ways of life into which one could be drawn.[38] If the theocrat were to suppose that conscience ought not to be free or if he were indifferent on the matter, he would show no concern for his deep religious values and seriously risk relegating himself to the spiritual misery that he seeks to avoid. For on the theocrat's terms, most people fail to follow the right religious doctrine, living deficient lives and stultifying their pursuit of otherworldly ends as a result. Conscience must be free to escape that fate, if it is an evil that one should endeavor to eschew.

Here one assumes that the theocrat does not necessarily hold that a constrained or unfree conscience is bad in itself. In that view, the normative requirement that conscience should be forever free would mitigate the strength of the claim that the theocrat's doctrine and conception of the good could make on its adherents. Whether or not any theocrats actually hold such a view, namely, that conscience ought always to remain free, the more challenging case appears to be the one in which theocrats propose that conscience should be free at the outset but may forgo its freedom once the right religious doctrine and conception of the good is confirmed. It is not an implausible view empirically that conscience can confirm and attach itself to comprehensive doctrines in ways that make the bond difficult to break. I have noted that one observes conscience constrained in this sense in devout religious practitioners, inasmuch as they experience great difficulty in separating themselves from their religious beliefs, practices, and communities. Locke makes this point, if in a more emphatic way, in *A Letter Concerning Toleration*. Naturally, the theocrat may take no objection to such attachments. In a qualified view of that sort, conscience would be understood to be rightly free until such time as it commits to the proper conception of the good, with the range of details concerning religious authorities, institutions, and practices that a comprehensive conception implies,[39] all according to the teachings of the appropriate religious doctrine. These are the more difficult cases, so I shall deal with them in what follows, proceeding on the assumption that the theocratic understandings of conscience allow that conscience may, and sometimes ought to, bind strongly to a religious doctrine and conception of the good.

The second normative principle of liberty of conscience I call *the principle of affirmation*. The theocrat is committed rationally to the principle that conscience must be free to accept the right religious doctrine and an appropriate conception of the good related to that doctrine so conceived. In this, freedom of conscience is further implied as a normative principle that strongly holds for him. The theocrat takes on this commitment in supposing that conscience must be free not just from the chains of false doctrine but also to accept and affirm the good. It is a normative principle that conscience must be free to affirm the right religious doctrine and conception of the good, set by the theocrat before himself and his fellow travelers as a principle that a person ought to follow generally, to honor otherworldly values and advance otherworldly ends. For the principle is not just meant to hold for some particular person but for people generally, at least for those who are similarly situated.[40]

Third, the theocrat supposes that conscience must be free to distinguish between the good and other, deficient religious doctrines and conceptions. This supposition serves as the basis of a third normative principle of conscience to which the theocrat is committed rationally, which I call *the principle of distinction*. The theocrat's dedication to the pursuit of particular otherworldly values commits him rationally to the principle that conscience must be free to distinguish among the variety of religious doctrines that simple pluralism implies and to find the good within them. Without this freedom to distinguish before accepting or rejecting doctrines, there would be no way for conscience to pick out the holy from the unholy or the good from the bad, both of which are crucial for the theocrat. That is, one would have little assurance that conscience affirms the doctrine that is properly connected to otherworldly powers and ends if there were no allowance for discrimination among the many competing, contrary doctrines vying to attract conscience in the modern liberal polity and in the world at large. Conscience must be free to distinguish among rival doctrines so that it can refuse the bad and begin to gravitate toward the good. Without that freedom, conscience risks attaching itself to a secular doctrine or an inferior religious doctrine, either of which theocrats would find disastrous. As with the first and second principles outlined above, this principle is also normative, holding for all theocrats, at least across their respective religious communities.

REASON TO AFFIRM LIBERAL INSTITUTIONS

To this point, I have argued that the theocrat is committed rationally both to the notion that conscience has the capacity to be free and to three normative principles of liberty of conscience. Conscience must be free, for the theocrat, to reject errant faiths where they may arise, to gravitate toward the good, and to have the ability to distinguish among competing alternatives. What bearing does this have on the larger question at hand, namely, whether there exist reasons for theocrats to affirm liberal institutions? The answer to this question lies in the matter of what is implied by the theocrat's commitment to normative principles of freedom of conscience. If theocrats are committed rationally to the notion that conscience must be free, there follow important political implications regarding the nature of governing institutions that they can advocate and abide.

A rational commitment to the three principles of liberty of conscience requires theocrats to take political and other institutional matters under consideration. Their commitment to the normative principles would be vapid otherwise, for it is political institutions that protect freedom of conscience, and a refusal to take account of this fact puts religious practice seriously at risk. First, the theocrat's commitment to freedom of conscience implies that, in his view, he requires some measure of liberty in social and political affairs. What does this mean? If theocrats find the best religious doctrine they will naturally need to practice the teachings of that doctrine as a matter of honoring otherworldly powers and advancing otherworldly ends. Furthermore, in order for conscience to gravitate toward the good, religious practice will need to be permitted in a polity; otherwise, conscience will not have exposure to religious doctrine and will have no way to accept or reject it accordingly. Now, some authoritarian polities do not allow for any form of religious practice, so those political orders the theocrat must avoid. Communist conceptions of the good life disavow the claims of religious practitioners, viewing religion as merely indicative of a defect, an unfortunate outgrowth of problems at the level of forces of production.[41] Anyone committed to the principle that conscience must be free to accept the best religious doctrine will have to reject those political theories and institutional arrangements that disallow religious practice altogether. Not all conceptions of the good life are religious, one must remember, and not all are friendly to religion. Whereas communistic and other authoritarian orders may take on a similar guise to theocratic polities, nevertheless they are fundamentally distinct in their nonreligious views of how life should be lived, in their lack of a strict and comprehensive religious doctrine, and in their hostility toward religious practice.

A commitment to the three normative principles of freedom of conscience disallows one from sanctioning or endorsing authoritarian ways of life such as communism.[42] But that is not all that such a commitment implies. In the theocrat's case, his commitment also requires that conscience be free to reject errant faiths and conceptions of the good with which people may be presented. The theocrat must therefore avoid political arrangements forcing him to conform to the teachings and practices of inferior religious doctrines. If the theocrat were to be subject to the institutional authority of a polity with a strong, single religious establishment, for example, one that did not allow for the pursuit of any religious conception of the good except for that sanctioned by government, he would find himself unable to meet this requirement. For the institutions and authorities of such a polity would not allow theocrats to disown the exalted doctrine in the event that they may determine it to be deficient and would thereby violate the principle of rejection.[43] Such institutional arrangements would also violate the principle of affirmation, because they would not allow one to move toward any other religious conception of the good life than that which authorities sanction. Also unsatisfactory would be polities allowing their subjects to have latitude in their beliefs on condition that they refrain from practicing religious rituals and execute practices of political allegiance instead. Those polities might not incorporate institutions that run afoul of the principle of distinction, but they would fail to allow the theocrat to gravitate toward the good. For the theocrat's religion embodies practices and does not just consist of otherworldly beliefs; under institutions that do not permit them to worship freely, theocrats will not have religious freedom in the way they require, even if they are ostensibly free to hold their beliefs without formal reprisal. Theocrats could reasonably view such requirements as tantamount to a demand that they follow another religion altogether, under government that they may well consider worse than anarchy.[44] Polities with strong religious establishments and those with other types of authoritarian institutions and structures violate the principles of liberty of conscience to which each theocrat is committed rationally and therefore must be excluded as unacceptable modes of governance on their very terms.

But in this there is a heightened concern. Under theocracy, those who try to diverge from the authoritative conception of the good risk denunciation and censure, facing punishment for heresy, apostasy, and other religious crimes. The theocratic polity does not allow subjects to reject, without punishment, its religious institutions, values, and ways; nor does it permit subjects to gravitate toward other religious practices and convictions so long as they live within the grasp of the polity's institutions. This appears to violate the principle of rejection to which theocrats have a strong, analytically prior commitment. Does this mean that there can be no theocracy for theocrats?

It would certainly be a curious result if it were to turn out that prior theocratic commitments require theocrats to disavow theocracy. That would seem to imply that all theocrats simply are confused in the various commitments they hold or that theocrats' adherence to freedom of conscience, a strict, religious conception of the good, and otherworldly values forms a strange and disjointed piece. Nothing that I have suggested here supports such a conclusion, however. For while the theocrat's commitment to freedom of conscience requires him to avoid theocratic polities, nevertheless he could consistently endorse theocratic government for smaller religious communities internal to a larger polity, provided that surrounding political institutions and mechanisms were to protect liberty of conscience to an extent that satisfies his three normative principles. A measure of liberty, consistent with the various principles and commitments of theocrats, would permit theocratic strictness within a wide array of communities. It could also allow for the rejection of faith, the gravitation of conscience toward the good, and the freedom to distinguish authentic from fraudulent or irreligious doctrines and rulers. Religious authorities of theocratic communities would not be able to have complete political or legal autonomy if their governance were to harmonize with the principles I have described. But no wish for complete autonomy is implied by the nature of the theocrat's otherworldly commitments, and complete autonomy for theocratic communities would not be justified for other reasons independent of the theocrat's particular beliefs and commitments.

Here one might object that it is simply not true that liberalism and liberal institutions are the only ones that there is reason for the theocrat to affirm. Whether or not liberal institutions can uphold the three normative principles of liberty of conscience, the objector may claim, another form of government than those discussed above, such as a polity with more than one established religion, could do equally well or better than liberal institutions at abiding and supporting the theocrat's commitments. A multiple establishment of religion would involve government in favoring and supporting several religious communities, so it could appear to do very well by the three principles of liberty of conscience. But multiple establishment cannot suffice to meet the theocrat's requirements, for a polity with a multiple religious establishment need not guarantee the liberty of persons to reject their faith, and so it would not reliably uphold the principle of rejection. What is more, minority groups often are not well treated under multiple establishments. Theocrats tend to be viewed with mistrust or are unpopular with citizens at large, as various examples of historical persecution show. Furthermore, polities with multiple religious establishments can have those establishments change with the natural competition arising among different religious groups. Where those polities tend toward the establishment of a single religious doctrine or a strong civil religion, the theocrat will be faced with the particular problems of a single establishment mentioned above. And so there is reason to doubt that a polity with a multiple establishment would provide a stable environment for any theocrat's religious practice. A multiple religious establishment does not cohere well with the theocrat's commitment to freedom of conscience, and there seems to be no reason for theocrats to prefer that government to liberalism.

One might agree that the theocrat must reject multiple establishment, authoritarian governance, and theocratic polities that exalt the wrong religious doctrine. But this does not seem to bear on theocrats' reasons, or lack thereof, to live in a theocratic polity under their *own* doctrine, rejecting liberal institutions and developing rule according to their religious dictates. Here there is another objection, and a vital one: Why should theocrats not try to bring about a powerful establishment of their own religious doctrine? Is there not most reason for theocrats to live in a theocracy of their own specifications, as opposed to a liberal polity that would place limits on religious practice?

Given theocrats' commitments to otherworldly values and understanding their desire to avoid government under the wrong religious doctrine, there appear to be three independent reasons why they ought not to try to create a theocratic polity of their own in which to live. First of all, for theocrats living within liberal democracies, such a feat would be very difficult to accomplish. Legal and other institutional obstacles stand between those who wish to impose one particular religious doctrine on nonmembers of a faith, and the barriers are strongly supported by citizens in pluralistic liberal democracies. Since theocrats will not likely be able to convince voters and legislators to turn their country into an actual theocracy, the theocrat bent on achieving full-blown theocratic rule would have to seize control of government or undertake to overthrow liberal institutions, both of which are losing propositions.

Second, even if a group of theocrats were to manage to create theocratic political institutions, empowering religious authorities and prioritizing a strict comprehensive doctrine, that would still not suffice to satisfy their demands. For most theocrats live under the wrong doctrine or denomination, according to any theocrat's reckoning, and so theocratic institutions without the qualification that they promote the right doctrine will not be enough. This is no mere ethereal problem for the theocrat: after all, even the institutions that theocrats have themselves created need not be holy. Some theocrats might transform their interpretation of doctrine in the laborious process of building the institutions they require for rule. Or they may determine that many of their fellow theocrats have departed from the exalted conception of the good in the course of constructing social and political institutions. Any such case would prove to be disastrous for the theocrat, given his commitments, since an errant religious doctrine or conception of the good would to his mind be deeply counterproductive for him and his community.

Third, even if theocrats were able to overcome these external impediments and doctrinal stumbling blocks and were in fact to find themselves dwelling within a theocratic polity of the sort they seek, their problems would not be solved. For a theocratic polity would be ever able to fall away from its divine proximity by virtue of the continuing prospects of corruption. This is a notion that the theocrat is rationally required to accept, given not only his requirement of strict governance but also the care that he takes in reproving subjects who try to depart from the chosen path. And the point holds whether one believes that conscience is the product of right doctrine or one maintains that conscience is antecedent to religious doctrines and conceptions of the good. The theocratic polity is not a utopia, after all, insofar as strict rule under a comprehensive doctrine constrains subjects and inasmuch as laws are required at all. Theocrats' advocacy of strict institutions attests to the fact that they understand how corruption is a continuing problem in the temporal realm: they are not simply concerned that individual subjects may try to depart from their religious course but also that the wayward may take other mutineers with them, scuttling the theocratic ship. In addition, not only would there remain the peril of individual subjects going awry or of factions emerging; once created, the very institutions of theocracy could be led astray as well. For the temporal institutions of theocratic governance shall promote piety, but they may do so practically without regard for the particular otherworldly values that theocrats intend for them to promote. The political institutions of theocracy must be avoided by theocrats, because those institutions can be turned against the particular otherworldly values, aims, and ends in whose name they were created, placing theocrats perpetually at risk of religious oppression.

What is more, theocrats from various religious traditions might agree with the value of the three principles of conscience outlined here. The Old Order Amish, for instance, display at least a partial commitment to the principles of distinction and rejection. They allow their youth to depart from their agrarian quarters before baptism in hopes that the young members will return to Amish communities after a flirtation with worldly doctrines and ways of life.[45] Iranian scholars and youths battling to break the Ayatollah Khamenei's theocratic grip on power might also agree with the principles of conscience outlined here. For the youth of today in Iran do not only want to break down the walls with reformist and less restrictive policies; they wish also to gain the ability to pursue, in their own ways, strict Islamic conceptions of the good different from those the Khamenei regime allows.[46] Even Qutb's view harmonizes with the sentiment of this idea, to the extent that he proposes that "[Islam wants] to abolish those oppressive political systems under which people are prevented from expressing their freedom to choose whatever beliefs they want."[47] No one wishes to live under oppressive government or to have to fight for justice in a war zone. Where conscience is not free to reject deficient doctrines and ways of life, to affirm the good, and to have the liberty to distinguish between good and deficient, it risks being forced to live under decidedly ungodly authority. Whether authorities take the form of ayatollahs, Puritan rulers of the Bay Colony, or some other manifestation, even theocratic aspirations seem destined to wreck and splinter on the rocky shores of polities unbounded by principles and institutions of conscience.

The argument I provide here is notably distinct from the case made by Chandran Kukathas in his recent book *The Liberal Archipelago*. In that work, Kukathas contends that the fundamental principle that describes an open society is freedom of association.[48] To this he adds a salutary, corollary principle of freedom of dissociation from groups and associations and a principle of mutual toleration of associations, each of which he attempts to ground in freedom of conscience.[49] Kukathas then proceeds to articulate six principles of free societies that would give broad liberties to "the variability of human arrangements"; none of these directly mentions conscience or its liberty, but each is meant to have important connections to, and reliance on, freedom of conscience.[50]

The high importance Kukathas places on free conscience is admirable, but his conceptualization of liberty of conscience stands decidedly inferior to the one I supply here. Kukathas argues that there is "a core human nature," a "universal humanity,"[51] which involves living in accordance with the demands of conscience.[52] As he puts it: "If there are any basic human interests, that interest is *at a minimum*, an interest in living in accordance with the demands of conscience. For among the worst fates that a person might have to endure is *that he be unable to avoid acting against conscience*—that he be unable to do what he thinks is right."[53] Kukathas notes, quite correctly, that people do not wish to act against conscience.[54] He emphasizes the fact that individuals will endure deprivations to avoid acting against dictates of conscience as they see them; they do so based in a kind of motivation by principle, namely, a "desire to do what is right."[55] For Kukathas, freedom of conscience is just living in accordance with what one's conscience says and not being forced to act against it.[56] He illustrates his view with the example of a Muslim woman named Fatima, who is a mother, the wife of a Malay fisherman, and a member of a simple fishing village community. Fatima does not desire to live elsewhere or otherwise, but she could leave her community if she were to prefer to do so. Kukathas proposes that Fatima is free because she enjoys an "inner freedom" that is liberty of conscience; she "is not forced to live a life she cannot accept."[57]

The central problem with Kukathas's theory is this: merely because a person's conscience binds him to ideas of what is good and bad does not make his resultant actions permissible, deserving of legal protection, or consistent with principles of conscience. Consider the enraptured father whose conscience demands that he must perform child sacrifice, or take the religious zealot whose conscience tells him to war against heretics so as to save their souls. What can one say to them, if Kukathas is correct about the basic interest of a person not to be made to act against conscience? He proposes that "one should not do violence to other consciences,"[58] but he offers no clear or significant argument to defend the notion, either on moral or legal grounds. Kukathas does suggest that it is wrong to persecute those with different "conscientious beliefs" because so doing fails to respect conscience, insofar as it demands that people act against conscience.[59] But this is an odd argument, since preventing the religious zealot from burning a heretic at the stake also asks someone to act directly against what his conscience tells him to do. If it is undesirable or wrong to ask another to act against conscience, as Kukathas sees it, the point should hold with respect to the religious zealot, the rapt father, and others who would perform similarly objectionable actions. Kukathas goes on to contend that one needs to give people the right to *reject* liberty of conscience as a value.[60] But that stands in tension with his other claims, and it is also philosophically suspect because the argument attempts to make the value of liberty of conscience the very ground for its own rejection. Elsewhere Kukathas appears to favor equal liberty of conscience, but it is neither obvious what grounds he has in mind where he advances the claim nor clear how he can argue as much without rendering his view incoherent.[61]

Kukathas's theory is inadequate because it does not distinguish principles of conscience from what individuals believe their consciences tell them to do. Not all the principles, values, and ideas to which conscience binds one are moral, rational, or worthy of respect. There are grounds on which to distinguish what one merely thinks is right from what is right in fact, and theorists can and should draw that distinction where there is warrant. The three principles I have articulated allow that conscience can be incorrect, if, for instance, one forms a conception of the good aiming to have strict, theocratic institutions that will not allow for the rejection of faith, or if one does not affirm that conscience must be free in the ways the three principles describe. The principles thus provide guidance for what is and is not permitted, abstracted from the actual dictates of conscience that people believe they have. The principles stand apart from the existing attachments of persons, which vary widely, and structure right action in that regard. I have given reason to hold that these are principles to which theocrats are committed rationally and that they should accept.

One might express concern that the three principles of conscience I have identified appear to occupy "a single public or impartial point of view," whereas in reality they are deeply partisan.[62] The principles actually stem from a particular liberal conception of the good, one could contend, and they are insidious as well, not least because they are unaware of their destructive design. There are many variations on this objection, launched by theorists skeptical of the possibility of providing principles for affirming liberal institutions that are impartial or freestanding. For example, Stanley Fish insists that there is no position exterior to the discord among people in liberal society where one can discover freestanding principles of the sort I have articulated.[63] Charles Larmore offers a more sophisticated objection that could also be applied against the view I have developed, namely, that a hidden comprehensive, liberal conception of the good is at work here, one faithful to the "philosophy of individualism" displayed by Immanuel Kant and John Stuart Mill.[64] According to such a philosophy, as Larmore describes it, people "should always maintain a contingent allegiance, revisable on reflection, to any substantial view of the good life" that they might embrace.[65] The predicament is that there are other reasonable versions of the good life that are also permanent features of Western culture, and they emphasize "custom and belonging" instead of individualism.[66] With this in view, Larmore states, conceptions of liberalism like those of Kant's or Mill's "are not adequate solutions to the political problem of reasonable disagreement about the good life"; indeed, he contends, the philosophy of individualism has itself become "simply another part of the problem."[67]

The three principles of conscience I have identified might be claimed to be neither freestanding in any meaningful sense nor helpful, since there appears to be little reason for various religious and other persons to affirm them. But that would be incorrect. For a theory of governance grounded in the principles I have articulated has the potential to achieve a more adequate standard that goes above and beyond the partisanship of existing liberal views. There are three reasons for this. First, the principles do not require people to bracket their beliefs in order to adopt them; instead, the principles embody reasons that religious practitioners should, even must accept, given their commitments to pursuing otherworldly values and ends. Second, religious practitioners can affirm their own doctrines fully, freely, and within the boundaries of reason and right religiosity, if they act accordance with the three principles.[68] The three principles are not Western, as such, and should not be thought of as undermining non-Western religions.[69] Third, the principles have a broad and cosmopolitan applicability, appearing to hold up well across empirical variation.[70] Consider how the principles fit the views of classical, comprehensive, and political liberals: they gird views that give autonomy high priority in life as well as positions of political liberals who differ with comprehensive liberals in that respect. And the principles could be extended to cover religious and nonreligious people alike, given that the nonreligious display commitments of conscience, too; Roger Williams's comments on the many varieties of conscience are instructive in this respect. This being so, there is reason to believe that the three principles could meet Larmore's standard of cardinal political principles "that citizens can affirm together, despite people's inevitable differences about the worth of specific ways of life."[71]

With respect to the extent of the applicability of the principles I have articulated, I suspect that there is good reason for all persons to affirm that conscience must be free to affirm the good, to reject the bad, and to distinguish between the two.[72] There are few points of convergence where theocrats and liberals can come together, and principles of conscience look like promising grounds on which to unite, the principles I have articulated outstripping other principles and values in that respect. Theocrats, liberals, and others may affirm the three principles for different reasons, but their differences are another matter.[73] I will not attempt fully to defend each of these suggestions at this juncture, since doing so would require an extended treatment beyond the scope of the present work. I will state, however, that inasmuch as persons have and pursue conceptions of the good, religious, moral, or otherwise, there appears to be reason for them to affirm the three principles of conscience I have articulated here.

FIVE OBJECTIONS CONSIDERED

I shall address and forestall five possible objections at this juncture. First, one might object that I have misconstrued the special nature of liberty of conscience. Insofar as conscience is a faculty with a capacity to bond strongly to ideas of right and wrong, the objector may claim, its liberty is inviolable in the Lockean sense that one cannot compel another to believe anything through the use of outward force.[74] Penalties are not able to convince the mind, in Locke's view; as he says, they are "no ways capable to produce such Belief."[75] Locke puts it thus: "It is only Light and Evidence that can work a change in Mens Opinions; which Light can in no manner proceed from corporeal Sufferings, or any other outward Penalties."[76] One can throw another in prison, torment him, or confiscate his property, but one cannot change that person's mind about his religious convictions. "Nothing of that nature can have any such Efficacy," Locke proposes, "as to make Men change the inward Judgment they have framed of things."[77] Many historical examples show how extreme coercive measures fail to destroy religious beliefs, testifying to the recalcitrance of religious convictions; the Poor of Lyons, the Cathars in France, and the Old Order Amish are all examples of heretical groups that persisted through lengthy and grinding persecution.

The problem with this objection is that Locke's argument does not adequately consider the phenomenon of altering beliefs by modifying practices over time. Notice this distinction: whether it is possible directly to change the beliefs of individual persons with coercion, threats and the use of force can be very effective in bringing about gradual modifications in religious groups' practices, at times even catalyzing the demise of religious communities. The use of legal strictures against polygamy in the United States, for instance, stopped most early American members of the Church of Jesus Christ of Latter-day Saints from engaging in that practice. For decades, the Mormon Church had not formally renounced the belief in polygamy, yet by the 1960s most Mormons did not believe in it. If government is able to stifle or outlaw a religious group's practices, and if it can ensure that children and young members of the group are not taught the objectionable points of the doctrine in question, it can indirectly alter or liquefy the religious group's beliefs. Locke did well to distinguish between religious beliefs and practices, in the *Letter*,[78] but he failed clearly to acknowledge the fact that suppressing or forcing modifications in practices can result in changes in belief.

There lies a hidden force in this first objection, however, beyond the notion that conscience enjoys a special, epistemologically inviolable kind of freedom. The more powerful objection rests instead in the contention that conscience *can* be affected over the long term and that moderate coercion may in fact be right and godly. And this objection has its champions: Jonas Proast defended the use of tempered coercion in religious matters, in his *The Argument of the Letter Concerning Toleration, Briefly Consider'd and Anser'd*, of 1690. Proast agrees that reason and arguments "are the only proper Means" to induce the mind to accept any truth but observes that coercion can effectively bring people to deliberate on arguments "which, without being forced, they would not consider."[79] There is a need to use outward force to draw people to the true religion and to salvation, Proast claims, especially with "all the false Religions now on foot in the world."[80] He reflects that people normally start learning their religious doctrines in childhood and then proceed to become stubborn, unreflective, and conceited with regard to their beliefs. For those who end up off the path to salvation, Proast contends that the use of penalties is practically the only thing that can get them to act in a more godly way.[81] He thus advocates empowering the civil magistrate to use moderate and "duly proportioned" force when instructions and admonishments fail, although he agrees with Locke that prosecution with fire and sword is inappropriate.[82] He proposes that the civil magistrate's penalties should not be sufficiently severe to make people renounce religion altogether but rather "only such as are apt to put [them] upon a serious and impartial examination" of religious doctrine.[83]

Locke's responses to Proast, in the ensuing exchange between the two, fail to do away with this powerful objection; liberals may lay hands on the Lockean touchstone, but no compelling argument will materialize to vanquish the spirit of Proast's protestation. Jeremy Waldron has picked up on this point, contending that Proast's attack on Locke "completely and effectively demolishes the substance of [Locke's] position."[84] And the question remains: why, if at all, is it wrong to employ moderate coercion to change someone's religious beliefs? The three principles of conscience provide an answer here. The principles of affirmation and distinction do not recommend such measures, first of all. The former specifies that conscience must be free to accept the good and as such does not countenance constraining or forcing conscience to bond to inferior principles and values. The latter principle, the principle of distinction, could only be observed if "duly proportioned" coercion were not simply used to prompt confrontation with a single religious doctrine but employed instead as part of a system that fostered encounters with a healthy variety of other views. The principle of rejection is decisive here, however, forbidding the use of force to compel persons to consider views in the manner described by Proast. For one who wishes to use coercion will need assurance that he has the right doctrine and conception of the good in view. Otherwise, people will be placed at serious risk of being coerced into accepting ungodly practices, which would be a self-defeating outcome on the religious adherent's very grounds.[85] Because conscience must be free to reject lesser religious doctrines and conceptions of the good, those who would use tempered coercion would have to demonstrate that they have the right path in mind for present and future persons. They would need to establish this in conjunction with demonstrating furthermore that they have uncorrupted institutions and authorities, where they wish to institute coercive inducements or penalties for those whose conscience does not fit with accepted views. For conscience to be free, theocrats should affirm liberal institutional arrangements of the kind I have outlined. Those institutions would allow for conscience to gravitate toward the good, permit rejection of the bad, and allow properly for persons to draw distinctions between the two.

A second objection might be expressed here in the form of the following question: does liberty of conscience not involve more than negative liberties and also require a free *mind*? One might readily agree that liberty of conscience requires religious free exercise, which in turn necessitates institutional considerations such as guarantees that government shall not continually molest persons in their religious pursuits. The problem remains that there would also be need for freedom from *internal* obstacles such as fears, superstitions, and false understandings in order for conscience truly to be free. Here, the objector takes the lead from Charles Taylor, who argues that "internal bars to freedom" clearly count among the significant obstacles that people face in life.[86] Taylor suggests that some such internal obstacles to freedom are not even known to those who suffer them; people can come to have "false appreciations" that they do not detect.[87] Building on Taylor's account, the objector could contend that theocrats are confused and mistaken about their purposes because of various internal obstacles to reasoning set up in their minds. Do those obstacles not need to be removed for conscience truly to be free?

A response to this second objection is also available. First, some internal obstacles are surely salutary to the mental life of persons: one need only imagine what life would be like were people to have no compunction regarding lying, stealing, or killing. Merely granting that theocrats have "internal obstacles" alone is not enough to justify the thought that such barriers should be removed. One needs to go beyond the basic idea of mental obstacles to distinguish desirable from undesirable varieties. Second, to argue that theocrats need to have their internal obstacles removed for conscience truly to be free, one needs to provide some assurance that the obstacles those people face are in fact harmful barriers as opposed to guiding constraints that augur well for their pursuit of the good. This point is crucial: merely to suggest that theocrats' internal constraints are undesirable obstacles is to beg the question of whether they are.[88] By way of example, Orthodox Jews may appear merely superstitious and internally blocked where they insist on the importance of enclosing their communities with an *eruv*, but such insistences are not obviously irrational, unreasonable, or incorrect.[89] I am not proposing that theocrats cannot have desires that frustrate their purposes; to the contrary, I have suggested that theocrats who seek unmitigated theocratic governance are indeed misguided, based on a careful analysis of theocrats' rational commitments conjoint with the reasons there are for them to affirm liberal institutions. I have adduced reasons and argumentation to support the view, however, instead of simply declaring that theocrats are unfree because they suffer from internal obstacles hampering their liberty of conscience.

A third objection might proceed on the observation that I have so far only adduced prudential reasons for theocrats to avoid theocratic polities. What if the theocrat were to hold not only that it is best to achieve a particular theocratic polity but also that none other should be suffered in the event that his efforts fail? For some theocrats, at least, the objector may propose, the best option would be to bring their theocratic polity into being and the second-best option would be to die. Such was the view of Qutb, who contended that Muslims must firmly enjoin the good and forbid evil, "[struggling] for Islamic rule even at the expense of life itself."[90] Louay Safi elaborates Qutb's proclamation as follows: "To die in the cause of Islam . . . is considered martyrdom . . . which the Qur'an recognizes as the ultimate honor for the believer in this life, leading to paradise in the hereafter."[91] With a theological view of this kind, the objector may say, the reasons given here for theocrats to avoid a theocratic polity surely do not have much strength at all.

Theocrats who take the view that their second-best option is death will naturally distill that notion from an interpretation of religious doctrine, or they will receive it from the pronouncement of a recognized religious authority. If one simply accepts such an interpretation, there will be little with which to argue. But the theocrat ought not to hold that dying is the second-best option, and there is good reason for him to reject interpretations of religious doctrine that support such apocalyptic visions. For there is a fact of *varia lectio* that the theocrat must acknowledge; it is a truth on which his very theological view trades. Religious doctrines can be interpreted in a variety of ways, and so the theocrat needs assurance that his own reading of doctrine, or that of his religious authorities, is not mistaken. The mere fact that an established religious authority states that death is the second-best option, for instance, hardly can suffice rationally to satisfy the theocrat that such a command is in fact God's own. For one finds widely across religious traditions persons and institutions claiming to have a true interpretation of doctrine, many making a variety of declarations contrary to those of others, about what religious doctrine commands.

Furthermore, it is an implausible suggestion that the best religious doctrine should command such an apocalyptic stance toward temporal life. For even a theocratic polity can never be perfect while it remains earthly, a problem that requires it to retain its strictness and its sanctions as long as the polity exists. Since even the best governmental option for temporal life will always result in inferior social constructs, theocrats would do far better to consider which, of the inferior governmental forms available, are the institutions that best allow for religious practice and a stable environment for religious communities, without high risks of subjection to irreligious rulers, institutions, and laws. Liberalism and liberal institutions are best suited to the task, since the liberal form of government is not hostile to religious practice and is better than others at protecting liberty of conscience for theocrats and others alike. Liberal institutions may not themselves be divine, but they are nevertheless the least-worst option available to theocrats in the temporal realm.

At this point, the objector may concede that liberal institutions will be the best ones under which to live, for *some* theocrats. For liberalism can indeed best protect liberty of conscience and religious free exercise, and nervous or uncertain theocrats may thereby find such institutions to be a great asset. The objector may note, however, that there would still remain the substantial proportion of theocrats with a reply to this argument: they insist that the quest for a pure theocratic polity simply is what God commands. These theocrats claim to know that they have found the good, and in their understanding, the good life includes a strict, denominational polity, set up in a particular way, without liberal institutions promoting liberty of conscience or other liberal freedoms. Theocrats such as these might believe themselves "bound to obey a set of overriding and totalizing obligations imposed upon them by their Creator,"[92] as Christopher Eberle puts it. They may well be prepared neither to reason about nor to compromise their conception of the good, and they may add that their doctrine does not even permit them to question such matters. Here, there is a fourth objection. The argument that attributes to theocrats a rational commitment to liberty of conscience fails to apply to self-assured theocrats in particular. This is important to notice, one observes, since it shows how the argument does not take the full range of theocratic assumptions and commitments seriously enough.

This fourth objection is very serious indeed. It is here, however, where natural theology critically assists the endeavor to identify the reasons that exist for theocrats to affirm liberal institutions. It is important to be clear that if the theocrat were to claim that a pure theocratic polity is what God commands, he would put forward two distinct propositions: first, that he has found the good and, second, that God commands that liberty of conscience is not part of it. Consider first the theocrat's first claim. Other things being equal, there is at least a prima facie reason to doubt that the theocrat has found the right conception of the good, by dint of the fact that so many religious practitioners are, by the theocrat's own admission, living drastically deficient lives. The strength of his conviction in the truth of his doctrine and the fact that some putative religious authority has given him a rendering of God's commands together cannot suffice to give the theocrat adequate reason to believe that God's doctrine requires unmitigated theocratic governance. Other theocrats similarly are convinced of the truth of their interpretations of doctrine, and their authorities assure them that God's teachings are quite different. Moreover, even if one could reliably be said to know that God commands strict observance of his doctrine, it would not follow that God does not recognize a moral right of persons to reject errant doctrines and conceptions of the good with which they may be presented, under institutions that protect liberty of conscience. Since a requirement of unmitigated theocratic governance is not *entailed* by God's commanding strict observance of his doctrine, the burden will be on the theocrat to demonstrate why God commands theocracy without a framework of liberty or liberal institutions.

The theocrat therefore needs to furnish a reason in favor of the view that God commands that liberty of conscience shall have no place in the best earthly community. But such a reason will be very difficult to find, for it is decidedly implausible that God would issue such a command. If God were to command theocrats to live under strict religious governance, he thereby would ask theocrats to deny that which their commitment to achieving otherworldly values seems rationally to require. For in order that they might properly pursue their doctrine, even after finding the good, theocrats will still need to reject the bad and distinguish it from the good. Liberal institutions allow for this possibility, but theocratic institutions do not do at all well in this regard, as they put theocrats at continuing risk of being forced to practice another doctrine or conception of the good than their own. There is therefore strong reason for theocrats to reject unqualified theocratic governance and to affirm liberal institutions, given their wish strictly to promote and pursue otherworldly ends. For institutions of the latter kind are the only ones that appear to be able to protect their religious practice sufficiently by allowing them to reject deficient religion without serious penalty. On the theocrat's very terms, it would be irrational for him to deny that conscience ought to continue to be free to reject the bad and to distinguish between bad and good, even after the good is in view.

The fifth and final objection I shall consider here concerns the idea of a rational commitment. In particular, one might object that it is grossly unfair to attribute to theocrats a rational commitment to the three principles of liberty of conscience since theocrats simply do not accept those principles in any significant way. Whether or not there are reasons for theocrats to avoid a theocratic polity, one could say, the argument presented above fails since most theocrats simply would not accept it. Many theocrats do not think about their religion in the way that a commitment to liberty of conscience requires: they do not reflect on their religious beliefs, and certainly they do not subject their sacred institutions to a calculus of practical reason. And so the objector may claim, first, that theocrats just are not committed to liberty of conscience in any meaningful sense. Second, the objector may add, requiring theocrats to commit to the three principles of liberty of conscience would be to demand that they disavow their religious values. For theocrats will damage their religious conceptions of the good if they are made to think about their religious institutions as the objects of practical reason or if they are to conceive of themselves as free to choose among a variety of governing institutions. Even worse, the objector may propose, the argument in favor of a rational commitment to the value of liberty of conscience seems to ask theocrats to doubt the sacrosanct nature of their sacred institutions. A rational commitment to liberty of conscience, if it were to apply to theocrats, appears only to be tenable if their religious beliefs were set aside or dramatically liberalized in some way.

This fifth objection appears powerful, but a proper response to it can be provided. First, the idea of a rational commitment to a principle, value, or norm is logically independent of one's belief in that principle or value. One can be committed rationally to a principle without actually believing in the principle at all.[93] Clearly, many theocrats would not agree with what is implied by this conclusion, and the argument itself may appear ethnocentric or culturally imperialistic, in part because theocrats would vigorously disagree that they are committed in any way to such seemingly liberal principles of rejection, affirmation, or distinction. But just as one does not have to agree with a rational commitment in order to hold it, one does not have to have that commitment in the front of one's mind for it to apply. Rather, a rational commitment involves that which rationality itself requires: it is not identical to one's current and often conflicted set of beliefs, desires, and ends.[94] It is of course true that many theocrats will not readily concede that liberty of conscience should be important to them. But in saying that the theocrat is committed rationally, one goes beyond the theocrat's present beliefs to that which rationality itself requires of him, whether or not he is aware of it.

It is true that a rational commitment to some principle or belief does not itself provide a reason to follow that principle or to hold the belief in question. One can be rationally required to follow a plan of action, for example, for which no reason to follow the plan exists.[95] In the case of the theocrat, however—and here is the second response to the objection—his rational requirement to uphold principles of conscience is derived from entirely reasonable beliefs: that otherworldly powers and ends exist and that pursuing a path of worship in their regard is a good thing. The form of reasoning that I have brought to bear is thus hypothetical only in part.[96] For if one allows that the theocrat can reasonably and rationally believe in the deep value of otherworldly powers and ends, it appears that there is good reason for him to avoid theocratic polities on his own terms. The theocrat may not readily accept that such is the case, but that is a separate matter from his rational commitment itself, just as it is distinct from reasons for him to affirm principles of conscience.

Third, I do not mean to suggest here that if one is committed rationally to some notion one must thereby be continually aware of either the commitment or the notion itself. Rather, a rational commitment requires that one's plans of action not run afoul of the commitment but does not demand that the commitment must always be in the front of one's mind. It would indeed damage the fabric of theocrats' lives if, for instance, they were required repeatedly to question the authority of their religious leaders, or called on to doubt the propriety of their religious institutions, or required continually to reflect on whether they had found the good. But here it is crucial to note that the argument I have given concerns the question of what sort of governing institutions theocrats should have rather than how theocrats' individual lives should be lived. It does not follow from the fact that a rational commitment binds theocrats to liberty of conscience that theocrats are required individually to doubt the propriety of their authorities and institutions. Nor does the argument imply that all religious functioning must be individualistic, in the sense that "the individual regards herself as an independent and self-willed member of the religious group."[97] The overarching institutions of liberal government might allow theocrats to live in strict, theocratic communities within liberal polities, satisfying their need to practice their religion while also ensuring that theocrats could reject wayward conceptions by protecting religious free exercise; I shall consider this possibility in chapter 3. A reason to affirm liberal institutions does not translate into a reason perpetually to question or doubt one's own religious beliefs, just as a reason or a rational requirement to reject theocratic polities does not imply that one must think instrumentally about one's religious beliefs and commitments.

CONCLUSION

If the argument I have provided to this point is sound, there is reason to think that the prospects of liberal government could truly be made more appealing to theocrats. The theocrat's rational commitment to freedom of conscience implies that he must demand a measure of liberty from government; not all theocrats may be aware of this fact, but an effort to present them with the case could change that situation. Liberal government appears to be the only sort of government that meet the criteria that theocrats hold in this regard; other kinds of government are hostile to religion, or they do not have the resources to protect religious free exercise to the extent that the theocrat requires. Communicating the value of liberty of conscience to theocrats and considering carefully their complaints and concerns with regard to liberal rights and freedoms could allow theocrats to develop both an understanding of the value of liberal institutions and an attachment to government that protects and honors those commitments. Liberal theories of government have not responded especially well to concerns respecting ambitious and retiring theocrats, but there are rational grounds on which liberals can devise a sound, defensible political theory that could appeal deeply to people from a wide variety of religious traditions.

It would be unfair to conclude simply that theocrats are unclear about the commitments they hold or to emphasize that theocrats are unaware of the reasons for them to affirm liberal institutions. For a similar obfuscation holds true for liberals: liberal government has also faltered on certain of its most fundamental commitments, just as liberal political philosophers have failed to advocate government that protects freedom of conscience to the extent that is warranted. I develop in chapters 3 and 4 the prospects of a liberal theory more attuned to the problems raised by ambitious and retiring theocrats, one able to improve on the prudential and moral failures of liberalism I have described.

3. How Should Liberal Democracies Treat Theocratic Communities?

CONTEMPORARY POLITICAL AND LEGAL THINKING languishes when it comes to discovering and constructing workable standards for treating religious convictions, and the predicament of theocratic communities within liberal democracies bears out this observation. Advocates of separationist principles and proponents of accommodationist standards alike have endeavored to build a solid foundation for law that respects religion in its various forms, but none has been successful in so doing. While separationist principles and certain accommodationist insights provide guidelines for handling the wide variety of religious convictions within liberal democracies and existing legal standards serve the majority of religious citizens quite well, they fail to provide for a significant sector of religious persons. Members of theocratic communities within liberal democracies do not receive appropriate treatment under popular legal standards, and they need a new framework under which to be treated by law.

In chapter 1, I described four moral problems that ambitious and retiring theocrats raise for liberalism and liberal government. In particular, I argued that: (1) there is no appropriate legal standard by which to treat theocratic communities; (2) liberals and liberal government have failed to provide grounds for interfering with theocratic practices, even though liberals repeatedly advocate such interference; (3) theocrats are owed an explanation as to why liberal government may regulate their practices; and (4) this explanation should be provided in terms that theocrats should accept, employing reasons that hold for theocrats given their quite reasonable basic commitments and beliefs regarding otherworldly powers and ends. I provided rudiments of a response to the fourth problem in chapter 2, where I distinguished reasons for theocrats to affirm a liberal institutional order. I argued that theocrats are rationally committed to three cardinal principles of liberty of conscience and proposed that, given theocrats' other deep commitments to otherworldly powers and strict religiosity, there is indeed reason for them to affirm

71

liberal institutions as well. In this third chapter, I aim to take on the first of the four problems noted above and consider the prospects of a new legal standard for treating theocratic communities in liberal democracies. Standing arguments against religious establishment, I argue, are instructive but inadequate to address the question of religious free exercise for theocratic communities. I shall examine different versions of the legal standards of strict equality and religious accommodation and show that those standards are fundamentally flawed or otherwise unable to handle theocratic commitments in an appropriate way.

The failures of popular legal structures are sufficiently serious to warrant a new approach and legal classification for theocratic communities. For the free exercise problems pertaining to theocratic communities appear to be amenable to a distinctive solution. I propose that perhaps the only legal structure able to handle theocratic communities appropriately that could be adapted to fit with the overarching legal structure of modern liberal democracies would be one that allowed those communities to gain semisovereign status. To elaborate this suggestion, I will undertake to describe some of the main elements of a standard of semisovereignty, and I shall provide reasons as to why a standard of that kind could be a significant improvement for theocratic communities. For the sake of argument, I assume that the demands of the three principles of conscience I have articulated support a moral right of persons to religious free exercise. I shall use this idea as a point of departure for the argument that follows. If it is the case that persons have a moral right to religious free exercise, I propose, liberal government presently treats members of theocratic communities in ways that are unjust, and a framework of semisovereignty for those communities may be warranted.

LEGAL CHALLENGES OF THEOCRATIC COMMUNITIES

The wide diversity found across theocratic communities could lead one to suppose that those communities cannot be identified by any set of necessary and sufficient characteristics; for my purposes here, a more general characterization will suffice. A theocratic community is one in which persons endeavor to live according to the dictates of a religious conception of the good that is strict and comprehensive in its range of teachings.[1] The strictness of religious teachings normally is promoted by religious leaders, who do not tolerate dissent among community members and try to prevent or disallow competing religious views from emerging. Since religious authorities in theocratic communities do not have political authority with which to enforce their views, they attempt to maintain religious order using other means. Theocratic communities also are generally nonliberal, not inasmuch as they all reject liberal values equally or in the same fashion but in the sense that they undertake to maintain the tenor of their religious communities by discouraging or forbidding outright many liberal values and practices. The comprehensiveness of theocratic religious conceptions pertains to the range of life practices to which those conceptions apply. Religious doctrines of theocratic communities are widely or fully comprehensive in the sense that they extend to cover "all recognized values and virtues within one rather precisely articulated scheme of thought."[2] Theocratic conceptions of the good do not apply merely to some areas of members' lives; rather, those conceptions range across nearly all life practices, covering personal associations, familial structures, institutional arrangements, practices of ritual and worship, ideals of character, and so on.[3]

Not only members of theocratic communities hold religious conceptions of the good exhibiting the features of comprehensiveness and strictness. The lone ascetic, for instance, also displays these traits. What sets theocratic communities apart is the communitarian aspect of their religious vision: theocratic communities are comprised of persons coexisting in tight-knit groups, distinguished in their various roles and functions, living interdependently in a particular area or a territory. A theocratic conception of the good is in this sense other regarding in its strictness and its thoroughness, looking to regulate the lives of a community of persons and not only focusing on the life plans of a particular individual who holds such a conception. The group of persons to whom a theocratic conception of the good applies may be a small assemblage of devout believers, or the whole of humanity may lie within the regulative vision of the theocrat's conception, if, for instance, the doctrine is strongly in favor of proselytizing. This other-regarding, communitarian feature of the theocrat's conception of the good, along with the particular structures and institutions of community life that he envisions, leads him to make associational and institutional claims to free exercise, complementing the religious free exercise claims of individual theocrats.[4]

The U.S. theocratic legacy has its beginnings in the strict religious life of the Puritans of New England, but the theocratic ways of the Pueblo Indians and other native peoples antedates the arrivals of Europeans. Along with certain Pueblo Indian villages, examples of theocratic communities within the United States include Old Order Amish settle-, ments, the Village of Kiryas Joel, members of Mormon polygamist communities, and citizens of the former city of Rajneeshpuram. Pueblo Indians living in the western pueblos of New Mexico have centralized, religious governance involving rule by priests.[5] The Hopi and Zuni tribes, notably, continue to work to resist assimilation, attempting to persist in living according to religious tradition.[6] Old Order Amish communities reside in twenty states in the USA, with the oldest settlements existing in Lancaster County, Pennsylvania. The Amish are well known for their disciplined, religious life: members of Amish communities live under the Ordnung, a comprehensive but unwritten set of regulations that governs their daily affairs.[7] The Amish live close to the land, under what has been called a patriarchal-democratic form of government, with a powerful bishop at the head of a church to whose counsel he is subject.[8] Citizens of Kiryas Joel, a small village in New York State, very nearly exclusively belong to the Satmar Hasidim. The villagers follow a rigid interpretation of the Torah, segregating sexes outside the home, wearing special clothing, and speaking Yiddish primarily.[9] Both political and spiritual authority is unified in a hereditary rabbinical leader, who is the mayor of the village.

The Mormons, whose religion was founded in 1830, were forced to trek across the United States in order to escape persecution for their unusual religious beliefs and practices. Under the leadership of Brigham Young, Mormons set up a religious society in what is now Utah, in 1847; Mormons authorized the practice of polygamy and developed a governmental structure that was hierarchical and impermissive in its regulations. Polygamy was outlawed in the United States in 1878, but polygamous Mormon communities still exist, refusing to concede that the practice of polygamy must cease.[10] The theology of these groups has evolved significantly since the days of the early Church of Jesus Christ of Latter-day Saints, but members are required to give near-total obedience to the particular leaders of their communities and so qualify as theocratic communities in the sense described above. Followers of Bhagwan Shree Rajneesh, an Indian guru, incorporated Rajneeshpuram as a municipality in Oregon in 1982. The Rajneeshees claimed that their religious vision required municipal incorporation: to practice the tenets of Rajneeshism, they argued, only incorporation as a city could properly provide essential services for devotees.[11] Religious life in Rajneeshpuram was strict and nonliberal,[12] as well as comprehensive, but it was also unstable, and the community fell to pieces after criminal indictments were handed down against leaders.[13] Even the Bhagwan was convicted of conspiring to defraud immigration authorities; he was fined and deported.

These five American theocratic communities elicit a variety of challenges to courts and legislators in the United States, as do similar groups in other liberal democracies. Four of the five communities have raised problems reaching all the way to the United States Supreme Court: the Amish were prodded to defend themselves against numerous challenges to their educational practices;[14] the Pueblo Indians were taken to task over their criteria for tribal membership;[15] Mormon polygamists were forbidden from living in uncommon family units;[16] and state law creating a school district for the citizens of Kiryas Joel, corresponding to the territory of their religious village, was deemed unconstitutional on grounds that it was a kind of special legislation giving favoritism to a particular religious sect.[17] The case of Rajneeshpuram was no less problematic. The state of Oregon successfully attacked the legality of the incorporation of the city of Rajneeshpuram, on the grounds that the action violated the establishment clause of the United States Constitution, and article I, sections 2, 3, 4, and 5, of the Oregon Constitution.[18] Those who appreciate the value of religious free exercise realize that at least some of the judgments in cases such as these should come down in favor of theocrats, presumably. Where regulation seriously interferes with the religious practices of religious communities, they propose, legislation should be altered or members of religious communities exempted from applicable laws, within reason. But when it comes to actual legal standards under which to provide such treatment, sympathizers and defenders are at a loss. What sort of treatment should theocratic communities receive? What sort of legal framework would delineate proper boundaries of governmental interaction and interference with those groups, and on what grounds would these be justified?

LIMITATIONS OF ANTIESTABLISHMENT ARGUMENTS

One might think that existing arguments against religious establishment suffice to respond to the challenges of theocratic communities since those communities appear to be ruled by religious authorities under a form of religious establishment. But this is mistaken: antiestablishment arguments do not themselves provide a complete answer to the question of how to treat theocratic communities. Perhaps foremost among the problems is this: theocratic communities simply are not religious estab-lishments in the legal sense of the term. The theocratic communities are sub-groups within liberal polities, after all, receiving little to no special treat-ment at the hands of state and acquiring government aid and assistance under neutral criteria. What is more, the regulative autonomy of theo-cratic communities is highly qualified: religious rule does not apply to outsiders and neither does it allow for extreme forms of coercion against its membership. Antiestablishment arguments are calibrated instead for pluralistic polities wherein most citizens have access to membership in a variety of groups and where one also finds an array of different, ex-clusive religious faiths to which people strongly adhere.[19] Under condi-tions of pluralism, where citizens are divided in their beliefs and convic-tions, antiestablishment principles of separation of church and state are strongly justified: principles of separation enjoy strong moral support and have a firm footing in such constitutional bases as the First Amend-ment of the United States Constitution, as I have argued elsewhere.[20] Those principles do not apply especially well to theocratic communities, however, and the peculiar nature of those groups elicits distinct questions about the moral impropriety of requiring tithes, the inevitability of seri-ous, political discord in societies exalting one religious doctrine, the harm that may be done to the church in commingling secular and ecclesiastical institutions, and the relevance of reasonable pluralism to these matters.

Just because liberal antiestablishment arguments have been con-structed with government establishments of religion in mind and with a pluralistic body politic in view, of course, does not mean that they do not suffice to provide a sound and complete framework through which to treat theocratic communities. What is it that undermines the suitability of antiestablishment arguments to theocratic communities, exactly? Be-yond the issue of the basic inapplicability of antiestablishment argu-ments to theocratic communities, there exist four independent reasons to think that theorists will need to build arguments that go beyond anti-establishment principles in order to meet theocratic challenges. First, in arguing against religious establishment, one may point to the unfairness of giving priority to one religious denomination over another, by reason of the fact of reasonable pluralism. This argument takes wing under con-ditions where one finds a variety of reasonable comprehensive doctrines and conceptions of the good, which, as Joshua Cohen, John Rawls, and others have noted, is the very condition of modern constitutional democ-racies.[21] That condition does not obtain within theocratic communities, however: the theocrat from an Old Order Amish community, for example, may point out that no pluralism is found is found in his village, putting the brakes on that liberal argument and bringing it to a halt. For the theocrat gives no priority to one religion over another, in the relevant sense, where there is doctrinal homogeneity within her community.

Second, liberals follow James Madison and Thomas Jefferson in proposing that nonmembers of a religion ought not to have to pay tithes to that group.[22] Under conditions of pluralism, this argument is also very powerful, but here one must distinguish carefully between compulsory tithing within religious communities, on one hand, and state funding for the various activities and practices of such religious groups, on the other. The theocrat from Kiryas Joel, for instance, will point out that virtually all people in his village are Satmar Hasidim, and he may contend that, among the villagers, there is a near uniform desire to support religious institutions. If the theocrat were correct, it is quite possible that the liberal argument respecting the impermissibility of compulsory support within religious groups will have to be transformed. For there may be points where specific dissenters or refractory members of a theocratic community object to particular tithes or to the very practice of tithing but where the authority structure of the theocratic community would be undermined if the objector's claims were upheld by an authority external to the community. The question of whether state funding may be provided to theocratic groups is also left unresolved by existing antiestablishment arguments. Theocratic communities are marked by a comprehensive religious existence guided by religious authorities, making the question of providing state funding to those groups more complex and delicate than one may have anticipated. In one sense, providing theocratic communities with government aid would seem to count as an establishment of religion, since the aid would appear purposefully and unavoidably to fall into the hands of religious leaders and would therefore advance religious purposes or otherwise show that government endorses such communities or religious doctrines.[23] Whether theocratic communities could rightly receive any state or federal funding must be clarified, given these concerns, since traditional antiestablishment thinking does not provide a decisive answer.

Third, liberals often gesture to the sort of public discord that comes with the establishment of one religion over another. Where individuals of different faiths are not treated with something like equal concern and respect, liberals contend, one will find not just unfairness but also disaffection and unrest. Here, too, the argument does not respond directly to religious devotees in theocratic communities. Instead, it is intended for, and mainly applicable to, polities and governments representing multiple religious denominations and widely contrasting comprehensive doctrines and conceptions of the good life. The argument from public discord speaks well to the problem of strife between groups, but it does not easily address the theocratic situation wherein one particular doctrine is held high within a particular community, where religious authorities try to foster and maintain some specific religious conception of the good and where members of the community appear strongly to approve of the practices.

Fourth, one who takes the lead of Roger Williams may be worried that an especially close relation between church and state would damage religious institutions and do a disservice to religion itself.[24] This notion the liberal joins with a similar argument: that governing institutions will be compromised in their function if they commingle closely with religion. These arguments may be sound, but they need to be examined more carefully in the context of theocratic communities. For the theocrat may propose that her community's religious vision asks for little to no interference from government. Concerns regarding damage to her community or to government institutions, she may say, are therefore unfounded.

Standing arguments against religious establishment do not suffice to solve the special problems and challenges pertaining to theocratic communities within liberal democratic polities. Antiestablishment arguments and principles of church/state separation have a sound moral basis under contemporary conditions of reasonable religious pluralism, but those principles and arguments do not combine to provide a complete answer to the question of how liberal democracies ought to treat theocratic communities. While antiestablishment principles are instructive to those who consider the matter of how theocratic communities should be treated, they do not properly extend to cover the complexities of religious authority, practice, and institutions within theocratic communities, and these are critical issues requiring careful attention indeed.

DEFICIENCIES OF STRICT EQUALITY

Antiestablishment arguments do not provide enough equipment to tackle theocratic communities, contrary to what one might expect, so one must set one's sights beyond them in searching for a standard that can appropriately accommodate those communities within liberal democracies. Since I am here considering an appropriate legal schema for treating theocratic communities, I will examine both existing and proposed legal frameworks for handling those religious groups. I shall call currently used and past standards, as well as those notions proffered by commentators, *existing standards*.

Judicious, workable principles for dealing with religious convictions are not easy to uncover. The United States Supreme Court complains about this fact on occasion. It has proven very difficult to construct a framework for handling religion that consistently respects liberal values of toleration, liberty, fairness, and autonomy. Where a schema seems to work well for one religious group, it often fails in regard to others. This is perhaps most clearly seen in light of theocratic communities, since they are groups that are improperly served by prevalent standards. Existing legal structures subsume theocratic communities under the broad category of religion and religious affiliation, failing to make special allowances for those communities when the integrity of religious practice is at issue, even though proponents of the respective structures are often motivated by a desire to create a legal framework that would allow theocratic communities to flourish. Popular legal structures available for treating religion break into two basic standards: *strict equality* and *accommodation*. Actual and proposed frameworks for dealing with religion are variations on these types, with the accommodation standard enjoying a good deal of vogue. Both kinds of legal structures can incorporate separationist principles, although many accommodationists are unreceptive to the idea of strong separation of church and state. Each of these kinds of structures is seriously flawed, I will argue, and no variation on either form could serve as an adequate basis for handling theocratic communities in modern constitutional democracies.

One possible way to deal with the variety of religious traditions and communities in liberal democracies would be to demand strict equality before the law as a legal corollary to the view that religious differences deserve equal treatment under liberal ideas of governance. This standard I shall call *strict equality*. Strict equality is supposed to be fair in its demand for equal treatment for all groups and individuals, religious and secular, and it has the virtue of legal simplicity since it avoids untidy complications by flatly refusing to validate particular religious claims for special treatment.[25] Strict equality also has an apparent prudential benefit: with different religious groups all receiving the same treatment, that is, with all people living under the same public regulatory code, citizens arguably will enjoy an absence of religious disquietude and discord. Legislation would need to be facially neutral to be acceptable, according to this standard, neither discriminating against any group of citizens nor targeting any group for special protections or benefits. Under strict equality, it may seem, the absence of special treatment for any particular religious group or for religious groups generally will be understood as an absence of favoritism, and religious adherents will happily comprehend that their government treats them all in a way that is essentially fair.

On closer examination, however, strict equality proves to be seriously deficient from a moral and legal standpoint. If government were to enforce a standard of strict equality, it would by that fact disallow exemptions for members of particular religious groups. Minor exemptions, while of little consequence to liberal government and the citizens of a liberal polity and in no way compromising the integrity of the law, are of major importance to religious adherents. Many of the wide range of religious practitioners in a pluralistic polity require small exemptions in order to be true to the dictates of their doctrines: here, one need not gesture to theocrats but rather to the less exotic, regularly participating religious citizens of liberal democracies. Because it may not allow members of minority faiths to observe their specific religious holidays without penalty, display modest religious symbols as members of the military, or stand exempt from certain requirements of due process, strict equality shows itself hardly to be tolerant of religion at all.[26] The liberal state must be at least accepting of religious difference, but strict equality does not take such difference seriously; the proponent of strict equality does not acknowledge the fact that religious pursuits and attachments reasonably may be important to people's lives.

Strict equality is also an unrealistic standard, as its opponents have noted. For the law shows itself to be partisan on many religious matters. Institutionalized laws and practices in the United States originated in Protestant doctrine and still retain their partisan trappings.[27] In other liberal democracies, the case is similar, as with Anglicanism in England or the diffuse Protestantism of English Canada. United States law codifies observance of Christian holidays and the Christian Sabbath; one finds Christian reference on coinage and in the Pledge of Allegiance; and both the Declaration of Independence and the Articles of Confederation include mention of God. In requiring strict equality before such a legal code, there would be no counterbalance for minority faiths.[28] Under such circumstances, where religious traditions are not even equipollent in regard to the body of law before which they stand, strict equality cannot provide an ethical, liberal handling of religious practitioners' claims.

While the standard of strict equality is inappropriate and flawed, it contains within it an important element: strict equality is motivated by a perceived need for a fair and common basis of principles according to which liberal government can adjudicate on tricky and potentially divisive controversies. That strict equality embodies the wrong principles, I submit, does not change this fact. What liberal democracies require are principles that will properly allow for religious exemptions and other accommodations for religious groups, where they may be necessary, and that would fit with a schema properly suited to the free exercise requirements of theocratic communities as well. Without an appropriate basis for treating religion, one that may be principled, reasoned, and moral, the laws of a liberal polity will amount to little more than an arbitrary hodgepodge of regulations.

FAILURES OF RELIGIOUS ACCOMMODATION

A more sophisticated and fair-spoken standard for treating religious convictions in liberal democracy, and one that has a host of contemporary defenders, is known as *religious accommodation*. The standard of religious accommodation picks up on the moral scantiness of strict equality, proposing that members of specific religious groups may have claims to be *exempted* from certain generally applicable regulations (negative accommodation) or that, under limited conditions, particular *benefits* ought to be extended to them (positive accommodation). Justification for religious accommodation normally takes the following form: positive and negative accommodations ought sometimes to be provided to members of religious groups, since (1) people may require these measures to practice their religion, (2) religious practitioners deserve certain exemptions or benefits, and (3) accommodations do not come at a great cost to government or citizens generally. Nearly all advocates of accommodation favor exemptions for members of religious groups, but some argue for a host of benefits as well; this reflects the fact that the accommodation standard is scalable, with some proponents contending that a panoply of benefits should be given to religious groups and others proposing, for example, that religious groups ought to have positive measures provided to them only to compensate for disadvantages caused by government.[29] Accommodationists who favor small sets of exemptions are sometimes advocates of separationist principles, but those who favor greater levels of accommodation tend to view the idea of strongly separating church and state as a misguided notion.

Proponents of religious accommodation do not claim that legislation generally applicable to the majority of citizens would be inappropriate where a particular religious group has a claim for accommodation; nor do they maintain that any specific law would be unacceptable or unconstitutional in the area of law in which a religious community may seek a positive or negative accommodation. Rather, the proponent of accommodation simply argues that individuals or groups sometimes deserve differential treatment with respect to generally applicable statutes when laws conflict with their religious beliefs or practices. Most accommodations take the form of exemptions, and most exemptions are granted legitimately so that members of religious groups may freely exercise their religious practices.[30] Negative accommodations are widely found in many areas of the law, from zoning and taxation to legislation "directly implicated in liberal practices and dispositions," as Nancy Rosenblum puts it, including antidiscrimination law, employment law, and requirements of due process.[31]

Michael McConnell and Richard Posner, advocates of a robust version of accommodation, suggest that *Sherbert v. Verner* is the "paradigmatic case" of negative exemption; in that dispute, an American textile worker maintained that she had been forced unjustifiably to choose between her religion and her employment, as she was a Seventh Day Adventist and thereby could not work on Saturday.[32] The Supreme Court held that the worker could not be refused unemployment benefits, since the denial of those benefits was tantamount to a "fine" for her religious convictions.[33] Legal exemptions such as the one granted in *Sherbert* are, in the main, designed to allow liberal-minded religious individuals to take part in the political and economic clamor of life in their modern democracy without having to sacrifice some important element of their religious convictions. Will Kymlicka characterizes these exemptions as "group-specific measures" and classifies them as what he calls "polyethnic rights," measures intended to aid ethnic groups and religious minorities to "express their cultural particularity and pride without . . . hampering their success in the economic and political institutions of the dominant society."[34] When devotees have an inclination to participate in the business and politics of liberal society, religious exemptions remove weighty burdens from their shoulders.

This point deserves further elaboration. Inclusion usually motivates accommodation arguments, in the sense that normally their end is the creation of means for religious adherents to participate in the workplace and in public affairs. Canadian Sikhs who have rallied successfully to join the Royal Canadian Mounted Police, for instance, certainly are devout religious practitioners of their faith, but they do not shrink from public life, and neither do they desire to overthrow liberal government or convert society to their way of living.[35] Exemptions serve members of these and other religious groups very well, allowing them to participate in the armed forces, enabling them to hold employment, or permitting them to partake of modern life in numerous other ways. For that matter, a positive accommodation can be salutary for deserving religious adherents, providing chaplaincy where soldiers have been uprooted,[36] for instance, or compensating some similar disadvantage, where government has been its cause. Not all accommodations serve inclusive purposes, though: exceptions may also be granted where people desire to opt out of the conventional business and culture of a liberal polity. These exemptions, such as exceptions from military service or compulsory education, are "atypical," as Kymlicka says, but they apply to nonparticipatory groups such as the Old Order Amish.[37] Insofar as they observe constitutional boundaries and as long as they do not run afoul of principles of religious liberty, accommodations rightly provide much-needed relief to many religious citizens of liberal democracies.

An accommodation framework goes further than the strict equality standard in providing a more stable, morally sound basis on which to treat the variety of religious conceptions of the good found in vibrant contemporary liberal polities. However, the accommodation standard cannot properly extend to theocratic communities existing within liberal democracies. This is a critical matter that political and legal theorists have overlooked: even the popular legal model of religious accommodation cannot properly handle theocratic communities, though it works well to include other religious adherents within liberal-democratic legal structures and despite the fact that the standard is motivated to be sensitive to the demands of faith.[38] Why is this the case?

Consider first negative accommodations in a theocratic context. Every exemption corresponds to a particular regulatory statute, with these statutes combining to form the myriad federal, state, and local laws of a liberal polity. Since theocratic conceptions of the good life are religious, strict, and thorough, broadly covering the theocrat's religious institutions, principles, values, and life practices, mere exemption from a few applicable laws will not suffice to permit theocrats properly to pursue their conceptions of the good. Theocrats' uncommon ways of life and their nonliberal manner of dealing with their adherents will invariably conflict at many points with the standing and proposed legal codes of a liberal polity. Exemptions would therefore be required in most places where the laws are not silent,[39] proving to be an awkward solution and moving well beyond the idea of exemption as it is normally conceived. Exemptions may serve as finishing tools in constructing an appropriate legal standard for theocratic communities, but they cannot be expected to do the principal hewing and carving.

Allowing theocratic communities to weave a panoply of positive and negative legal accommodations would also not suffice to enable their members to practice their religion as they ought to be able to do. Four weighty reasons support this contention. First, an accommodation standard implies that theocratic communities will often be made to solicit different branches and offices of government for exemptions or positive accommodations, since the law of the liberal polity will not apply only where they request special treatment. With all the ways in which laws touch their lives, this tends to result in the continual and excessive involvement of theocrats with legislators, courts, and government, since existing and new legislation regularly affects their uncommon practices. To force theocratic communities to fight for exemption statutes one at a time would hardly amount to a workable outcome, as Douglas Laycock notices.[40] Second, under an accommodation standard, theocrats are made vulnerable to a wide variety of challenges to the legality of their practices and institutions. Exposed in this way, theocrats will not know where the next lawsuit may come from. This unfortunate condition obtains for many theocratic communities in the United States. Fellow citizens who object to the idea of anyone using hallucinogenic drugs, for instance, could demand that peyote and other materials used in religious rituals be classified as controlled substances.[41] For that matter, parties may object to the implications of genealogical structures in theocratic communities, their possibly polygamous familial arrangements, or the seeming unanimous and unquestioned support of a single religious leader who exercises control over a theocratic village.[42] Under the legal accommodation standard, nearly any of the theocrat's practices can become the site of legal contest, where those practices distinguish theocrats from mainstream liberal citizens. Legal battles are time-consuming for theocrats and legislators alike,[43] given the myriad places at which exemptions and positive accommodations would need to be sought and religious practices defended. For that matter, the court battles are often difficult to win.[44] What is more, with the interference brought by other citizens and government, such legal imbroglios may prove to be prohibitively expensive to theocratic communities as well. Staking legal claims, rallying support, and defending against lawsuits hardly are inexpensive endeavors.

Third, a series of legal contests may unwillingly turn theocrats into litigious or disputatious individuals, implicating theocrats in a way of life that their religious doctrines would rather they avoid. Religious doctrines often provide teachings about ways in which to resolve disputes among members, but continual interference from the legal institutions of liberal polities erodes those important elements of doctrine.[45] Members of theocratic communities also wish not to be drawn into the adversarial legal systems of liberal democracies and tend to dread the spotlight when it is turned on them. As a matter of religious principle, theocrats generally consider the embroilment to be *infra dignitatem* or even proscribed outright by doctrine. The Ordnung, for instance, forbids the Amish from taking recourse to U.S. courts where legal conflicts arise: Amish who file lawsuits may be excommunicated, defending against lawsuits is disallowed, and appealing decisions to higher courts is similarly prohibited.[46] The Amish have understood that some involvement with the American legal system is necessary for their continued survival, but they abhor the ceaseless entanglements in which they find themselves.[47] Whereas many theocrats by their nature long to escape from the politics, law, and society of liberal polities, and though the accommodationist wishes to allow theocratic communities to flourish, the accommodation standard unwittingly draws theocrats into the very legal fracases that they are out to avoid.[48]

Fourth, and perhaps foremost, the very spirit of theocratic authority would be defiled if the community's authority were construed to be subject to the will of the liberal polity. Unfortunately, this is the situation that obtains for theocratic communities within the United States and in other countries as well. The expectation that theocratic communities will be subject to laws unless they have permission otherwise and the understanding that legal action may be brought against them at practically any juncture pervade the normative worlds of theocratic communities and unjustly hamper their members' pursuit of religious teachings. Shifting interpretations of the free exercise clause of the First Amendment have not helped this problem: the Supreme Court has interpreted the clause to state that a right of free exercise does not relieve persons of their obligations to comply with valid and neutral laws of general applicability if the laws in question conflict with religious dictates, even though the Court's decision in *Wisconsin v. Yoder* clearly suggested that parents cannot violate compulsory education laws for nonreligious reasons.[49] Members of a theocratic community need to be able to have their own religious leaders, make their own institutions and regulations, and develop their own *nomos*, that is, their own normative universe, if they are truly to pursue their religious conceptions of the good. Those committed to protecting the right of persons to form small religious communities tend to understand that this is the case, but they err in thinking that present standards do well in this regard or in arguing that the First Amendment puts up a solid bulwark against maltreatment of religious communities, as recent interpretations of the amendment seem to show. Under a framework that accommodates theocratic communities within the towering legal edifice of the liberal polity, theocratic groups can hardly help feeling jeopardized; in the United States, theocrats are subjected to shifting and at times fickle liberal institutions, suffering a fractured sense of regulative autonomy as a result. American theocrats live encaged in a free country under present standards, shackled by the politics of legislative procedure, the free exercise of their religion well beyond their reach.

It bears mention that there is something peculiar that makes theocrats so different and difficult to accommodate. It is not just the strictness, nonliberality, and thoroughness of their conceptions of the good that make them troublesome. For each one of these features of a theocratic conception of the good is consistent with that of the lone ascetic, the eremite, or the Garrisonian perfectionist,[50] all of whom would be well served by the accommodationist's schema. Consider Luke the Stylite, the tenth-century ascetic perched atop a column at Chalcedon.[51] He holds a strict, nonliberal, comprehensive, and religious conception of the good; the stylite's way of life allows for little movement, forbidding him to associate with others and prohibiting him from joining with the hustle and bustle of public life.[52] A small set of exemptions, with regard to taxation and conscription, may relieve the pillarist almost completely from any involvement with the rest of the polity.[53] The stylite might welcome liberalism and its legal institutions, since existing legal standards could allow him to live his life as he believes he must without interference from those who would prefer to make him conform to social ideals or try to drag him into public life. But the theocrat will be much more uneasy with the prospects of liberal governance, since his nonliberal, comprehensive vision applies to his entire community, including its various institutions, traditions, educational practices, values, familial structures, criteria for membership, peculiar systems of religious roles and divisions of labor, and the like. Friends of the Old Order Amish made this point with regard to Amish beliefs, in the respondent's brief for *Wisconsin v. Yoder*,[54] contending that the spiritual strength of the strict and peculiar Amish community lies in "the bonds of a common, lived faith, sustained by 'common traditions and ideals which have been revered by the whole community from generation to generation.'"[55] For people whose conceptions of the good are communitarian, nonliberal, strict, and comprehensive in range, an allowance of legal exemptions simply will not suffice to include or exclude them from living out their visions in a liberal polity.

THE IMPLAUSIBILITY OF FULL ACCOMMODATION

To try to save the accommodation standard, one might be tempted to adopt a framework for treating theocratic communities that would give them great liberty. Beyond mere exemption, and at the other end of the accommodation spectrum, lies a theoretical standard that I shall call *full accommodation*. Under this standard, liberal government would allow for religious free exercise very nearly without qualification, with government ready to provide benefits wherever it stands in the way of religious practice and where it may give aid or assistance to religious practitioners otherwise. As a combination of positive and negative accommodations, full accommodation yields, for members of religious groups, a condition of general liberty with regard to the laws of a polity, motivated by an attempt to harmonize the practices of the devout with those of other citizens. Full accommodation thus has two sides, the first of which is nearly unbridled free exercise. On this side, the proponent of full accommodation gestures toward commonly held reasons for allowing people to have freedom from interference in their religious pursuits. Government ought not to create barriers with respect to its citizens' religious practices, the proponent may say, because conscience has an absolute right to freedom or because the purpose of government is only to help—and never to hinder—individuals in their pursuits.

The second side of full accommodation consists of benefits, such as financial aid or other assistance, that government would be ready to provide to religious practitioners. These benefits would come not just where government seems to have caused a hindrance but also where government could act to aid or assist members of religious communities when they request this. Full accommodation would provide funding for sectarian schools,[56] aid to churches' counseling services,[57] special transportation and other services where religious adherents are loath to partake of public provisions, and so on, along with general negative liberty regarding secular legislation that does not fit with adherents' religious doctrines. Under full accommodation, government could significantly help theocrats in their religious endeavors, or so it might seem: the defender of full accommodation may contend that her standard would disentangle problems that strict equality or exemption standards cannot resolve. Since liberal government clearly provides obstacles to the political realization of theocratic doctrine, and since theocrats would benefit greatly from financial aid for their institutions or from symbolic endorsement, the exponent may suggest, there is merit to the claim that liberal government should accommodate theocrats to such an extent. Full accommodation would do very well by such communities as the Old Order Amish, she may say, as they are a hard-working, peaceful, self-reliant, law-abiding group,[58] whose inspiring practices would flourish under a full accommodation framework.

However, full accommodation would be an unmitigated disaster as a standard for treating religion and religious association in liberal polities. First, if positive accommodation were to extend to the provision of financial aid to religious institutions, within theocratic communities or not, establishment and fairness concerns would immediately come to the fore. Were a system of benefits to religious groups to come at a cost to nonmembers of those groups, that system would violate fundamental moral principles of church/state separation, and those principles certainly apply in such instances. Nonmembers of a religious group ought not to have to pay to support others' religious institutions or practices, and to entangle religious and governmental institutions is a dangerous thing in a pluralistic polity, risking both the corruption of church doctrine and discord among religious groups over questions of state favoritism.[59] Principles of separation of church and state may not apply well within theocratic communities, but between those communities and the other citizens and institutions of a liberal democracy, the principles are very robust. The provision of financial aid or other benefits specifically to members of religious groups would have to be very limited to be moral: government would violate principles of right in extending the wide range of benefits advocated under full accommodation to theocratic and other religious groups.

Nor is this stalwart establishment objection the only problem facing full accommodation. Deliverance from secular, liberal legislation, where such regulation grates against the teachings of a religious doctrine, could easily devolve into a nightmarish scenario. Ironically, it is here that theocratic communities provide some of the strongest examples of the shortcomings of full accommodation. Reclusive theocratic groups, if they were given free reign over their subjects, would be at liberty to mete out severe corporal and capital punishments for such crimes are heresy or apostasy; many theocratic communities have done such awful things in the past, and theocrats continue to do so in communities outside standing liberal democracies.[60] Certainly, not all theocrats are principally opposed to violence, and neither do theocrats all display virtues that resonate with liberal citizens. The case of Rajneeshpuram serves as a good example here: thirty-four of the group's top leaders were charged with a variety of state and federal crimes, including attempted murder, assault, arson, burglary, racketeering, electronic eavesdropping, and criminal conspiracy.[61] Whereas the Old Order Amish provide convenient examples of tame theocratic communities, they are atypical among theocrats; it is only fortuitous for proponents of full accommodation that the Amish have accepted, developed, and continue to hold many of the values that liberals recognize and cherish. To those objecting to the nastier tendencies of theocratic groups, Isaiah Berlin's reflection will seem astute: "total liberty for wolves is death to the lambs."[62] Even if the proponent of full accommodation were to limit her endorsement where theocrats may feel compelled to be forceful or violent toward nonmembers of their faith, she would still face the problem of justifying, in a coherent, principled way, reasons for disallowing members of insular religious communities from treating their members illiberally in following their religious doctrine.

Further, full accommodation would not circumvent the very serious problems outlined above, namely, that an accommodation standard by its very nature subjects theocrats excessively to liberal legal structures and codes. The ways in which that subjection damages the regulative autonomy of theocrats are several and grave. Even under full accommodation, theocrats will have to toil for many exemptions and positive accommodations, even though they may detest such actions and despite the fact that the contests could turn theocrats into the sorts of disputatious persons against whom their religious doctrines warn. Full accommodation also does not protect theocrats from the wide range of legal challenges brought to bear in a liberal polity, both from government and private parties, and so it abandons theocrats in that regard. Furthermore, only a large, awkward, and vexatious set of positive and negative accommodations could allow theocrats to begin to believe that they were free from the clutches of the liberal polity's legislative grip, but at that point theocrats would have an excess of liberty, and they would be free from regulation preventing them from taking part in illiberal behavior both within and without their communities.

With these failings in view, one sees that the accommodation standard, along with other existing legal frameworks, cannot do as a standard for treating theocratic communities in liberal democracies. Strict equality is an inappropriate model generally, since it does not appreciate the value of even small exemptions to participating citizens. Whereas many variations of accommodation standards may have noble motivations, they do not provide satisfactory frameworks with regard to theocratic groups. Mere exemptions cannot adequately exclude or include theocratic communities in liberal polities, full accommodation is too lax a standard to take seriously, and other accommodation designs damage the spirit of religious communities by neglecting their claims to autonomy. If theocratic communities are to be treated at all properly by liberal democracies, and if those communities are to be able to exist as they should, some other standard will have to be constructed.

THE PRECEDENT OF SEMISOVEREIGNTY

The legal standards that I have canvassed and addressed above seem to exhaust the possibilities by which to deal with theocratic communities in liberal democracies. If theocratic communities are not to be treated under a framework of strict equality or religious accommodation, what remains? I cannot hope to delineate and justify here a complete and detailed schema for handling theocratic communities ensconced in liberal polities, but in what follows I shall try to point to a way forward on the problem, introducing the idea of semisovereignty for theocratic communities, discussing its basic elements, and providing reasons why a legal framework for semisovereignty could make for a better, more workable standard through which to treat theocrats.

Legal standards for handling theocratic communities will fail if they end up penning theocrats within the laws of a liberal polity, but liberal polities could go too far in providing theocratic groups with regulatory autonomy as well. Granting theocratic communities full sovereignty, allowing them to secede from their respective polities so as to become sovereign bodies internationally, would be an alternative but deeply problematic solution. First of all, a theocratic community may not have an entitlement to secede from the larger liberal polity in which it is found, if the claim to that entitlement were made simply by virtue of the fact that many or most of its members desire secession. The liberal polity may not want to compromise its territorial integrity, for instance, but secession often leads to such a result. Second, theocratic communities normally do not wish to secede from the liberal polities in which they live. Theocrats receive a host of benefits from liberal government: they are protected from hostile groups, their trade with other citizens is regulated, and theocrats are normally provided with access to basic welfare and social services, which they do not wish to forgo. Third, religious authorities of fully sovereign theocratic polities often treat their subjects in illiberal ways and even strike out against other polities where their authoritative structures devolve or where their respective religious conceptions of the good are especially virulent. In most cases, it appears, conferring sovereignty on theocratic communities, and making them into independent, autonomous polities unto themselves, is not the answer.

Semisovereignty, in contrast, could prove to be very useful for treating theocratic communities ensconced within liberal democracies. But what is "semisovereignty" exactly? The very general implication that the idea of semisovereignty conveys is this: a semisovereign body has a significant measure of political or legal autonomy, with respect to some greater political order, but its sovereignty is not entire. Normally, semisovereign bodies are subunits of larger polities, either ensconced within a polity or adjunct to one. To say that a political unit is semisovereign is not to imply that it is exactly halfway to being sovereign or even partway there in every respect. Rather, semisovereignty (or "quasi sovereignty," as I shall alternatively refer to it) can take many forms. A semisovereign body or community could be the ultimate recognized political authority within the territory that it occupies, for instance, but unequal or even unrepresented politically in the larger polity in which it may be found. A semisovereign community could also be sovereign in some areas of jurisdiction but not in others; this is evidenced in cases where, for example, a community is unable to apply its laws to persons who are nonmembers, even though it may have complete jurisdiction over its membership. Quasi sovereignty is a concept that allows for a variety of possible legal relations between the partway sovereign community and its individual members, as well as between the semisovereign community and the polity in which it is located.

Semisovereignty might seem like a fanciful or outlandish notion, but it is not an unprecedented standard historically. The millet system of the Ottoman Empire granted a fairly robust form of self-governance to theocratic communities, for example. Recent scholarship on the millet system indicates that the communal autonomy it allowed was not only territorially based but also limited to religious matters, with individual members of millets apparently able to choose between religious and civil jurisdictions when disputes in marriage law were at issue.[63] In the United States, Indian tribes have held a quasi-sovereign status for well over a century, since the Supreme Court's decision in *Cherokee Nation v. Georgia*, in 1831.[64] Chief Justice John Marshall described the Indians' status, in that case, as that of "domestic dependent nations," with their tribal relations to national government being similar to "that of a ward to its guardian."[65] In three opinions authored by Justice Marshall in the course of nine years, from 1823 to 1832, the territory of Indian nations was declared to have been incorporated within the geographical limitations of the United States.[66] In 1871 the U.S. Congress ended its treaty relationship with Indian tribes and under new legislation decided that tribes were no longer to be considered independent nations with which treaties could be struck.[67]

Indian tribes are neither states of the union, in their quasi-sovereign status, nor are they foreign nations. In the United States, the relation of Indians to federal government remains "both pre-constitutional and extra-constitutional," as Charles Wilkinson expresses it.[68] The Constitution and its amendments refer to Indians,[69] but the Indians command special status. The Supreme Court has held that the Bill of Rights has "little application to Indian law," with individual members of Indian tribes unable to make Bill of Rights claims against their tribes and Indian tribes standing unprotected by the Bill of Rights from federal decisions as well.[70] Instead, the Indian Civil Rights Act of 1968, which imposes federal rights on the relation between tribal members and tribes, creates statutory rights that apply to Indians and has a content similar to that of the Bill of Rights.[71] Even though they may seem daunting, these measures have given Indian tribes the ability to maintain their own forms of law and legislation, with some tribes enjoying the opportunity to create and preserve their own normative worlds, living under their own regulation, and directing themselves as they see fit. Indian tribes gain certain other specific benefits in their quasi-sovereign status as well, such as the right to sovereign immunity from lawsuit.[72]

Two serious problems haunt the semisovereign status presently held by Indians, however, chief among which is confusion over just what the present standard should and does involve. Two doctrines in federal Indian law have battled against each other for prominence very nearly since the Supreme Court began hearing cases concerning Indian tribes, the first being the "doctrine of inherent sovereignty," and the second the "plenary power doctrine" or the "doctrine of trust responsibility."[73] Indian tribes are understood to retain full sovereign powers, through the doctrine of inherent sovereignty, unless they give them up through treaties, or they are taken by limited acts of Congress. The plenary power doctrine, in contrast, holds that Congress has the rightful ability to abrogate or abolish tribal powers of self-government.[74] Each of these standards is based partly on Supreme Court jurisprudence respecting Indian tribes and partly on other normative considerations about how tribes should be treated, but the standards conflict, and it is not obvious which should take prominence. This is one of the main weaknesses of the tribal sovereignty paradigm, especially with regard to its usefulness and applicability to theocratic communities: the standard is confused, characterized by "doctrinal incoherence and doleful incidents."[75] It will be important to be clear about the range and extent of legal autonomy to be given to theocratic communities, as well as the relations that individual theocrats and theocratic communities have to federal legal structures and statutes, if a quasi-sovereign status is to be made available to them.

A second defect of the tribal sovereignty model is this: it has proceeded from an ill-conceived and insulting understanding of the nature of the relation that a liberal polity ought to hold with respect to tribal communities. The history of the United States' dealings with Indian tribes is one of "conquest, exploitation, and eradication," as Judith Resnik suggests.[76] That rationale permeated the early Supreme Court decisions regarding tribal sovereignty, such as *Cherokee Nation*, wherein Justice Marshall described the quasi-sovereign status of Indian tribes as "[resembling] that of a ward to its guardian."[77] It was also at work in *Johnson v. McIntosh*, where the Court depicted tribes as neither Christian nor civilized.[78] If a semisovereign standard is to work for theocrats, there will be a need to go beyond the notion that the relation between theocratic communities and the federal government ought to be one of mere guardianship, as if theocrats were little more than Aristotelian slaves in need of a master.[79]

BASIC ELEMENTS OF A NEW STANDARD

Theocratic communities are obviously quite different from Indian tribes in several respects: unlike Indian tribes, most theocratic communities have not made treaties with government, for instance.[80] Theocratic communities are also not mentioned in the constitutions of liberal democracies, whereas the U.S. Constitution, for example, refers explicitly in three places to Indians and the Fourteenth Amendment mentions Indians as well, reiterating the exclusion of "Indians not taxed" for purposes of apportionment.[81] Further, Indian tribes are nearly all long-standing communities, existing before liberal government was conceived. But theocratic communities often are formed in fairly short order, and they crop up continually, as exemplified in the cases of Rajneeshpuram or Kiryas Joel. These differences, along with the problems of the tribal sovereignty paradigm identified above, highlight the need to avoid adopting indiscriminately the version of semisovereignty to which Indian tribes are subject.

The tribal model is instructive, however, and here I shall try to sketch some of the basic elements of what a quasi-sovereign framework for theocratic communities likely should include. I will focus on the following five considerations: preconditions of quasi sovereignty; educational, human rights, and exit requirements that liberal government must demand of theocrats; the appropriate extent of legal autonomy for theocratic communities; government funding and taxation for theocrats; and protective measures that could be used to defend the framework from corrosion.

In order to become semisovereign, first of all, a theocratic community would have to meet the following preconditions: (1) The religious community must be virtually homogeneous in its religious affiliations and have ownership of the property in the area to be made semisovereign. This requirement would help to circumvent a number of serious objections that could otherwise be raised by nonmembers not wishing to live in the prospective community. (2) The theocrats' territory must be distinct, free from and clear of neighboring districts or communities. A quasi-sovereign theocratic community could not be part of a city block, for instance, but would need to be an easily separable unit with regard to zoning and municipal regulations.[82] (3) The community would have to provide a basic plan for its social institutions, showing the ability to take care of members' basic needs and requirements. The plan of a prospective theocratic community would have to be presented to appropriate governing bodies, so that government could ensure that theocrats had a generally workable blueprint for their religious community, one that would not quickly dissolve into confusion when put into practice.

Stipulating that theocratic communities must take care of their members' basic needs and requirements leads naturally to the question of what, exactly, those requirements and needs happen to be. It seems reasonable to require that theocratic communities honor members' wishes to exit from their communities, in cases where they may decide to enter into the larger liberal polity.[83] Freedom of exit seems to be necessitated by an appropriate consideration of the value of freedom of association, as Chandran Kukathas has argued.[84] It also seems reasonable to oblige theocratic communities to meet educational and human rights requirements: theocrats will need to provide food, shelter, and clothing for members and will need to respect a minimal set of basic rights and interests for their entire cohort, without exceptions for women, children, or any vulnerable community members.[85] Extreme practices such as child sacrifice would be prohibited under that minimal set of rights and interests; as William Galston suggests, any defensible liberal order could not countenance, without qualification, "free exercise for Aztecs."[86] Education is a more tricky matter, however. While there are good reasons to maintain that any defensible framework for quasi sovereignty will need to be firm on exit and human rights requirements, one notes that there is great contestation over the kind of education that liberal government can rightfully promote or require for members of religious communities. I shall assume for the sake of argument that no satisfactory answer has yet been given to the question of just what the requirements should be. Even so, it is important to appreciate that liberal government will need to demand some form of education for children of theocratic communities, just as it must make such requirements of parents and guardians generally. For the education of children of theocratic communities cannot be left entirely to the devices of theocrats, since that risks some children acquiring virtually no education at all.[87]

Under a well-formed schema for quasi sovereignty, the educational baseline that liberal government may justifiably require of theocratic

communities would be considerably less comprehensive than that advocated by such liberals as Amy Gutmann or Stephen Macedo.[88] Here, it
is important to be chary, however, since quasi-sovereign communities
may by their nature wish fully to prevent their children from having con-
tact with outsiders. Prospective educational standards need to take this
into consideration, therefore: the reclusive nature of semisovereign communities will make chances for collaboration with public schools un-
feasible, even though, as Jeff Spinner-Halev reflects, greater cooperation
between public and parochial schools in larger democratic life may be
fruitful and judicious.[89]

First of all, the intellectual baseline for curricula in quasi-sovereign
theocratic communities would need to include requirements for basic
literacy, mathematical competence, and civic knowledge.[90] Second, educators in theocratic communities should be enjoined to teach students
about the nature of their rights and how the liberal polity's institutions
support them, as part of an effort to provide children with what Eamonn
Callan calls "some secure grasp of the meaning of their own culture of
birth."[91] Educators could bolster this understanding by impressing on
young members how principles of liberty of conscience support rights
and freedoms permitting their community to exist, prompting students
to consider why liberty of conscience may be important to them. Further,
well-formed curricula for children in theocratic communities would
likely include teaching about the importance of institutions securing citizen liberties at the federal level, such as constitutional protections for
freedoms of speech and association. For institutional guarantees with respect to liberty of conscience require freedom of speech at the federal
level of a democratic polity, as well as freedom of association for citizens,
although this is different from promoting or upholding those freedoms
within theocratic communities. The same holds true for the "value of political participation,"[92] which has robust importance in liberal democratic life, although it need not enjoy even a moral toehold within semisovereign theocratic communities.

Third, a schema for semisovereignty might usefully require educators
to teach children in theocratic communities about the values of toleration and respect for people outside their territories. Children in theocratic communities might, for instance, be taught about the integrity of
other ways than their own, while at the same time being free to learn
about the shortcomings and pitfalls of those whose lives are morally op-
probrious. Under such a structure, children would be educated to un-

derstand that there are other religions and conceptions of the good in the world; according to Spinner-Halev, this could trigger students' understanding "that occasionally there are good reasons for [people's] different convictions, and so they are worthy of respect."[93] Spinner-Halev's point is well directed, but it misses the mark here. For with a proper inculcation of the three principles of conscience, a more minimal, solid ground for respecting others can be fostered in children of theocratic communities. That ground is this: whether or not there is good reason for others to believe the particular convictions they hold, principles of conscience themselves give cause to respect the fact that others can come to their beliefs conscientiously and thoughtfully, maintaining their convictions with integrity. Importantly, the aim of inculcating such an understanding would not be to prompt or persuade young members of theocratic communities to endorse the life plans of others outside their territories. But no logical or psychological entailment seems present in that respect, and an educational schema incorporating the curricular elements I have described could be quite auspicious, with children in theocratic communities benefiting from a relatively fair and considered inclusion of the "great variety of lives," as Callan describes it.[94]

One might voice concern that children of theocratic communities will be left to lead a stunted existence if subjected to the more minimal educational structure that quasi sovereignty would allow. Here, the objector could champion instead a demand for education aiming to foster "sympathetic and critical engagement" with beliefs and ways of life at odds with those of one's own theocratic community.[95] Callan argues for such schooling in *Critical Citizens*, contending that children should not be denied "a sympathetic understanding of ethical diversity."[96] He suggests that any morally defensible educational schema must overcome the specter of "ethical servility": a nasty, set antipathy toward other ways of life, a vicious and degraded social status wherein one displays "ignorant antipathy towards all alternatives to [one's own] ethical ideal."[97] In Callan's vision, children in liberal-democratic polities would be empowered to engage imaginatively with ways of life that are "strange, even repugnant," doing so with interpretive charity.[98] Does more need to be required of the education of children in theocratic communities to ensure they develop their capacities to engage with other views sympathetically and critically?

First of all, theocrats might not object to educating youth in ways that promote sympathetic engagement with ethical diversity if principles of liberty of conscience were inculcated respectfully and conscientiously in members of theocratic communities. For the principles lend themselves naturally to such a treatment, since they emphasize the importance of conscience being free to accept the good, to reject the bad, and to distinguish between the two. Second, several theocratic communities encourage thoughtful engagement with a modest array of ethical diversity already. Consider, for example, Christian theocrats who contemplate Old Testament stories about polygamy or the concubines of King David but issue no immediate or thoughtless condemnations there, working instead to understand the religious and moral complexities of the Bible. In addition, many theocrats are well able reflectively to respond to criticisms from outsiders when questioned about their practices, values, and ways of life, which simple engagement with them demonstrates. Theocrats do not forfeit the ability to think critically, reflectively, or sympathetically merely because of the religious beliefs and values they espouse, and a sensitive treatment of the issue must take account of this fact.[99] What is more, however, Callan's understanding of "ethical servility" would need to be carefully reconsidered before attempting to apply it to members of theocratic communities. For simply because some theocratic practice or disposition appears to relegate believers to a servile position does not mean that it does. It is easy to deride the practices of theocrats by contending that they are shot through with superstition or to slight theocrats' attitudes by characterizing them as having a vicious, "ignorant antipathy" toward ethical diversity.[100] But so doing merely begs the question of whether theocrats' attitudes, understandings, and dispositions *are* false, harmful, or ungodly. And in that respect, the objector's argument remains unmade.

I wish to emphasize that, although the exact standards of appropriate educational requirements are still undecided,[101] the lack of a resolution does not militate against the usefulness of a framework of semisovereignty. For quasi sovereignty would be compatible with many of the educational conceptions on the table, allowing expanded autonomy for theocratic communities meeting basic educational requirements. Under a quasi-sovereign framework, liberal government would need to be lucid in its educational demands, and those demands would need to be met in turn by theocratic communities. But beyond those central requirements, theocratic communities would be able to provide teaching as they believe their religious doctrines require and could do so without being hampered by the many obstacles to religious free exercise that existing legal standards bring to bear.

In meeting the preconditions for quasi sovereignty, a theocratic community would be permitted to gain a significant measure of legal autonomy. But here it will be important to avoid giving theocratic communities broad or unqualified legal sovereignty, for a number of reasons. Broad legal sovereignty would imply the following features: (1) jurisdiction over a wide range of persons, in both civil and criminal realms, covering people with very little involvement with the community; (2) the capacity for theocratic authorities to punish people whom they prosecute to the extent that they please; and (3) an ability for theocratic authorities to create whatever laws they believe they should regarding education or concerning basic human rights, even where those laws may lead to a disavowal of these basic criteria. Educational, human rights, and exit responsibilities may be delegated to theocratic communities but must be superintended by the liberal polity; under a semisovereign framework, government would be enjoined to seek the least invasive way of ensuring that these conditions are met but would need to be prepared to act where the requirements are not fulfilled.[102]

A quasi-sovereign standard would need to open zones of legal autonomy for theocratic communities in a much more discriminating way. On civil matters, the standard would allow communities to decide internal laws and regulations for adherents, including conditions of membership, regulation regarding property,[103] rules pertaining to marriage and the inclusion and exclusion of outsiders, and other civil matters affecting their community.[104] Semisovereignty would also permit criminal punishment of theocrats by their communities' authorities. Semisovereign theocratic communities ought to be permitted to punish those members whom they find wayward; were they not allowed to discipline their adherents at all, theocrats would hardly be able to develop their normative worlds, with the tenor of life in their communities set mainly by liberal government and not by their religious conceptions of the good.[105] But it would be wrong to allow authorities in theocratic communities to inflict serious corporal or capital punishments, or excessively cruel discipline, or punishments such as extended isolation or imprisonment that may extend for a long duration and whereby members may be denied their freedom of exit. Quasi-sovereign theocratic communities also should not be permitted to pass binding judgment on felony crimes; this adjudication is not delegable by liberal government, and neither can the prospects of felony punishment be left to the discretion of theocratic authorities.[106] Federal government must protect its citizens in an even-handed way, especially on these issues, and will therefore need to ensure that felony crimes will be dealt with in a reliable manner.[107] There are two related reasons for placing these limits on punishment: first, while theocratic communities may initially present a design for stable social structures and institutions, their conceptions of the good remain significantly changeable. Small changes to a community's leadership or authority structure can have a critical impact on the prioritized conception of the good; this means that individual members in theocratic communities will have a difficult time predicting, at the outset, how the rules and structures under which they live might change over time. Second, authorities in theocratic communities could turn to excessive punishments for such crimes as heresy or blasphemy if left to their own devices or in instances where their prioritized rules or structures change. The same holds true for more mundane felony crimes such as assault or fraud, where community authorities may mete out excessively harsh judgments if a semisovereign standard were to allow it. It also appears that a quasi-sovereign framework should not allow theocratic communities to exercise legal powers over nonmembers, since it is difficult to see how jurisdiction over nonmembers would be needed to create or maintain a religious *nomos* or "to control internal relations" otherwise.[108] That is, theocratic communities probably should not have criminal or civil jurisdiction over nonmembers, and a sound framework for semisovereignty would presumably need to limit jurisdiction in these respects.

Off-community dealings and taxation will also require close attention for an appropriate schema of quasi sovereignty for theocrats. Taxation is a thorny issue, to be sure, since government normally does not tax religious institutions in the United States and allows for tax respite to religious organizations under the rubric of tax breaks for all nonprofit institutions and organizations. The Supreme Court upheld a statute allowing tax exemptions for "religious, educational or charitable purposes" by any nonprofit organization in *Walz v. Tax Commission*.[109] Where liberal polities benefit from the presence of nonprofit institutions, in the variety of forms that they take, tax breaks are rightly credited and a fine idea. Without government intervention, the public goods that nonprofit organizations yield would be underproduced;[110] a small tax break helps those organizations flourish.

Theocratic communities do not normally produce public goods, however, because of their exclusive and often reclusive nature. The reason for declining to tax them would seem to lie in a free exercise objection to taxation, if anywhere: taxing theocratic communities would impede their ability freely to exercise their religion, one could suggest. The problem with such an argument is that liberal government needs to be able to sustain governmental organizations and institutions that protect and support citizens living in theocratic communities and elsewhere. Unlike other citizens, whom government may reach with taxes in a variety of ways without taxing the religious institutions to which they belong, refraining from taxing theocratic communities could mean that members of those communities could hardly be taxed at all. Members of semisovereign theocratic communities could easily spend most of their lives in their communities, after all; theocrats tend not to exhibit the changing attachments and shifting involvements of most liberal citizens.[111] Furthermore, if many religious groups were to apply for quasi-sovereign status and became exempt from taxation once semisovereign, the ability of government to accrue sufficient revenue for its most basic operations could be jeopardized. For these reasons, it seems reasonable to suppose that theocrats should face some form of taxation under a quasi-sovereign framework.

Financial aid and endorsement issues appear to be quite complex with quasi sovereignty; how would these matters be handled with respect to semisovereign theocratic communities? It would be a mistake, first of all, to prohibit government from providing any aid whatsoever to theocratic communities. To the contrary, government should provide some assistance to citizens who live in theocratic communities; here I can only provide an outline of the acceptable boundaries for funding and endorsement, but there are certain principles that a sound framework for semisovereignty would need to incorporate. First, principles of separation ought to be observed in government dealings with semisovereign communities, both with regard to financial aid and in terms of symbolic support or endorsement. Theocrats have no moral right to receive state funds for their religion,[112] and neither should semisovereign theocratic communities have symbolic endorsement from government, since that may reasonably give citizens the impression that government endorses or prefers one religion over another or religiosity over unbelief, which it ought not to do.[113] Importantly, semisovereignty for theocratic communities would not logically imply symbolic endorsement of those groups' religious beliefs, nor would it need to involve the provision of government revenues for their religious practices; strong separation of church and state should be maintained even with a quasi-sovereign innovation. It is true that governments of many democratic countries around the world do not observe separationist principles, but that is a shortcoming of governance in those respective polities. For those governments fail to honor their moral obligation to refrain from aiding or assisting religious organizations at nonmembers' expense.[114]

Nevertheless, religious significance is sufficiently pervasive in theocratic communities that separationist principles, if misconstrued, could wrongly prohibit government from providing any aid or assistance to community members. It is surely reasonable to suggest that what government provides to citizens generally, it should make available to members of theocratic communities. If this is so, neutral goods such as basic health care and social services should be made accessible to citizens living in theocratic communities. This could include funding to semisovereign communities for medical purposes, along with allowances for the handicapped and other similar neutral services that government provides for all its citizens. With regard to schools, government could justifiably fund at least building and infrastructure, along with textbooks, salaries, and school lunches. Since liberal government will place educational responsibilities on theocratic communities, it would seem fair for them to aid communities to that end, as it aids school-going children generally.

One might wonder how the basic elements of quasi sovereignty for theocratic communities, as I have described them, are any different from the standard that many accommodationists would advocate. The accommodationist could agree completely that theocratic communities must not be allowed to punish their members severely, for example, and also maintain that liberal government must protect freedom of exit for members of theocratic groups. The accommodationist could further accept that the state should protect children within theocratic communities in much the same way that it protects children within families from extreme and unreasonable acts that are injurious to children's interests; some educational baseline for children might count as part of this protection, or the accommodationist could wish to require it on other grounds. Further, the advocate of accommodation might suggest that theocratic communities ought not to have jurisdiction over nonmembers and that community authorities must not be entrusted to adjudicate on serious crimes. With these stipulations in view, the accommodationist could propose that government may not otherwise interfere with the relations between members of the group or with the group's procedures for selecting members or leaders and must accord the group and its members the full range of rights and privileges enjoyed by other groups in civil society. How would a semisovereign framework differ from such a well-constructed accommodationist standard, and how would it be better?

First, a quasi-sovereign standard would be notably distinct in the way it protects theocratic communities from the corrosive effects of liberal legal systems. Accommodation standards cannot prevent public or private parties from bringing suit against theocratic communities and their practices, and those standards also require that religious groups continually must fight for exemptions from existing and imminent laws. As such, accommodation proves to be unworkable for theocrats, for litigation against religious practices strikes in a wide range of zones and issues forth from a variety of public and private corners. Battles fought in court are expensive and time-consuming, but, more seriously, continued involvement of theocrats in litigation and public battles is anathema to their religious doctrines, and it can lead them to become the sort of disputatious persons their doctrines condemn. Accommodations are given piecemeal to theocratic communities and normally only after a serious dispute has damaged the consistency of their religious lives. Semisovereignty would alleviate these problems significantly, since with it theocratic communities would not have to petition state and federal government for a host of exemptions or constantly worry about new legislation that may impact their religious ways of life. What is more, under a semisovereign standard, government and private parties both would be limited in the kinds of legal procedures they could bring to bear against theocratic communities. With this protection, theocratic communities would not become embroiled in lengthy and expensive legal disputes as often or as long as they are at present, they would not be forced continually to represent themselves publicly in an adversarial legal system that they may deplore, and their members would not be cajoled to take on an adversarial disposition with regard to liberal citizens, institutions, and government. Quasi sovereignty thus could provide much-needed assistance for theocratic communities, one suspects, and an appropriate commitment to religious free exercise requires relief for theocratic communities, since it is unjust for government to grind down religious practice and stultify free exercise in the way that existing legal standards allow.

In giving communities more robust protection from outside interference, quasi sovereignty would allow theocrats to create more stable zones of legal autonomy within their communities. This is a second way in which the standard differs from accommodation. The particular features of a framework for semisovereignty, once devised, could allow for little to no scope for interference from state or federal government on intracommunity matters, apart from the requirements that liberal government would be charged to oversee. The accommodation standard is not well equipped to enrich and expand zones of autonomy for theocratic communities, even where it is so motivated. For an accommodation framework proceeds on the assumption that citizens will be subject to laws unless granted exemptions or positive accommodations to the contrary and so does not present a sufficiently solid bulwark against the ravages of overarching regulation. Quasi sovereignty would place the burden on government to show why prospective legislation should apply to members of theocratic communities, instead of forcing theocrats continually to battle for exemptions, as an accommodation framework leads them to do.

Third, the protections that quasi sovereignty can afford and the zones of expanded autonomy delineated by such a framework would capacitate theocrats to build their normative worlds without the jarring intrusions and overpowering regulations that continue to pervade and weaken their frames of reference. As opposed to living under the extensive and intrusive house rules that liberal government now foists on theocrats, members of theocratic communities would be able to build their own *nomoi*, constructing their full range of institutions with an appropriate sense of autonomy that is lacking under other standards. Semisovereignty would impose some liberal legal requirements, as I have suggested, but the standard would allow theocratic communities to incorporate them into their worlds as they choose or desire. This would make for another qualitative difference in intracommunity rule for theocrats, and a good one, since it would empower theocratic communities to be governed largely under their own capacities, having codified protection in specific legal zones and permitting theocrats to practice their religion as they believe their doctrine requires. The accommodationist may wish to so capacitate theocratic communities as well but cannot accomplish the goal with a scheme of exemptions and positive accommodations alone. Under an appropriate schema for semisovereignty, theocrats will be enabled to build their communities within space marked out by a few legal fenceposts, each of which would stand as part of a village that they may identify, plan, and construct.

It is true that theocratic conceptions of the good are strict, often strange, and comprehensive in their range of teachings, but it would be wrong to dismiss quasi sovereignty for theocratic communities simply because theocratic ways of life might differ from one's own notions about how life ought to be lived or because government may be suspicious of the value of theocratic practices. A quasi-sovereign schema, if properly constructed, would respect the moral right of persons to religious free exercise, disallowing government from defiling the spirit of theocratic communities as it does at present. Honoring that right is a matter of justice, and it will benefit theocrats, since through it they will be endowed with the ability to develop the sorts of communities and the kinds of religious personalities that are important to them. But what is more, it would also be good for liberals and liberal government to acknowledge the value of quasi sovereignty for theocrats since, in so doing, liberals will show that their commitment to the value of religious free exercise is authentic. In constructing a framework of semisovereignty for theocratic communities, liberal government will show that it respects its theocratic citizens, that it understands the value of their normative worlds to them, and that it shall not allow legal machinery simply to abrade and destroy those communities. Despite urges to object generally to theocracy or suspicions that theocrats live deficient lives, respectful liberal government would resist its more perfectionist tendencies in creating a quasi-sovereign framework of which theocratic communities could take advantage.

BUILDING AND PROTECTING THE NEW STANDARD

Determining how to build a framework for semisovereignty and implementing measures to ensure that a plan for semisovereignty remains intact and protected will be pivotal to the standard's success. American theocratic communities could have quasi-sovereign status shielded by Congress; that is an option, and it is very nearly the situation that obtains for Indian tribes in the United States. One problem in this regard is that congressional authority has proven to be very powerful in its ability to diminish Indian sovereignty. As Scott Gould remarks, there have been several occasions on which Congress has sought to pare down the sovereignty of tribes, and in those instances the Supreme Court "has never failed to find the necessary power" in Congress to accomplish its goal.[115] The peculiar and unclear status of Indian tribes has also been used by both Congress and the Supreme Court to alter the condition of tribes over time or to "wage a continuous attack" on tribal sovereignty, as Alex Skibine puts it.[116] Perhaps to its credit, over the past three decades Congress has seen itself as holding a trust responsibility with respect to Indian tribes, a responsibility that obligates Congress to protect tribal sovereignty, even though understandings of the form of tribal sovereignty have changed.[117]

A more extreme option would be to forge a constitutional amendment for quasi sovereignty or a civil rights act for theocrats; both could yield a basis for formal protection for persons living in theocratic communities. I suspect, however, that the protection of a quasi-sovereign framework may be properly achieved without having to resort to drafting a civil rights act for theocrats or taking drastic measures otherwise.[118] For the free exercise clause of the First Amendment stands tall in defense of religious liberty and could provide formal protection for a semisovereign framework for theocratic communities in the United States, cover of a sort that would not require a new amendment and would naturally be distinct from the extraconstitutional protections afforded to Indian tribes.

Formal protection, of course, has its limitations; even where the law seems to be a staunch ally, its interpretation by courts can at times be counterproductive. For that matter, courts may not heed the intent of other governmental bodies, and this has certainly been a problem for Indian tribal sovereignty. The Supreme Court has extended state taxing authority on reservations, diminished territorial boundaries of tribes, and forbade Indians from regulating hunting and fishing by nonmembers in Indian territory, even though Congress quite clearly did not intend for those abatements to occur.[119] Like Indian tribes, theocratic communities also have a history of improper treatment by government, so confidence here cannot be high. Other indicators, however, bode well for the political and legal implementation of quasi sovereignty: courts, legal scholars, and political practitioners seek a better, more defensible standard for treating religious communities; moral and legal arguments recommend an option of semisovereignty for theocratic communities; and legal scholars have begun elaborating arguments helping to demonstrate how such a framework might be squared with the American constitutional tradition.[120] One finds in America greater deference to residential and other private associations, and trends toward careful and qualified devolution continue in liberal democracies around the globe. These factors lead one to think that the case for quasi sovereignty need not remain a merely moral, *ex ante* argument regarding the sort of treatment theocratic communities ought to have. Perhaps the best way to introduce and protect a framework for semisovereignty, at least in the American example, would be through congressional legislation supported by state and federal government and defended to the Supreme Court under First Amendment jurisprudence.[121]

Constitutional boundaries for quasi sovereignty will need to be considered judiciously in thinking through a schema of quasi sovereignty. There is a threshold at which quasi sovereignty would threaten the stability of the polity's overall liberal structure; that threshold should not be reached. The citizens and institutions of the larger liberal order will need to be free to work to honor and protect liberty of conscience for all citizens, along with defending citizens' other rights and freedoms, social and political institutions, secondary associations, and the like. These important institutions and participatory activities would be put at risk if excessive allowances were made to quasi sovereignty, since not only the very framework for semisovereignty would be jeopardized but so would the status and security of the overarching liberal democracy.[122] Since semisovereign communities will be largely nonparticipatory, they will require a robust liberal polity as a backdrop, one whose citizens and institutions need to be empowered to protect their communities appropriately.

With this in view, a well-crafted framework for quasi sovereignty could only allow for state and local semisovereignty up to certain level. The structure and number of quasi-sovereign communities would not justifiably be permitted to destabilize the majority population, the political and territorial integrity of the larger polity, or the country's constitutional foundations. Furthermore, the framework should permit the fluid and proper functioning of life and liberal institutions in the larger liberal polity. And so, while the precise parameters of quasi sovereignty remain underdetermined, one expects that a baseline of 5 to 10 percent of the entire territory of a liberal polity would be an approximate measure of the limits of quasi sovereignty. Optimal distribution of quasi-sovereign communities and their territories would likely be best accomplished through dispersion, as a quiltwork across states and provinces, with no theocratic community being excessively large either in area or population. International security issues will also be important to weigh here; they militate toward spotting a liberal polity with quasi-sovereign communities, instead of concentrating the communities in some large, particular area, setting aside a state or province for that purpose, or permitting merely one or two large communities to exist within the polity's borders.

A framework for quasi sovereignty might run the risk of creating a "separate but equal" dilemma. The Fourteenth Amendment provides a sobering lesson on this matter, one could argue: putting people in different categories and handling them separately is a recipe for domination and oppression, since so doing regularly leads to the de facto superiority of one group over another. Here one could assemble the scads of negative examples of Indian reservations and the legacy of poverty, separation, and injustice those constructions have left to Native peoples. Why would quasi sovereignty for theocratic communities not merely recreate those problems? Should a liberal polity not aim at integrating theocrats over the long run instead?

That the Indian case is on balance a negative example does not mean that the standard of quasi sovereignty is unusable or doomed to failure. I have drawn on the positive attributes of that standard while considering how to mitigate or excise the negative elements therein. To that end, I have stipulated the need of candidate quasi-sovereign communities to provide a plan of action to government, one that would include a design for the structure of members' quotidian affairs. The framework would grant specific jurisdictional allowances and other delegations to semi-sovereign theocratic communities, but that does not yield a recipe for disaster. For the liberal state would be charged to be vigilant about ensuring that theocratic communities met requirements for basic human rights, living standards, education, appropriate treatment of women and children, and rights of exit. None of this would need to be especially taxing or burdensome, and, combined, the factors suffice to ward off Veit Bader's fair-minded concern that quasi sovereignty for theocratic communities could lead to systemic illiberal or antidemocratic outcomes.[123] Furthermore, the standard I am advocating would be superior to those currently used: liberal governments at present tend to burden theocratic communities beyond what is reasonable or leave those communities to their own devices where they should not be so abandoned. In addition, government remains unclear on what it should ask or require of members of theocratic communities, with the result being treatment of those communities in an unprincipled and ad hoc manner, allowing the communities to be weighted down with lawsuits and other attacks. For the objector who divines prospects of injustice where legislators consider granting quasi sovereignty to theocratic communities, here he must reckon with the historical record: existing standards have themselves re-sulted in serious injustices, and this is part of the motivation for consid-ering an option of quasi sovereignty for theocratic communities.

With respect to the debated goal of integrating theocratic communi-ties into the fabric of the larger democratic tapestry, the liberal state has no clear moral claim. Provided that a framework for quasi sovereignty were able to satisfy requirements regarding education, taxation, political stability, and the other elements I have discussed, it is difficult to see what sort of argument for integration might even reasonably be ad-vanced on this front. For to contend that the liberal state has a right to integrate theocratic communities would be to suggest that conscience ought not to be free to pursue the good to the extent that the three prin-ciples of conscience require. Theocrats' moral right to religious free ex-ercise is a right largely to be left unmolested in daily life; working to in-tegrate or assimilate theocratic communities into a larger political unity would come at the cost of the reasonable ability of theocrats to pursue their very conceptions of the good, whether the integration were forced, legislated, or merely encouraged by government. It is true that integra-tion can take many forms, but those versions aiming to bring theocratic communities into a "larger political unity" would unjustifiably alter the pursuits and practices of religious communities and risk homogenizing people's conceptions of the good.[124] I have provided reasons that theo-crats should, even must, accept to affirm liberal institutions, and I have shown how theocrats are rationally committed to three principles of lib-erty of conscience. Those reasons and arguments help to justify the right of liberal government to apply a modest and appropriate legal code on the theocrats within its borders, but more extensive integration appears to be entirely without warrant.

If a framework for quasi sovereignty for theocratic communities were built so as not to run afoul of the basic legislative and moral require-ments of liberal governance, it could presumably warrant strong support under the First Amendment, especially given the failings of existing standards. For the rest of the standards that exist, including strict equal-ity, variations on partial accommodation, and full accommodation, cre-ate serious and unwarranted governmental intrusions on religious prac-tice, or they are severely deficient otherwise. A sound understanding of the First Amendment and the moral principles that it embodies prompts one to acknowledge the general value of a framework for semisover-eignty.[125] The details of such a schema will be of the utmost importance, naturally, and would have to be crafted so as to cohere with the Constitution and its amendments and inspire extraconstitutional confidence as well. But there is no obvious reason why the details could not be worked out accordingly; instead, there seems to be good cause to hold that quasi sovereignty for theocratic communities might be a success.

FIVE OBJECTIONS CONSIDERED

Before concluding, I shall consider five fairly weighty objections to the argument that I have presented in this chapter. First of all, one might object that the claim that theocrats are treated unjustly under the legal frameworks of contemporary liberal democracies is overstated. The objector could concede that existing legal standards impede members of theocratic communities in their religious pursuits and agree that these impediments hamper theocrats' religious practices; certainly, one could say, theocratic communities do seem to face some adversity in liberal democracies. But is that adversity sufficiently serious to constitute an injustice?

Three factors combine to indicate that members of theocratic communities are handled unjustly in contemporary liberal democracies under present legal frameworks. First, the obstacles facing theocrats are not negligible; they are not small or insignificant problems that merely pester theocrats as they try to live in accordance with their religious doctrines. Rather, theocrats' very ways of life are at stake, with their ability to live according to their most precious ideas of the good hanging in the balance. Under existing standards, theocratic communities are burdened sufficiently heavily to make their religious visions practically impossible to pursue, whereas the free exercise of their religion is something to which persons have a moral right. The seriousness of the damage seems to be a necessary component of injustice: where the damage caused to some party only amounts to a minor inconvenience, one normally does not say that some injustice has occurred. With respect to members of theocratic communities within liberal democracies, this criterion is satisfied.

A second component of injustice must also be this: that the serious obstacle, injury, or impediment to a party has not befallen them by mere chance or misfortune alone. For where one suffers some considerable harm simply because of bad luck, it hardly seems sensible to say that an injustice has occurred, since nobody is to blame. Such situations can elicit anger in injured parties,[126] but they would not properly constitute an injustice, except perhaps from a cosmic point of view. One sees that this element of injustice, too, is satisfied when it comes to theocratic communities: the relevant barriers to religious free exercise that theocrats encounter are not mere products of vast impersonal forces. It is the laws of liberal polities, created and amended by human actors, that impede theocrats in their pursuit of the good life. This leads to what appears to be a third component of injustice: the harm or impediment in question must not be unavoidable. For there are many instances where, it seems, any choice of action will have some fairly serious adverse impact on persons. Rawls speaks to this point in *Political Liberalism*, in discussing the outcomes of an appropriately oriented public conception of justice, namely, one with neutrality of aim.[127] It is an unavoidable and sad fact that some ways of life simply die out over time, Rawls maintains, because not all ways of life can rightly be saved.[128] For instance, reasonable educational requirements may lead to some forms of life withering away, when those requirements are put into practice.[129] Rawls borrows an apropos notion from Berlin, suggesting that there "is no social world without loss."[130]

The problem in this respect is that the withering away of theocratic communities often is not unavoidable. Whereas it is true that many religious groups will rise and fall in the historical course of a well-ordered liberal polity, existing legal standards generally stifle and choke out the efforts of persons who endeavor to live in theocratic communities. With some innovation, one suspects, this problem could be rectified, in accordance with reasonable requirements that would respect theocrats' moral right to religious free exercise, heed principles of separation of church and state, and not excessively involve government in protecting or supporting such groups at the expense of nonmembers. Present legal standards impede theocrats' religious free exercise, but those standards could be changed. I suspect that a new standard could be devised in a manner consistent with a very defensible version of liberalism, grounded in the cardinal principles of conscience I have articulated and building on the successes and failures of the Indian tribal sovereignty model. Providing a schema of semisovereignty for theocratic communities probably would not have to be especially burdensome for legislators and government, and it would not obviously require liberal government to forsake its principles, by any means.

A second objection could be levied here concerning the extent to which liberal rights and values other than religious liberty would be respected under a quasi-sovereign schema. The objector may suggest that little has been said about the value of personal autonomy, for instance, which surely liberal government ought to consider very carefully in determining how to handle the claims and requirements of theocratic communities in liberal democracies. The legal autonomy afforded to quasi-sovereign theocratic communities could undermine the personal autonomy of individual members of those communities, the objector may contend, and so any defensible case in favor of a quasi-sovereign schema would have to justify the apparent priority given to the moral right to religious free exercise in this respect.

In response to this second objection, first of all, I should like to note that at the outset of this chapter I proposed to take it that there is a moral right to religious free exercise, but I did not suggest that no other rights exist or claimed that personal autonomy ought always to lose out in cases where it conflicts with religious liberty. Religious free exercise is indeed a moral right among others, and any well-constructed schema for quasi sovereignty would have to take other rights and values under careful consideration. I wish simply to suggest here that personal autonomy ought not to be valued so highly as to undermine entirely the religious free exercise of strict religious devotees. There are good reasons to hold that personal autonomy should not dominate religious free exercise, on any proper reckoning, and the arguments I have provided with respect to liberty of conscience strongly support this position. Second, it should be emphasized that it is not due to conflicts with the value of personal autonomy that theocrats find their religious free exercise hampered. Rather, it is the savagery of the law that undercuts theocrats' religious free exercise, with existing standards allowing wanton destruction to be wreaked on theocratic communities' pursuit of the good.[131] The very motivation for examining the viability of quasi sovereignty springs from an assessment of the deficiencies of existing standards, not from a desire to impair personal autonomy or a lack of concern for that value in particular. Third, a schema for quasi sovereignty would not necessarily demand or allow that personal autonomy be undermined in theocratic communities. The particular framework I have advocated in this chapter, for example, would expressly require theocratic communities to meet educational criteria, but these elements could be expanded if necessary, just as other criteria for personal autonomy could be added, without vitiating the quasi-sovereign standard generally. Since a quasi-sovereign framework could be fashioned in a number of ways, one expects that its requirements would not inevitably run afoul of an appropriate valuation of personal autonomy.

A third objection could be made regarding the degree to which quasi sovereignty would successfully alleviate the stresses of legal action on theocratic communities. The objector might reckon that litigation would be necessary at a variety of stages simply in order to set up a quasi-sovereign framework, not to mention the political involvement that may be required initially to implement the schema. Furthermore, it could be argued that members of theocratic communities would have just as many, if not more, occasions to sue their groups or their leaders as they do at present. To this one could add that parties external to theocratic communities, such as parents or other relatives of community members, citizens from neighboring areas, or regulatory bodies and government agencies, also may attempt to take legal action against theocratic communities. What reason is there to think that quasi sovereignty would effectively reduce the legal pressures that currently weigh on theocratic communities in liberal democracies?

First, quasi sovereignty would stabilize patterns of litigation by preventing lawsuits from being initiated against theocratic communities as they are at present, namely, from a wide spectrum of public and private parties on virtually any issue or concern. Quasi sovereignty could incorporate procedural limitations making legal action more difficult to initiate against theocratic communities meeting the basic criteria set out by liberal government, by narrowing the scope of issues on which suit may be brought and reducing the range of parties able to take legal action against theocratic communities as well.[132] *Ceteris paribus*, this would likely reduce the pressures of litigation. Second, unlike the accommodation standard, quasi sovereignty would not make theocratic communities wait until they are attacked before providing them with exemptions or other legal accommodations. This is worth noting here since it is not just the quantity of litigation that is problematic; the very structure of accommodation standards is also a burden to theocrats, allowing for lawsuits very nearly without discrimination and providing relief, if at all, only after proceedings have been litigated. Existing standards damage the *nomoi* of theocratic communities not simply with the amount of litigation that they allow but also with the oppressive context they create. Third, a reduction in litigation would not be the only thing recommending semisovereignty for theocratic communities, since a quasi-sovereign framework could also serve to clarify relations between theocratic communities and governing bodies. By being clear on what government will require of theocratic communities and by delineating well-devised requirements in a public, accessible manner, liberal government could show it respects the right of theocrats freely to practice their religion and pursue their conceptions of the good, affirming the liberal commitment to religious liberty as well. One might even dare to hope that such a framework could help to cultivate a more favorable disposition between theocrats and liberal parties, with the mutual respect that may be developed in such an arrangement. Reducing the pressures of unnecessary litigation will help members of theocratic communities to pursue their conceptions of the good, but that abatement would not be the only aim or benefit of a quasi-sovereign standard.

One could marshal a fourth objection here, focusing on the question of whether quasi sovereignty should be limited to theocratic communities instead of making the option available to a broader range of groups. Here, the objector could distinguish two particular kinds of communities that might be well served by quasi sovereignty. First, the objector may point to communities that are religious but have no comprehensive conception of the good. These would include the town, for instance, whose people believe that God affirms a "No work on Sunday" rule but the townspeople are latitudinarian on other elements of beliefs and practices.[133] Second, one could distinguish groups that have comprehensive conceptions of the good and the wish to withdraw from society but are not religious; this kind of group would include Thoreauvian naturalists.[134] Any of these groups could surely be true believers in their ways of life, the objector may point out, able to satisfy whatever authenticity test one might wish to apply.[135] Why should quasi sovereignty be granted to theocratic communities but not to communities such as these?

Consider the first sort of community first: namely, the one that has a religious but not comprehensive conception of the good. In the example I have provided, the issue would be whether to consider granting quasi sovereignty to a town to enable its membership to require store closings on the Sabbath, even though the townspeople are largely indifferent to people's pursuits otherwise. Importantly, the request at issue is not extreme: the townspeople do not wish to gain quasi sovereignty so as to be permitted to deny some of the town members their basic rights and liberties, to disadvantage and deny right of exit to townspeople who fall out of favor, or something of a similarly invidious nature. A well-formed schema of quasi sovereignty would not allow those practices in any community. Nevertheless, three points must be made here. First, legal accommodations would suffice to satisfy the demands of the townspeople. This does not run afoul of the argument I have provided, for I have not argued that accommodation is by its nature unjust or insufficient for religious practitioners generally but rather that it is that not workable for theocratic communities ensconced in liberal democracies. Second, a community of this nature would not likely be interested in quasi sovereignty. Quasi sovereignty has a list of requirements that applicant communities would have to meet, regarding a complete institutional plan of action, educational requirements for children, taxation, and the like, all of which would likely be viewed as burdensome and undesirable by the people in question. Furthermore, communities of this sort would have no reasonable concern about the corrosion of their *nomos*, provided they were allowed a reasonable accommodation, and this applies not just to prospective Sunday closing rules but to a wide variety of practices and prohibitions that a noncomprehensive religious community might wish to enact. And so if this sort of community were to seek quasi sovereignty, they would have no obvious claim to it.[136] For government would not be standing in the way of their prospective "No work on Sunday" rule if it gave the townspeople a modest allowance of accommodations to that end, and refusing them access to a quasi-sovereign schema would not limit their religious free exercise. Accommodations fit reasonably and well with such communities, but a quasi-sovereign standard does not.

Communities of the second sort are more difficult. Those communities' conceptions of the good are comprehensive and other regarding with respect to how life is to be lived. There are prima facie reasons for thinking that such communities should be candidates for quasi sovereignty: the spirit of the community may be defiled by excessive involvement and entanglement with law and society, such embroilment may be proscribed by the community's doctrine or conception of the good, and members could have not only a plan of action for their community but also the wish to withdraw from society for the sake of their nonreligious *nomos*. As such, it is not obvious why communities of this kind should be disqualified from quasi sovereignty, for they are very nearly identical to theocratic communities and merely lack a vivid religious color.

Nonreligious communities do not have a case for quasi sovereignty identical to that of theocratic communities, however. The reason is this: they identify a source of value different from otherworldly ends, ex hypothesi. Consider, for instance, Kent Greenawalt's description of the community that is naturalist and Thoreauvian, striving to live at one with nature: "Suppose two hundred 'Thoreaus,' less individualistic and obstinate than the actual person, establish an agricultural community . . . [and] all [members] agree that modern life is too hurried, stressful, and competitive. They live a simpler life and teach that to their children."[137] How is such a group relevantly distinct from a theocratic community and undeserving of a chance to acquire quasi sovereignty? I do not wish to contest that it is good and decent to live in harmony with nature; nor do I want to deny that this is something persons should endeavor to do. But there exist neither intrinsic dictates of nature nor practices of worship with regard to nature itself, in contrast to what one finds with religion. Nor does nature itself supply any ultima facie commands regarding how to live, in contradistinction to the dictates of divine commands and religious doctrines. For that matter, nature alone identifies no prospects of punishment awaiting in an afterlife for those who fail to comply with any putative natural dictates, just as it is silent on the notion of reward for the good and faithful. With this in view, to the extent that a naturalist community is not religious, it is in the end different in kind from theocratic communities;[138] and this militates against Martha Nussbaum's suspicion that one cannot distinguish "religious belief-systems from nonreligious beliefs and practices in any principled and systematic way."[139] It is true that various theocratic communities observe close bonds with the natural world—the Pueblo Indians and the Amish are examples—so having close communion with nature by no means disqualifies a community from being theocratic. But enjoying an intimate connection with nature itself does not suffice to make an individual or community religious.

The objector may retort that not all comprehensive nonreligious communities are naturalist in essence. Some communities could simply contend that their views of liberty and justice are very different from those of liberal government and society. Members of this sort of community might claim that conscience requires them to live a nonconformist life, one requiring withdrawal and quasi sovereignty. Persons with these conceptions of the good could seek to build a community freed from interference by government and society, as much as possible, or they might aim not to be required to conform to the world for the sake of their community's own experiment in living. Why should quasi sovereignty not be granted to this sort of community? Would they not deserve a chance to qualify, just as religious communities would? And do the three principles of conscience not support such an allowance?

First, comprehensive nonreligious communities have more accessible claims about liberty and justice that fellow citizens can consider and assess. By hypothesis, they do not appeal to transcendent values above and beyond political justice, and so their disagreement generally operates on the same plane as their fellow citizens. As William Galston suggests, nonreligious moral doctrines tend to "rest their claims on shared experience and uncontroversial canons of reasoning . . . [debates between] utilitarians, Kantians, perfectionists, particularists, and pluralists are conducted on common ground and are potentially resolvable in a way that disagreements between Christians and Jews are not."[140] Citizens across the board disagree variously with the policies and impositions of liberal government; some object to taxation, some contest the permissibility of abortion, others protest the corrupting influence of political officials. Their protestations alone are not grounds for quasi sovereignty, even where citizens may organize into a comprehensive community. For if they were, that would justify giving quasi sovereignty to a plethora of prospective communities, which would be unworkable for a liberal polity. Disagreement alone is not sufficient; a serious, sincere objection based in otherworldly values, consistent with principles of liberty of conscience, is different.

Second, requests for a robust, protected form of withdrawal issuing from nonreligious groups are few and far between in liberal democracies. One reason for this may be that while members of nonreligious communities often express concern for greater liberties, more extensive community health care, better education for all citizens, or lower or higher taxes, they do not normally seek complete withdrawal or secession unless they have other grounds such as nationalist ones. A second reason is that nonreligious groups tend not to object to liberal practices with the same fervor as their theocratic counterparts. Nonreligious communities are less likely to stand in favor of segregation of sexes, all other things being equal; they have no worship requirements, by hypothesis; they have no church to protect; they launch no educational objections regarding the ungodly teachings of certain books; and they have no otherworldly values or ends over which to fret, no sense of jeopardy in that regard. So they have less to reject in that respect. Third, the lack of demand for withdrawal from nonreligious communities may be explained in part by the fact that existing standards of associational liberty are largely adequate for their purposes. A fourth reason could be that many of these people also have an option to emigrate to countries with more amenable views on how to live, how extensive government should be, and how social and political inequalities are structured. A fifth reason is that where nonreligious comprehensive communities have sprung up in liberal democracies, the experiments have tended to be short-lived. It is true that inductive issues complicate the matter here, since opening the gate to quasi sovereignty could lead some nonreligious communities to desire to pursue that option and to do so successfully.[141] But private property and associational liberty allowances seem largely adequate to satisfy the concerns of nonreligious parties, at least at present; and the retiring nonreligious community remains a rara avis.[142]

I am not submitting that nonreligious comprehensive communities could never identify or adduce adequate grounds for quasi sovereignty for themselves; I am suggesting that the case appears difficult to make convincingly. Such an argument would likely have to proceed on a different footing from the case for quasi sovereignty for theocratic communities, perhaps via an argument for expanded associational liberty stemming from the need for liberal government and citizens to better respect claims of conscience. It is also worth emphasizing here that exemptions, accommodations, and differential treatment can indeed be warranted for nonreligious claims of conscience. In chapter 2, I noted that conscience is not limited to affirming religious conceptions of the good and proposed that nonreligious conceptions can be affirmed as well. Liberal government should make allowances for conscientious objection for individuals and groups, based on determinations that objections are sincere and the intrusions burdensome, among other considerations.[143] As for constitutional legal grounds for quasi sovereignty for nonreligious, comprehensive communities, there is slender cause to think that those groups have a case. Mark Rosen has argued that communities of nonreligious political perfectionists could be candidates for certain "extensive rights to govern their own affairs" in discrete territorial zones,[144] proposing further that those rights are required by "foundational liberal aspirations" articulated in Rawls's *Political Liberalism*.[145] The free exercise clause of the First Amendment provides legal backing for quasi sovereignty for theocratic communities, but it would likely be difficult to secure access to quasi sovereignty for nonreligious communities in the United States.[146]

Perhaps the most careful and judicious conclusion to draw is the following: while theocratic communities should be eligible as candidate communities for quasi sovereignty, there is cause for reluctance in thinking that nonreligious groups may so qualify. The fact that the issue of whether to grant semisovereignty to nonreligious communities is difficult to decide does not cut against quasi sovereignty for theocratic communities, however, nor does it militate against a framework for quasi sovereignty generally. For even if liberal polities were to include nonreligious comprehensive communities among groups eligible for the 5 to 10 percent of the polity's territory to be made into semisovereign regions, the integrity of the argument I have provided remains intact.

The question remains as to why liberal government ought to be called on to remedy the injustices done to theocrats living in liberal democracies. This could also be marshalled as a fairly serious objection: why do theocrats deserve action on the part of government to help make their communities semisovereign? One might grant that the damage presently done to theocratic communities amounts to an injustice, but even so this is surely not enough to show that government should be held responsible for rectifying the situation. For injustices are committed daily by private citizens in the harms they cause to one another; those injustices, too, are avoidable, in the sense that they need not come to pass, but it would be foolish to think that government could prevent them all. Government is not a panacea for all social ills, and it cannot reasonably be expected to prevent all injustices from happening or to rectify each of them when it occurs. Theocrats, however, are not hampered in their religious pursuits by simply any party; rather, they are impeded by existing legal structures, for which government is responsible and which only government can change. This critical point shows exactly why government ought to act to provide a new framework for theocratic communities: government has wrongly set up the obstacle in the first place, government can take it away, and no other party can do so.[147]

CONCLUSION

In considering how political and legal institutions of liberal democracies ought to handle religious attachments, it is critical to acknowledge the value of religious liberty; however, respect for religion also requires that the institutions of law and politics hold the values of religious toleration and autonomy in high regard as well. Where government flatly denies or dishonors the moral right of religious free exercise, it enfeebles religious lives unjustly and without cause; but if liberal law and governance could be reconciled with quasi sovereignty for theocratic communities, those injustices may be able to be resolved. Carefully crafting a legal schema that would allow theocratic communities to gain semisovereignty and treating members of theocratic communities under such a standard could improve dramatically the kind of treatment those communities presently receive.

I have argued that existing legal standards for treating theocratic communities are deficient and proposed that a framework for semisovereignty could much better enable members of those communities to practice their religions. Thinking through the prospects and possibilities of quasi sovereignty and trying to devise a workable, appropriate legal framework for handling theocratic communities are endeavors that ought to be taken seriously. The ways in which theocrats are maltreated under existing standards are serious and a remedy for their ailments is greatly needed. Semisovereign status would not liberate theocratic communities from the influence of other groups or institutions or free them from the influence of their neighbors, it is true, but no political bodies are free in that respect. What semisovereignty could do instead would be to deliver theocratic communities from the injustices of excessive entanglements that they presently endure, endowing their members with the capacity to build the normative worlds their religious doctrines require. If it is true that persons have a moral right freely to pursue their religious conceptions of the good, semisovereignty for theocratic communities might just be the way to bring that right to life for theocrats.

4. Inspiring Public Reason

THE PROMISE OF LIBERALISM

I ELABORATED IN CHAPTER 3 the idea of quasi sovereignty for retiring theocratic communities, completed an outline of the basic elements of a semisovereign framework, and provided reasons why a legal framework of that kind would make for a better, more workable standard for treating theocratic communities in liberal democracies. In this final chapter, I aim to achieve four remaining objectives. First, I identify implications that the arguments above hold for public reason and the role of religious argumentation in public discourse. Second, I focus on issues raised by religious extremists and other ambitious theocrats and advance suggestions as to how liberals and liberal government might better interact with them. Third, I briefly consider strategies for increasing domestic and international comity between liberal institutions and theocratic communities and polities. In the course of fulfilling these three objectives, I will tackle the remaining two moral problems that I identified at the outset. I consider how liberals and liberal government might provide grounds for interfering with theocratic practices and make a case regarding the kinds of explanations liberals and liberal government might give in that respect. I close by addressing and forestalling remaining objections to the argument presented in this work in its entirety.

PUBLIC REASON RECONSIDERED

Many philosophers and political theorists identify public reason as a property of citizens as a whole rather than seeing it as the mere personal or private reason of particular individuals or groups. As John Rawls describes it, public reason is the reason of free and equal citizens, and in that sense it is the reason of the public. The very subject of public reason is the public good, he suggests: public reason speaks to questions of basic political justice, including such fundamental matters as the nature of constitutional essentials and rules for their elaboration. Rawls considers the nature and content of public reason to be public, furthermore, inasmuch as public reason is expressed through a family of reasonable conceptions of political justice, each sincerely believed and reasonably understood to be acceptable to other reasonable citizens.[1] In Rawls's account, public officials of free societies are supposed to draw on public reason when debating and deciding on matters of broad social concern, in situations where they enact and repeal laws, amend constitutions, or forge the very political systems and governing institutions by which citizens will live. One could reasonably expand this notion of public reason to include contributions from citizens who do not hold public office, at least with respect to their voting or public backing for social and political policies and laws. In what follows, I shall refer to public reason in this expanded sense. Publicly valid reasons should be able to gain broad appeal by their nature, and for the sake of argument I take it that the reasons ought also to be accessible to all persons. While other conceptions of public reason exist, this is the one that I shall adopt for the discussion at hand.

Realizing the ideal of public reason has been no simple task. There remains wide disagreement on the very issue of what public reason allows in public debate and on the extent to which religious convictions and motivations can play a proper role in the public forum. Ambitious theocrats flag this problem colorfully. They are regularly critical of democratic life, speaking out on the inappropriateness of permissive legislation, the poor performance of political institutions, or the regrettable loss of morality in contemporary society. In chapter 1, I proposed that ambitious theocrats' political participation is a source of deep discordance in liberal democracies, with respect both to the views theocrats provide on policy issues and the ways they contribute to public discourse. Where theocrats give religious reasons for supporting or censuring policies and laws, in particular, secular parties contend that the reasons are inadmissible in public debate. Such responses frustrate theocrats in their efforts to be taken seriously in public discussion, fostering a sense of disenfranchisement among private religious citizens and religious associations alike. The same is true of particular policy proposals that zealous religious parties often try to advance. To theocrats, and to religious adherents broadly, secular parties can appear to be neither receptive nor respectful with regard to matters of profound concern to them. From the perspectives of secular citizens and religious moderates, ambitious religious devotees seem overzealous and simply unreasonable in their efforts to bring religious considerations to public debate, in both the policy proposals they make and the ways in which they make them.

A number of philosophers, including Robert Audi, James Bohman, Kent Greenawalt, Amy Gutmann and Dennis Thompson, John Rawls, Paul Weithman, and Nicholas Wolterstorff, have enriched philosophical deliberations on public reason by providing interesting and thoughtful contributions.[2] Much of the debate regarding public reasons, however, is narrowly calibrated for persons who already accept to a significant degree liberal principles of reciprocity and civility, who are "reasonable" in a Rawlsian sense, who adopt and abide burdens of judgment, or who affirm a list of primary goods similar to that which Rawls provides.[3] Ambitious and retiring theocrats reject to differing degrees such liberal principles and values and, to the minds of many, qualify as unreasonable people. If arguments respecting public reason cannot be demonstrated to be relevant to theocrats with nonliberal or antiliberal religious conceptions of the good, they risk disengagement from one of the most serious remaining problems of simple pluralism, a conundrum that the very debates over public reason were presumably intended to help assuage.[4] What is more, discussions of public reason remain quite abstract on the whole. They fail to identify or recommend ways in which liberals could engage not merely reasonable people who differ over narrowly defined issues within the framework of broadly held liberal principles and values but those roaming the theoretical space outside that structure. And there is a cost for such continuing detachment: namely, the prudential problems and moral failures I identified at the outset, those raised by theocrats whose ways of life do not harmonize with standing liberal institutions and laws.

I shall not take this occasion to analyze theories of public reason in detail; nor will I attempt to provide a precise ethics of civic virtue for liberal citizens. Instead, I shall furnish three suggestions regarding implications that the arguments above have for a more complete understanding of public reason. In particular, I focus here on what the content of public reason properly should include or exclude, to try to build on and improve existing understandings of public reason. I subsequently consider the more central and pressing political question: namely, what can liberals do about ambitious theocrats in liberal democracies and elsewhere?

First, the arguments from chapter 2 suggest an important connection between liberty of conscience and public reason. I have argued that the value of liberty of conscience is of high and common importance to theocrats, but it is clear that liberty of conscience is an important value for liberals as well, so long as one appreciates that freedom of conscience must be balanced against other liberal values such as equality, justice, autonomy, and fairness. This is noteworthy since there are very few values to which theocrats and liberals hold a common commitment, that are able to give the differing parties reason to affirm a liberal order and could be adduced in such ways as to meet publicity and reciprocity criteria of public reason. But beyond this, I suspect that liberty of conscience may be a quintessential value at the very heart of public reason, one that is of common importance to all citizens of liberal democracies and suitable for providing a strong foundation on which to justify a liberal order. While this notion requires further argument and elaboration to be justified fully, I expect that a cogent case could be made to this effect, drawing on the arguments of these chapters along with the resources of liberal political philosophy more broadly.

Here is a second consideration on public reason. I have suggested above that it will not suffice for liberals simply to have arguments regarding the justification of a liberal order; they will need to be prepared to give those arguments to others as well. To this extent, the view that I have offered is not novel: Rawls argued as much in *Political Liberalism*.[5] As I proposed in chapter 1, however, theocrats are owed justificatory reasons, morally speaking. Liberalism cannot back down from properly justifying its existence to its citizens, for the justification of a political order is antecedent to its enforcement, not in the temporal sense, perhaps, but rather in a logical sense.[6] One must not forget that theocrats object deeply to the structure and content of liberal institutions and laws. Their objections require a response, and one expects any liberal to agree that there is a need to provide such reasons where they are required. After all, it is the liberal state that sets up and polices legal boundaries for theocrats, and liberal institutions that coerce religious adherents where they transgress.

Principles of liberty of conscience will be integral to an adequate explanation on this front. Those principles provide strong requirements for theocrats to affirm liberal political institutions, while other values do not; theocrats are committed rationally to them; and the theocrat's rational commitment is derived from entirely reasonable beliefs respecting the pursuit of otherworldly value and ends. Principles of liberty of conscience cannot be expected to decide all possible policy controversies, of course. Nor would liberty of conscience be the only factor worth considering in thinking through the wide variety of controversial and divisive political issues that arise in the natural course of development of free societies. But I have not expected as much, and no hopes should be dashed by this concession. Rather, I propose more modestly that the value of liberty of conscience could serve in a broader, fundamental justification for a liberal order, one that could speak to the religious devotees of the world's multicultural and multifaith polities.

There is also a political reason for liberals to provide their arguments in favor of liberal institutions to theocrats, alongside the moral concerns I have described. The reason is this: simply having those arguments available will not help to assuage political discord within liberal democracies, allay concerns over the basic legitimacy of liberal government, or quell religious conflict that remains in other polities around the world. But here one must be careful since, politically speaking, it will not be satisfactory just to tell theocrats that they must not have theocracy or to declare that liberal government simply will not allow it. Those responses are politically unsatisfactory because people will not accept them, and replies of that kind have not helped resolve the problems of religious discord at hand in U.S. society, in other Western liberal polities, or in other areas of the world.

As a third and final thought on public reason, I propose that liberals should rethink the admissibility of religious reasons in democratic public debate, where constitutional essentials, policies, and laws are under discussion. Strangely, perhaps, it is ambitious theocrats and not more regular religious citizens who prompt realignment in this direction. The justification of a liberal order under conditions of simple pluralism requires natural theology reasons for theocrats, since there will remain no obvious reason for theocrats to affirm liberalism or liberal institutions unless naturally theological arguments are employed to that end.[7] As I argued in chapter 2, the only way to demonstrate to theocrats that strict theocratic governance is not for them is to consider the very nature of divine commands, addressing directly the question of what God would or would not command of his followers. Natural theology arguments of the kind I have offered will be required here, for without those theological arguments, theocrats will retain recourse to grounds on which to contest the putative reasons offered by secular liberal opponents to affirm a liberal order. And they will disagree seriously, vigorously, and all the way down. Reasons required for the justification of a liberal order surely must be considered admissible in public discourse; if religious reasons given to justify liberalism are admissible from liberals, then they must be acceptable from other parties as well. Which citizens give those reasons should be irrelevant, after all, when it comes to matters of broad public concern.

One could consider various other issues pertaining to public reason, such as whether one could ever work out an adequate standard for accessible public reasons, whether inaccessible reasons should count as admissible in public discourse on restrictive policies, the extent to which there is a duty of sincerity for those offering public reasons in favor of coercive policies or laws, or whether reliance on the dictates of religious authorities is acceptable for liberal citizens where they vote or participate in politics otherwise. I shall not address these issues with great specificity here, since that is not my central concern, but I would stress that liberal arguments about public reason could be joined with the three suggestions on public reason I have made and linked to the strategies for treating ambitious theocrats that I provide below. For the problem pertaining to narrow debates over public reason is that the discussion is in danger of disconnecting from some of the most serious problems of simple pluralism, problems that the very debates over public reason were presumably originally intended to help mollify. I am not arguing that people should not provide accessible arguments in public debate, nor am I suggesting that it is consistent with civic virtue for one to rely on religious reasons alone, or on the word of a putative religious authority, where one advocates or otherwise advances some particular policy or law. The question I want to ask is what can liberals *do* about the larger problems raised by theocrats, within the bounds of propriety and right?

RELIGIOUS EXTREMISM: STOPPING THE TURN TO VIOLENCE

Recent years have witnessed a surge of religiously motivated political behavior in the United States, in liberal democracies elsewhere, and in various other regions and nations of the world. Where this behavior confronts liberal principles and norms, it is at times overtly violent; as I argued in chapter 1, such ongoing issues testify to a series of moral and prudential problems for liberals and liberal governance, putting the very legitimacy of liberal government at risk. At the outset, I distinguished retiring from ambitious theocrats and suggested that the latter category includes violent religious extremists as well as religious practitioners working through more peaceful means to supplant existing liberal institutions and laws with stricter regulations and institutions. I shall now directly address ambitious theocrats and the problems they create, and I will first take the problem of extremist religious groups, those that pre-sent a high risk of violence or engage in violent behavior outright. I have mentioned that those groups present very real, serious concerns for lib-erals and liberal democratic governance. What, if anything, can be done to mitigate the problems they elicit?

I commence with empirical analyses of extremist religious groups and their formation. Much of that activity is considered within studies of so-called terrorism, an approach that has obvious drawbacks, not the least of which is that there is dispute over what should count as a terror-ist organization. For the purposes of this study, I wish to analyze groups that engage in religious violence instead of only those groups and or-ganizations covered under a more narrowly defined rubric of terrorism. It is important to be clear that while there are extremist examples among new or minority religions, there is "relatively little evidence" that the vast majority of those religious groups pose danger.[8] David Tucker has ar-gued that the problem with extremist religious groups is not religion per se but the "type" of religion.[9] The point merits agreement in part: it is true that religious extremism is not limited to Islamic groups, for in-stance, since extremism is identifiable from a wide variety of religious doctrines. But for Tucker's claim to be plausible, types of religion would need to be further disaggregated, and ambitious theocratic motivations of various kinds remain a central and persistent source of grief for liber-als and liberal democratic governance.

Analyses of religious extremism to date are scanty. In a study of ter-rorist group formation, Ami Pedahzur, William Eubank, and Leonard Weinberg found that new terrorist groups are largely religious in orien-tation.[10] They determined that of nearly four hundred identifiable terror-ist organizations around the globe, the number of terrorist religious or-ganizations was smaller than those of left-wing, right-wing, or nationalist groups. But religious terrorism is emerging more quickly: 71.4 percent of terrorist organizations established in the 1990s were religious.[11] There now exists "a constellation of [terrorist] organizations with religiously-inspired agendas," as the authors describe it, with militant Islamic groups constituting the lion's share.[12] These religious groups are dan-gerous, even though not much is "new" in their organizational or network structures.[13]

Can liberals or liberal government do anything to defuse the tendency for new and minority religions to turn to violence? Jonathan Fox argues that data from the Minorities at Risk project show that religious institutions tend peacefully to oppose legal or political impositions unless they perceive a threat to their institutional structure or to their religion itself.[14] He maintains that violent opposition tends to emerge where one finds a group-level desire for autonomy and independence resulting from perceived discrimination. Fox's analysis is consistent with that of Jean-François Mayer, who contends that the perception of an assault on a religious group is a key motivational factor prompting such groups to take extreme actions against liberal citizens and institutions.[15] Mayer suggests that both the Rajneeshees and Branch Davidians displayed an "obsession with persecution," noting that the same holds true for other religious communities that turned to violence, such as the Order of the Solar Temple, Aum Shinrikyo in Japan, and Divine Light Zentrum in Switzerland.[16]

It is worth emphasizing that each of these groups was theocratic, according to the definition of theocracy I have elaborated: each group promoted a strict, religious, and comprehensive conception of the good, advocating control of its community by religious authorities. Otherwise, the groups are interestingly heterogeneous. For example, not all these violent religious communities were guru based. Furthermore, only some held apocalyptic visions of the future,[17] and not all were millenarian.[18] Certain of these groups engaged in mass casualty attacks: members of Aum Shinrikyo, for instance, killed nineteen and injured sixty-one hundred people in two sarin gas strikes on Japanese targets in 1994 and 1995. Some commentators have argued that groups such as Aum Shinrikyo sit "sufficiently divorced from world" that attacks aiming to inflict mass casualties become a seemingly sensible proposition.[19] What, if anything, can liberals do about this?

Liberals could mitigate the tendency of such communities to turn to violence if they were able to lessen or remove the groups' sense of persecution, and this is within the scope of liberal capability. First, liberals could use forbearance here, being careful before countenancing claims that theocratic communities and other minority religious groups are backward, intimating that those groups are abusive to women and children, or suggesting that such communities are otherwise "irrational" or "mad and aggressive."[20] And yet there has been no shortage of such claims and intimations in academic and other liberal discourse.[21] Nongovernment parties have also employed "atrocity tales"—for example, of physical and sexual abuse at Waco—as one particularly effective method to prompt reactions from government.[22] It is important to resist temptations to smear new religious groups as bizarre, unjust, or violent, for doing so uses "attributions as social weapons," as Richardson puts it.[23] It matters how religious groups get labeled by others, because indelicate and untoward treatment can create a "context of violence," one marked by "interdependency, conflict, and the use of atrocity tales and labels as social weapons on both sides."[24] One finds support for this view in other research: John Wybraniec and Roger Finke noted a disturbing incidence of unfounded charges of child neglect and abuse levied against uncommon communal and family groups.[25] And government is hardly invulnerable to this tendency: the French parliament published an official report in 1995, entitled *Les Sectes en France*, that generously identifies 173 sects as displaying "dangerous characteristics"; the Church of Scientology, Jehovah's Witnesses, and even evangelical Protestants were tarred with their brush.[26]

These negative attributions are bad and undesirable for several reasons. First of all, they damage the reputation and standing of religious practitioners where the claims and attributions are undeserved. Casting aspersions in this way is therefore morally wrong. Second, evidence indicates that such attributions are more likely to spark problems by creating a sense of persecution, as when extremist third parties lash out where they believe government seriously mistreats theocratic communities. So there is a prudential reason to care about citizens or government parties throwing around undeserved, negative characterizations of theocratic communities. Third, the willingness to use such negative attributions without proper grounds testifies to a lack of civility and respect for religious practitioners and their conceptions of the good, whereas liberals should stand in defense of principles of conscience, religious liberty, and more vulnerable minority groups in liberal polities.

This leads to a second suggestion. Liberals could improve on the ways in which they defend uncommon religious communities, to demonstrate better respect for those persons and their ways of life. Here, liberals could speak with greater force and conviction about liberal principles of conscience and theocrats' moral right to religious free exercise. Liberals would do well to address the anticult movement, for instance, entreating it to refrain from using social and discursive networks to disseminate stories and rumors about theocratic communities. Liberty of conscience arguments could be of assistance here as well, since the arguments in favor of permitting conscience to accept the good should be acceptable to anticultists as well as theocrats. Furthermore, this case could be made to liberal government and courts: both government and courts have behaved in unacceptable and at times openly despicable ways when characterizing and treating minority religious practices, and liberals should fight against that tendency wherever it may exist. One must remember that very few uncommon religious communities begin violent or seek at their inception to overthrow liberal institutions, and there seems to be no reason for them to evolve in violent directions. These groups could grow to exist in harmony with liberalism and liberal institutions, and I daresay the world would be better off if they did so.

Third, liberals could work to disseminate and infuse principles of conscience in members of minority religious groups at risk of turning to violence, to reduce the likelihood that those people come to see themselves as being at odds with liberal principles and institutions. To reiterate, the three principles are as follows:

> Conscience must be free to reject lesser religious doctrines and conceptions of the good (the principle of rejection)
>
> Conscience must be free to accept the good (the principle of affirmation)
>
> Conscience must be free to distinguish between good and bad doctrines and conceptions of the good (the principle of distinction)

I articulated these principles in chapter 2, arguing not only that theocrats are committed rationally to these principles but that there is reason for them to affirm the principles as well. I shall not rehearse those lines of reasoning here, but I will suggest that if new terrorist groups are primarily religious in nature, then arguments from the three principles of conscience hold promise for informing the policies and actions government takes with respect to religious groups at risk of becoming violent.

Still, external pressures and attributions are not the only contributory factors prompting religious groups toward extreme actions. Mayer points out that internal dissent and protest can also trigger a turn toward violence, citing as an example David Koresh, who turned vehemently against defectors from the Branch Davidians.[27] The same is true of Aum Shinrikyo, whose leader, Shoko Asahara, was charged with murdering an uncooperative Aum member in February 1994. That slaying preceded a series of assaults, kidnappings, and murders,[28] and in February 2004 Asahara was finally convicted of having planned and ordered multiple killings. Another example one could adduce is that of the Mormon splinter group the Church of the Lamb of God, whose members killed numerous people connected with the group in the 1970s and 1980s even after their leader, Evril LeBaron, had died in jail. It seems quite correct to say that under conditions of greater internal pressures and intragroup instability, "even moderate external opposition is easily translated into a narrative of cosmic persecution."[29]

What can or should liberals do about dissent and protest within religious communities? This is a complicated question, but in the end one simply cannot expect to prevent internal dissent from occurring and recurring within religious groups. What is more, it would be a fool's game to try to do so. The legacy of the Reformation leads one to understand, if nothing else, that schism and dissent are facts of human existence. However, some of the pressure to engage in extreme actions against group members and nonmembers could be relieved if group members better understood their right to exit from their communities. Here, Susan Moller Okin's concerns about realistic rights of exit from theocratic communities could be addressed in part by liberty of conscience arguments: those arguments could be taught to children and youth, promulgated not just to women but to all members of theocratic communities, and enforced by law.[30] Members need to understand their ability to exit and their moral and legal rights to do so; that way, they will be less inclined to feel or be trapped. But more than this could be accomplished by a proper dissemination of principles of conscience to members of theocratic groups. For the effective teaching of those principles would lead group members to understand that leaving one's religious community, if conscience deems it necessary, is countenanced and supported by sound moral principles. Conscience must be free to accept the good, to reject the bad, and to distinguish between the two; this implies that one must affirm and reaffirm the institutions of social suasion and political control under which one lives, standing prepared to reject those institutions if necessary. In addition, if liberal principles of conscience were broadly disseminated and taught to all members of religious communities in liberal democracies, it stands to reason that there would be a lower likelihood that group leaders would contend that their own members must be forbidden from leaving if they dissent or defect, since if effective the teaching would impress on them the primary importance of liberty of conscience. To this end, it will be critical to teach children and youth to respect liberty of conscience as a primary educational principle in liberal democracies and to impress the common importance of that value on them.

This leads to a fourth suggestion. Allowing theocratic communities to acquire quasi sovereignty would help them to feel less threatened by liberal government, since it would show that liberal government is prepared to respect their religious practices and beliefs, giving members of those communities the option of greater religious autonomy and the ability to create a *nomos* of their own. It would also require clarity and fair dealing on the part of government if instituted and protected adequately; the lack of square dealing has done nothing to stave off the sense of persecution in those groups. A semisovereign option for theocratic communities will not prevent all internal or external violence from occurring, but it would help. And, what is more, properly providing that option would better respect the liberal commitment to liberty of conscience, to which every liberal democracy pays fealty and which is critically important to proponents of liberalism individually.

New religious communities tend to be more radical than established ones;[31] for those religious groups at risk of turning to violence against liberal citizens and institutions or their own membership, government should judiciously maintain careful relations. I suspect that new law enforcement techniques would be salutary here, since interactions with government and law will be mediated in part through the coercive arms of the liberal polity. Government will need to be sensitive to how social and legal contexts and interactions can prompt violent reactions from religious groups. But government will also have to be vigilant in watching for outbreaks of physical violence, the rapid acquisition of firearms and other weapons, and further warning signs. There tends to be a lead-up stage to serious violent reactions within theocratic groups: Aum Shinrikyo began by beating wavering and uncooperative members, with over thirty Aum followers believed to have been killed between 1988 and 1995;[32] David Koresh went through a process of buying firearms; and the Rajneeshees also acquired handguns early on.[33] Another group, The Way International, required expertise in marksmanship of their members and apparently started stockpiling weapons.[34] These are signs to watch out for, and government will have to be vigilant here, defusing such situations tactfully if groups start heading down those paths. Furthermore, such practices will have to be taken under consideration if communities wish to acquire quasi-sovereign status. Government would have to monitor potentially problematic groups closely once they are semisovereign as well and could not fail to act if such behaviors started occurring in quasi-sovereign theocratic communities. While government should be chary in attributing violent or abusive behavior to religious communities, actual negligence and abuse must not be tolerated.[35] That is to say, where communities successfully gain semisovereign status, violations of basic human rights by fellow members should not simply be something with which liberals will have to "learn to live."[36]

APPROACHES TO AMBITIOUS THEOCRATS: REASONS AND ARGUMENTS

I now turn to the second segment of ambitious theocrats described at the outset of this book. Here, I shall concentrate on persons who hold ambitious religious conceptions of the good but are less extreme than members of groups such as Rajneeshpuram, Aum Shinrikyo, or the Branch Davidians. While the case that I make will apply to those uncommon groups as well, I focus more specifically on elements of the Christian Right in America. The case I will provide can be extrapolated to the members of the Nation of Islam and other zealous Muslims, as well as similarly ambitious theocrats from other religious traditions. What is common to these theocratic religious practitioners is their political ambitiousness; still, ambitious theocrats are not all alike. They display varying degrees of extremity on a range of issues, they may or may not be evangelical, and their cultural and theological traditions vary significantly. Nevertheless, ambitious theocrats are different from retiring theocrats inasmuch as they fight variously to repeal laws on abortion, to contest homosexuality, to bring back other socially conservative values, or to revivify a closer relation between church and state. Ambitious theocrats are different from their retiring counterparts, in short, since they do not desire to withdraw from public life into their own nomic communities. With respect to these religious practitioners, what should liberals do?

Following the arguments given above, I propose that liberals should work to give ambitious theocrats reasons to affirm liberalism that they should accept. As a first step, liberals should provide general arguments in favor of liberty of conscience, articulating the reasons for ambitious theocrats to affirm liberal institutions and laws. One might immediately object that this places too much of a burden on reason and rationality, since ambitious theocrats seem famously able to ignore or deny what seem to secular parties to be very compelling arguments. But that objection is too quick: as I have argued, theocrats may be situated differently from liberals, secularists, or more moderate religious parties, but they are still receptive to reasons. And it is surely morally better to give good reasons to those persons than it is to refrain from doing so at all. When it comes to coercive impositions, government should have good reasons for interfering ready to hand, and here liberals can help by better outlining appropriate and justifiable principles and guidelines for government interaction with theocrats.

The provision of abstract reasons alone will not suffice to quell theocratic discord or to bring theocrats and liberals into a harmonious relationship. But there is evidence to suggest that providing abstract arguments in favor of freedom of conscience could successfully alter theocratic attitudes and behavior to a modest extent. This is supported by a study by Clyde Wilcox, who attempted to measure the amount of vertical constraint in mass publics, compared to elites.[37] He noted a positive correlation between people's attitudes and the abstract principles they affirmed; for example, in examining Americans' responses to abstract questions on establishment clause issues, Wilcox found a "moderately high degree" of vertical constraint in the mass public.[38] This finding bolsters the expectation that abstract arguments in favor of principles of conscience would help in the effort to prompt ambitious theocrats to affirm liberalism. And if liberal arguments could be used to modify theocratic attitudes even modestly, that would in turn hold prospects for altering illiberal theocratic behavior. The least that one can conclude here is that this view is not inconsistent with the data, and it coheres with other findings, such as those of David Leege and Lyman Kellstedt, who have noted that abstract beliefs about the Bible are "important predictors" of partisanship, vote choice, and attitudes toward abortion.[39]

Further support for this thesis comes from studies distinguishing moral obligations from attitudes, where the former are measured by the degree to which outcomes fulfill religious values and the latter are more properly likes and dislikes.[40] There appears to be a meaningful, demonstrable empirical distinction between moral obligations and attitudes so conceived.[41] But that is not all: Richard Gorsuch and John Ortberg Jr. have also adduced evidence to show that a sense of moral obligation adds to behavioral intentions over and above attitudes, where a short series of criteria is met.[42] The authors find that attitude and moral obligations are psychologically independent and that individual behavior can be changed by engaging religious values relevant to moral obligations, independent of attitude change.[43] They speculate that the "best approach to value change may be similar to, but distinct from, that used in attitude change."[44] As they put it, "[it] may be important to know not only what moral obligations people hold, but also which religious values may be salient to a given situation if behavior is to be changed."[45] In the end, evidence from the work of Gorsuch and Ortberg suggests that messages aimed at expectations of attitude as well as salient religious values can be powerful agents of behavioral change.[46]

The conclusion one draws is that liberals would do well to give ambitious theocrats in liberal polities arguments articulating the primary importance of liberty of conscience, proceeding from grounds of both moral obligation and theocrats' bases of religious values. Liberals could provide arguments against the viability of polities whose institutions fail to protect liberty of conscience: a turn toward theocracy should be simply out of contention, to help in cases where people begin leaning in that direction. These arguments could focus on theocrats' beliefs and attitudes, also looking to modify their expectations of positive and negative outcomes.[47] Such arguments could be joined with conciliatory, prudential, and other theological reasons to affirm liberalism, and while liberals may not be expert in the theological and religious traditions of various theocratic groups, more could be done to support liberal religious figures able to articulate doctrinal reasons for particular theocratic religious groups to affirm liberal principles and laws.

ENGAGEMENT

There is a substantial literature examining effects of social networks on individual attitudes, and facts of social interaction are crucial for understanding the nature and orientation of political and social attitudes alike.[48] Social networks influence religious attitudes and behaviors: they enhance religious participation and are "salient predictors of religiosity" even where one controls for race and various other factors.[49] Social networks do not merely reinforce norms and expectations about religious behavior; they also apparently "enhance religious expression" by fostering and maintaining the kinds of community that sustain religious practice.[50] Kenneth Wald observes that church members "[participate] in a social network," arguing that there exists a positive relation between church attendance and voter participation even though church attendance alone does not obviously encourage other forms of political involvement.[51]

The importance of social networks at the microlevel is affirmed in a recent study of religious practitioners' attitudes conducted by Peer Scheepers and Frans van der Slik, who looked at the "primary circle[s]" of a group of survey respondents—spouses, parents, and parents-in-law—finding that each sector of the circle affected respondents' moral attitudes. They argue that the effects of being involved in a religious community are stronger for males than females when it comes to attitudes on moral issues. Males' moral attitudes are more strongly influenced by public interaction with their religious community, whereas females' moral attitudes are relatively strongly affected by religious contemplation.[52] Scheepers and van der Slik's findings complement those of Kevin Welch, who has argued that "intracongregational friendships" are an important measure for predicting commitment to orthodox religious belief.[53]

Given the relative importance of social networks with regard to religious practitioners' beliefs, attitudes, and behaviors, I propose that liberals should involve themselves in ambitious theocrats' social networks, to enter into dialogic partnerships and provide arguments in favor of liberty of conscience. I call this entrance into theocratic social networks *infiltration*;[54] and by it I do not mean to suggest anything secretive, disingenuous, or untoward on the part of liberals. Rather, I propose that liberals should enter and enmesh themselves in theocrats' supportive social networks, discussing principles of conscience with them and giving them arguments they should accept in favor of maintaining and protecting liberal institutions. The voice and manner of communication will be important here,[55] and it will be crucial for liberals to be respectful and fair in communicating with theocrats, instead of merely trying to hammer them with liberal dogmas of their own.[56] To complement this effort, liberals could better support secondary organizations able to disseminate liberal principles of conscience through ambitious theocratic networks. Civil liberties groups and liberal religious organizations are fairly good candidates for endorsement by liberals,[57] but those organizations will need to be prodded and cajoled to be mindful of the importance of treating theocrats with the respect they deserve. In addition, liberals could do a better job of identifying, supporting, and assisting more liberal members of ambitious theocratic groups in liberal democracies, as I have suggested. By way of an international analogue, one need only consider the position of liberal mullahs or religious figures in theocratic countries to see how tactful and delicate support of those persons would be salutary.[58]

One might object that there are too few opportunities for dialogue with members of the Christian Right, the Nation of Islam, or similar groups, but that objection would be well off the mark. For where they are socially involved and politically determined, ambitious theocrats in liberal democracies will interact continually with citizens. This distinguishes them from retiring theocrats, since the latter withdraw from public life and retreat into their religious communities; opportunities to discuss liberal principles of conscience with retiring theocrats will therefore be limited.[59] Ambitious theocrats, in contrast, tend to be both politically involved and keen to proselytize nonmembers; there thus exist structural opportunities for dialogue and chances for liberals to communicate and reason with religious parties situated in those social networks.[60] For motivated theocrats of the ambitious variety, liberals should use more speech, not silence, as John Stuart Mill argued, and, specifically, liberals should employ reasons that theocrats should accept, instead of *pro tanto* reasons that elide theocrats' religious convictions or hold only for those affirming secular conceptions of the good. In short, liberals can both take and create opportunities to interact seriously with theocratic individuals, church officials, and other influential parties, making efforts conscientiously to communicate with them, moving well beyond the paucity of dialogue that exists at present or the quick and nasty position statements one encounters in mass media.

A second objection one could levy is that the social networks of ambitious theocrats are far too broad and powerful to be affected by liberal infiltration. But that objection is similarly misplaced: only 10 percent of Americans supported the seemingly broad-based Moral Majority in the 1980s, for instance, whereas two-thirds to three-quarters of citizens were critical of the organization.[61] Other research continues to show low levels of citizen support for and familiarity with the religious Right, so one should be careful not to overestimate the breadth of popular backing for such groups and movements.[62] Nor are ambitious theocrats territorially limited or otherwise unavailable: liberals can find them in the workplace, in churches, in their neighborhoods, and in other secondary associations. I am not suggesting that it is each liberal's duty to marry a theocrat in order to mollify and redirect his or her attitudes and beliefs; there are easier, more reasonable ways to do this with the power of reason, with conscientiousness and fair dealing, and through the strength of good example. Indeed, with the multiple belongings and shifting involvements characteristic of a liberal-democratic citizenry,[63] there exist good opportunities for people to get involved and ways for liberals to create dialogic opportunities of their own.

Furthermore, one needs to disaggregate evangelical Protestants by their theological convictions, just as one must for Catholics, Jews, and Muslims.[64] Theological convictions are not identical within those respective groups, and it is fortuitous for liberals that seemingly homogeneous theocratic movements such as the Christian Right are cloven by real diversity. Many Protestant evangelicals have rebuffed organizations such as the Moral Majority or the Christian Coalition; evangelical opinion is split, as it is for Catholics and members of other religious faiths.[65] The absence of a single, unified perspective for Protestants, Catholics, or Muslims enhances opportunities for liberals to infiltrate networks of ambitious theocrats and effectuate change with new liberal arguments. That is to say, religious people differ based on "the nature and motivation of their religiosity," as Wald puts it,[66] and liberals can use this to their advantage. Take the issue of abortion, for example: there is no unanimity of opinion among Catholics, and, contrary to what one might expect, the most intransigent opponents of abortion are white and black evangelical Protestants.[67] Interestingly, white conservative Protestants are more willing to grant civil liberties to homosexuals;[68] particular religious denominations are more of a mixed bag than many acknowledge, and it would be a mistake to think that the so-called culture war in the United States is marked with clearly defined positions or typified by staunch and steadfast adversaries and allies.

Where one finds divided denominations, there will be reduced political unity; and with no common front, ambitious theocrats will have a lesser chance of influencing public policy in illiberal directions. Successful modification of the views of antiliberal theocrats could change their political behavior even though, at the aggregate level, religion does not affect public opinion simply or consistently.[69] As for theocrats' receptivity to change in their beliefs or behavior, apart from the evidence of the efficacy of influence by members of people's social networks, a precedent for modification already exists: evangelicals and other major religious groups in the United States have been encouraged in recent years to modify their political patterns and increase their involvement in political affairs.[70]

Interactions and discussions between liberals and theocrats will undoubtedly involve continuing disagreement and controversy; that is a natural expectation. Stephen Macedo has done some interesting work bearing on the prospects of gently transforming theocratic attitudes and beliefs.[71] But these discussions and transformations need not lead ambitious theocrats to disengage from politics, nor should that be the liberal's aim in infiltrating theocratic social networks. Weithman has argued that criticism of religious practitioners' religious reasons for participating in politics or supporting particular policies and laws will force them to disengage from politics.[72] But that view is flatly implausible and surely false. For there is no reason to think that religious citizens will be pushed out of politics if their political positions or their reasons for them are questioned or criticized, even if they are newcomers to political participation. Those citizens could rethink their views, participate in different ways, or simply back off from attempts to codify in law their more illiberal external preferences. Indeed, challenging the contributions of those relying on exclusively religious reasons not easily accessible to others could enliven and charge debate, prompting change in stagnant pools of religious and nonreligious comprehensive doctrines and conceptions of the good.

What is more, for people currently active in religious institutions, there is evidence to indicate that civic skills they acquire at church simply do not increase political participation.[73] Those skills are superfluous with respect to political participation; they give religious devotees a chance "to practice skills gained elsewhere."[74] In addition, James Cavendish reports that the single most powerful predictor of traditional participation in traditional devotional styles is "social integration," tapped by measuring feelings of attachment to one's parish, the number of close friends a respondent has who are members of that group, and the frequency of conversations between the respondent and his or her pastor or fellow parish members.[75] Other work by Ronald Lake and Robert Huckfeldt lends weight to the view that personal networks generate politically relevant social capital and enhance the likelihood that a citizen will be politically engaged, at least where the citizen's networks are not laden with vehement disagreements over political matters.[76] This suggests that thoughtful criticism of religious practitioners by other members of their social networks will not require or entail "[withdrawal] from democratic politics"; nor will such critique make people shy away from political involvement with respect to specific issues, whether or not the criticism speaks to a person's reasons for participating in political life.[77] And the point holds even if liberals infiltrate and embed themselves in such networks so as to engage ambitious theocrats more directly, using appropriate and respectful methods of communication. Generally speaking, there appears to be no reason to think that ambitious theocrats or more common religious practitioners will refrain from participating politically if they face carefully and conscientiously articulated criticism from nonmembers of their communities, whether or not they are new to political participation.

AIMING TO INFLUENCE IDENTITY

The third strategy that liberals could take with respect to ambitious theocrats, building on the two suggestions I have provided, is to aim to influence their identities. What recommends this strategy is the fact that ambitious theocrats' identities are more malleable than one might expect, at least insofar as their attitudes, beliefs, and behaviors are concerned. This point requires explanation. First of all, Leege and Kellstedt have adduced evidence supporting the thesis that religious identity is a "strong source of political attitudes and orientations."[78] Whether one self-identifies as fundamentalist, Pentecostal, or post–Vatican II Catholic, they argue, one's religious identity is a good predictor of political attitudes and behaviors.[79] Other analyses similarly maintain that members of a religious group have a common identity drawn in substantial part from social networks.[80] Fellow congregants' religious values matter when it comes to an individual's acceptance of liberal or conservative politics, just as those values matter for liberal or conservative identification.[81] Controlling for social traits such as education, income, urbanization, ethnicity, and occupational status, differences among religious groups' attitudes remain.[82] With respect to white conservative Protestants in particular, a group that is less liberal than other white Americans or white Christians, longitudinal analysis of their attitudes on civil liberties shows that even regional effects are weakened by "greater transience and communication."[83] Sam Reimer and Jerry Park add to this finding, noting that committed, conservative Protestants are more prone to develop a shared sense of the existence of an ingroup and outgroup and are more likely to try to maintain a distinctive identity that allows for ongoing tension with outgroups.[84]

Changing even modestly theocrats' beliefs about their identities and the manner and extent to which they see themselves at odds with outgroups could bring positive political results: as Richard Rose and Derek Urwin have argued, countries with the strongest religious divisions tend to have more strain, violence, and political instability.[85] Liberals could work to modify theocratic notions of religious ingroups and outgroups and the non- or illiberal senses of identity that they imply. One way to make a positive impact here would be through the promulgation of the principles of conscience I have articulated. The goal would not be to stop ambitious or conservative Protestants from participating in their church communities or to cajole them not to belong to any religious organizations. Rather, liberals could engage members of ambitious theocratic groups in constructive dialogue, working to reduce the incidence of illiberal "activist corps" forming in churches and communities.[86] While liberals cannot prevent these illiberal subgroups from sprouting up, they could lessen the phenomenon of extremism with the sort of dialogue and involvement in religious networks that I have described. Here, it is helpful to mind the distinction between church involvement and other forms of commitment: church involvement is demonstrably separable from more abstract beliefs, such as beliefs about the Bible,[87] and it has no obvious bearing on political identity. Distinguishing between church attendance and church involvement, Leege and Kellstedt demonstrate that more intensive involvement in church has no impact on the political identity of a person, but it does strongly influence social traditionalism, moralism, and pro-life positions for Protestants and Roman Catholics alike.[88]

Second, if political elites were encouraged to refrain from propagating the view that liberal societies discriminate against so-called fundamentalist lifestyles, fundamentalists may be less likely to take positions more extreme than other evangelicals.[89] The distinction between fundamentalists and evangelicals is quite important: self-identified fundamentalists tend to be "more conservative than other evangelicals," but the differences appear to be significant only among those with a developed, politicized religious identification.[90] Liberals could counter messages of discrimination within fundamentalist networks by including more discourse on the value of liberty of conscience, by demonstrating the concordance of liberal institutional principles with demands of faith, and by endorsing a quasi-sovereign option for retiring theocratic communities. Cardinal principles of conscience could, in short, be employed as a central part of a larger effort to demonstrate the existence of common, fundamental interests among persons, whether they currently support liberal, nonliberal, or antiliberal forms of identity. For there are reasons for nonliberal and antiliberal ambitious theocrats alike to affirm liberal institutions that protect liberty of conscience, and liberals could promulgate those reasons while at the same time affirming and promoting institutions that rightly honor the liberal commitment to religious liberty.[91] And this is consistent with the nature of religiosity itself:

intolerance simply is not built in to religious commitment, despite the protestations of commentators such as Stanley Fish.[92] Clyde Wilcox and Ted Jelen have attributed narrow-mindedness to doctrine,[93] but as Robert Wuthnow points out, religious commitment is not always socially conservative by any means.[94]

Third, liberals might also modify the attitudes and beliefs of ambitious, antiliberal clergy if they effectuate changes in the beliefs and attitudes of members of their religious communities, since there is evidence to show that clergy are affected by what their membership desires.[95] And the relationship works in the other direction as well: pastoral cues are important for understanding church members' behavior and attitudes, especially for evangelical Protestants.[96] There is no shortage of exposure to political messages for American churchgoers: U.S. religious services have a "relatively high amount of political content,"[97] a finding consistent with numerous others that churches are important sources of political cues.[98] Wald notes that even doctrinally conservative Protestants do not report less political direction than others.[99] This leads one to expect that liberals could modify the identities of members of antiliberal religious communities by affecting both ministry and church members, not simply one or the other. As for the viability of such a strategy, Catholic pastoral letters such as *The Challenge of Peace* are a good example of how written works and arguments have been effective in changing attitudes of Catholic clergy and then other Catholics in turn.[100] This gives further reason to think that liberals would do well to support more liberal pastoral pens and voices in religious organizations and communities with theocratic leanings.[101]

One might accept this case in theory but object that any effort to affect ambitious theocrats' identities will be unsuccessful since those people tend to display psychologically or socially pathological characteristics.[102] That claim does not bear up under empirical scrutiny, however. Admittedly, a study focusing on members of the Moral Majority found 40 percent of respondents reporting feelings of "alienation" from society or stating that they live on social fringes.[103] Also, and interestingly, the majority of members polled did not report having positive self-images.[104] But while socially pathological characteristics may be important factors for recruitment into the Moral Majority or similar groups, activism in the Moral Majority was not generally attributable the same sources.[105] As Wilcox maintains, the single strongest predictor of active support was "a set of conservative positions on social issues."[106] Furthermore, the study found that both authoritarianism and feelings of inadequacy correlated significantly and positively with inactive membership in the Moral Majority, which might indicate that the Moral Majority attempted to keep members with those low self-assessments at the periphery of their organization.[107]

So liberals could encourage liberal views in churches and religious networks in order to modify non- and antiliberal religious practitioners' conceptions of ingroup and outgroup, their sense of the degree of difference between themselves and nonmembers, and by implication their understandings of their own identity. For communities of ambitious theocrats within liberal polities advocating and advancing illiberal views or policies, engagement and argumentation might produce very real and salutary effects. Even if zealous theocratic behavior were linked to lesser educational opportunities, lower socioeconomic status, or other factors, liberals could join treatment of those issues with new arguments and reasons and new, liberal institutions of conscience, to make a positive impact.

In advancing this case, I do not claim that liberal government should strongly promote a robust version of autonomy to retiring or ambitious theocrats, however. To the contrary, liberal government has no business promoting or enforcing any comprehensive conception of the good, be it secular, religious, or otherwise. For even if a thoroughly autonomous way of life were in some sense the best life for persons, government has no right to promote or enforce that way of life. And while one affirms the permissibility of liberals individually promoting autonomous ways of life, the advocacy of liberal principles of conscience is decidedly political inasmuch as it is not perfectionist. The principles of conscience are skeletal with respect to the identity of persons, but they could be publicly justified and affirmed as part of people's determinate conceptions of the good.[108] That is to say, the three principles can be affirmed by liberals as well as by persons striving to live what Wolterstorff calls a "religiously integrated existence."[109] In this way, they hold the promise of moving beyond rational or reasonable contestation, diminishing the need for compromise at the moral level that Bohman advocates.[110] Nevertheless, the three liberal principles of conscience are purposive only in part: they dictate no summum bonum or particular end for persons and so do not force integration or unity at the price of diversity.[111] As such, while the three principles structure reasoning and dialogue, they are not themselves discourse principles per se. By encouraging people to adopt prin-

ciples of conscience in their own lives, liberals could advance greater respect and understanding among persons of faith, between the faithful
and those marked by unbelief, and perhaps even between citizens of liberal democracies and other peoples and nations around the world.

Nor am I demanding, expressly or otherwise, that theocrats must be
made to accept some version of covenant theology.[112] To the contrary,
theocrats' theology and ways of life are up to them, within the particular
institutional limitations I have described. A liberalism of conscience pre-
scribes no specific codes; at most, it asks for the adoption of a small set
of specific beliefs and allowances regarding freedom of conscience and
the right of persons to reject inferior religion, none of which rises to the
level of a code in any meaningful sense. Is this tantamount to promoting
a new civil religion? It is not: there are no rites, no rituals, no requisite
practices or beliefs, so a liberalism of conscience would not be a civil religion in any standard sense.[113] A liberalism of conscience affirms meta-
physical principles of conscience, but it does not endow the country or
the nation with supernatural attributes.[114] Nor does the argument I have
given have any direct bearing on religious practitioners' images of God,
and it has few implications for the questions of obedience to God versus
skepticism and dissent.[115] For even if God were knowably stern and
vengeful, that would not eliminate the difference between strict pious-
ness in one's personal life and the imprudent and apparently ungodly attempt to foist a strict and pious conception of the good on an entire polity
using political institutions. Furthermore, even with the adoption of the
principles of conscience I have identified, theocrats would still retain the
theological and epistemological ability to claim coherently that other religions are misguided. And such claims are important to members of a
wide variety of religious faiths: Joseph Smith Jr. maintained as much,
contending famously that he was commissioned by God to prepare the
way for the "dispensation of the fullness of time."[116] With the affirmation
of the principles of liberty of conscience I have outlined, such views are
logically consistent and should be psychologically unproblematic.

This book does not preach liberty of conscience as a religious revival,
nor are its arguments constructed out of inaccessible religious reasons.
The arguments that I have provided are accessible, whether or not a precise set of necessary and sufficient conditions of accessibility for public
reasons is available.[117] However, promulgating a liberalism of conscience
honestly and conscientiously could be facilitated with rhetorical techniques, sparking enthusiasm for the principles and values I have articu-

lated. The Great Awakenings in America employed techniques of mass persuasion, using parades, tent meetings, and other means of conversion.[118] A liberalism of conscience could employ numerous possible means in this regard, provided that persuasive methods were tactful, appropriate, deliberative, and underpinned by solid reasons and sound arguments. Indeed, the American founders spoke openly and well of the importance of conscience and the need to respect it;[119] liberals could enliven people's motivations by appeals to great historical moments and insights of that kind. Furthermore, the U.S. example holds a rich Protestant social gospel tradition on which to draw and an auspicious history of liberal clergy involved in civil rights and other worthy causes, despite obstruction from theocrats and conservatives of various kinds.[120]

PROSPECTS FOR INTERNATIONAL COMITY

It remains to consider briefly some approaches that liberals and liberal government could employ in the international realm in hopes of making headway on the various problems of conscience and theocratic religious devotion that I have outlined above. There are several reasons to be attentive to the international components of theocratic issues, but a sufficient reason for concern presumably can be found in recent cases where extremist Islamic groups have lashed out at liberal institutions and citizens, motivated in part by theocratic aspirations and perceived maltreatment of their Muslim brethren.

I shall offer three tentative suggestions on possible directions for a new international approach. First, I suspect that international policy platforms and communications agencies could conceivably be transformed to help express reasons for theocrats around the globe to affirm liberalism. Parties speaking in those fora could try to offer, first of all, well-constructed arguments to support the policies that liberal governments employ, speaking to the concerns of theocratic religious parties in terms they might accept. In the course of those communications, liberal government could also encourage other governments, institutions, and religious practitioners openly to affirm liberty of conscience at the political level. That is, liberal governments could use their expressive organs to promote a healthy liberty of conscience internationally, encouraging theocrats to devise and build institutions protecting religious free exercise along with basic human rights and other values. To be sure, government would need to be careful and respectful in stating such messages, using an appropriate voice in communicating with theocrats and listening to their concerns as well.[121] What is more, government would have to take pains to promote its messages and ideas consistently across countries, instead of doing so in a partisan or merely cynical way.[122] As for agencies that may be of service in this respect, liberal democracies could perhaps employ institutions detached from particular governments to develop and strengthen international law.[123]

Second, this effort to give theocrats reasons to affirm liberal institutions need not be limited to government agencies or spokespeople. Liberal citizens might also strive to speak to theocrats through the channels of their various quotidian affiliations or by employing secondary organizations in civil society that have an international reach. International nongovernment organizations could be of crucial assistance here as well, as would be friends of religious liberty located around the world. Liberal religious figures within theocratic polities and traditions, for example, could be better recognized and supported in their efforts to provide theological reasons in favor of liberty of conscience or to promote institutions protecting freedom of conscience and basic human rights in their countries. In each of these three examples, nonstate parties might help to promote liberal institutions and liberty of conscience internationally; this is markedly different from liberal state agencies promoting such values and institutions themselves and would stand as an important addition to the endeavor I have outlined here.

Third, alongside arguments aiming to give theocrats moral and theological reasons to affirm liberal institutions, liberal government could provide prudential reasons for more militant theocrats to disavow full-blown theocracy, outlining the dangers associated with living under theocratic regimes. Included here could be benefits offered for nonliberal governments cooperating with liberal polities in their efforts to dismantle networks of religious extremists, as well as penalties for noncompliance where appropriate. It is worth mentioning that while I have argued that liberals and liberal government should rethink the ways in which they handle theocracy and religious extremism at home and abroad, such does not imply that the international effort to eradicate terrorism is misguided. Nor does it mean that liberal states must refrain from taking strong and decisive action against religious extremists who resort to terroristic means to achieve their ends. In fact, liberal government's preparedness to act forcefully where citizens and institutions are attacked by theocratic forces could indeed help to dissuade religious extremists from viewing such attacks as viable or worthwhile. The point I wish to emphasize is that such actions and policies could be joined with reasons that justify them, along with a demonstrated affirmation of religiosity plain and simple, an authentic willingness to help polities and peoples in the development of liberal institutions, and a disposition to be conscientious and fair in the promotion of these values.

Of course, shoring up the failures of liberalism by providing adequate, accessible, and acceptable reasons for theocrats to affirm a liberal order will not solve all the problems associated with zealotry in modern liberal democracies, and neither would it immediately or easily harmonize the values and practices of retiring theocrats with those of other citizens in a well-formed liberal order. It would be too sanguine to hold that the provision of such reasons will suffice to quell all religious discord, if only because new theocratic groups continually burgeon forth in democratic societies, as new flora in the simple pluralistic array. Nor do I wish to suggest that it would be desirable or reasonable to expect that theocrats and liberals ultimately converge on a shared conception of the good; conflict and disagreement are important conditions of politics itself, and free societies will never do away entirely with political and participatory discordance. Rather, the point is that theocrats' objections to liberalism appear to be serious and profound, but they are not irresolvable, and it is still too early to suggest to that the provision of reasons for theocrats to affirm a liberal order can only fail to mitigate the prudential problems associated with the legacy of theocracy in democratic polities.

There are good resources available for those wishing to develop a political liberalism of conscience. First, theocrats and liberals alike appear to share a commitment to normative principles of freedom of conscience. A political order constructed around shared principles of this kind could rise above a mere modus vivendi since in it liberals and theocrats would both be able to see the fundamental legitimacy of government in terms acceptable to them. Second, insofar as liberal government is itself committed to the value of religious free exercise, it could cohere well with central theocratic values and commitments as I have described them. Liberal government would need to refrain from its historically invasive tendencies with respect to theocratic communities, but one expects that government could achieve this. A commitment to religious free exercise would not rightly give theocrats carte blanche to enforce any practices or punishments on their members that they wish or sanction their liberty to strike out against citizens of the larger polity, however. There is no right to absolute liberty of conscience: absolute liberty of conscience would allow for no interference in one's pursuit of good, even in cases of conflict where one causes palpable injury to another, or where a religious conception of the good calls for extreme punishments, or where it would deny others' basic liberty to pursue dictates of conscience. Some modification of the existing views of both theocrats and liberals will be necessary, but I suspect that it may be possible to create a clear and well-reasoned case on this front, one that would lay out in greater detail the boundaries of acceptable religious practices and protections, to the satisfaction of liberals and theocrats alike.

FIVE OBJECTIONS CONSIDERED

I turn finally to five objections to the arguments that I have furnished in this work. First, one might object that promulgating the three principles of conscience I have described would be unacceptable. Advancing them would undermine the religious teachings and values of a wide variety of religious communities, the objector could suggest, such as those with doctrines contending that individual persons are not permitted to decide for themselves what is godly and what is not. Obligations of conscience cut against the principles I have articulated and defended, one could contend, and as such they are insensitive to the religious values they mean to protect as well as simply being unacceptable from a philosophical point of view.

This objection seems serious, but it is misguided: conscience is obligated to observe the principles of rejection, affirmation, and distinction I have identified if it is obligated to observe any principles or values at all. The principles enjoy at least a prima facie logically prior relation to any specific obligations or claims to conscience. To defeat the principles of conscience I have articulated, which require that conscience be free to accept the good, to reject the bad, and to distinguish between the two, one will have to marshal powerful reason, indeed. While that is not a logically impossible feat, it will be very difficult to accomplish, for freedom of conscience appears to be a demand of conscience itself, one that enjoys priority over any doctrine proposing that persons should instead subjugate or disavow those freedoms in order to follow a set of dictates. Furthermore, the adoption of liberal principles of conscience would not undermine the "religiously integrated existence" that many religious people seek.[124] Religious practitioners could treat the three principles of

conscience as maxims of civic virtue, continuing to act according to powerful religious motivations.[125] In the end, many religious motivations
and acts would be entirely consistent with the principles of conscience I
have outlined, since there is reason to think that those principles are
countenanced by God. With this in view, adopting and being motivated
by principles of conscience hold the promise of an ameliorated and no
less integrated existence for religious practitioners.

The view I am advancing may be caricatured as relying on an excessively Calvinist, Western, or liberal understanding of religion, but such
complaints do not show that the argument is deficient in any meaningful way. After all, the principles of conscience I have identified do not require thoroughgoing or continuous reflection on the part of each individual person and so do not amount to a version of comprehensive
liberalism that is somehow secretive or unaware of its design. Nor do liberal principles of conscience require self-abnegation on the part of those
who adopt them; to the contrary, those principles can be integrated with
robust principles of justice and equality, they allow for broad forms of religious practice and religious liberty, and they connect fruitfully with
people's own ends. As such, the three principles of conscience could be
adopted by theocrats and liberals alike, in ways enabling people to pursue their conceptions of the good freely and allowing them to live their
religion well and truly.[126] Promulgation of the principles also has
prospects for bridging gaps between persons, insofar as liberty of conscience arguments are compatible with various religious and secular
views, connecting closely to reasons differently situated people have to
affirm liberalism, in a context of legitimacy and political stability.

A second objection could be launched through a protestation that the
case I have presented asks for unacceptable modifications to liberalism.
The objector may aver that liberals who take the ideas of these pages to
heart will dilute or destroy the strength of their very views. In addition,
the objector could propose, liberals have traditionally emphasized the
importance of one's prerogative not to get involved in social and political
matters, whereas the suggestions for engagement offered here would
impose excessively on liberals' choices in that regard.

In response to this objection, first of all, it is true that liberals' positions and viewpoints may well change through the adoption of the arguments and suggestions in this book. But those prospects alone give no
cause for objection. For liberals should be prepared to modify their views
based on the moral prominence and political prospects of principles of

liberty of conscience. At a philosophical level, liberal theory will be well served by better affirming the value of liberty of conscience; there, modifications making a more prominent role for the three cardinal principles I have articulated would be salutary. I have given reason to hold that liberal theories are defective insofar as they fail to address successfully claims and challenges of theocratic religious practitioners. Unless one believes that liberal theory is complete, which it is not, progressive theoretical steps should be welcomed. The theoretical advancements and suggestions in this book aim to advance and complete liberalism in a more satisfactory way. Indeed, talk of transformation should not be surprising or especially unsettling, given the ways in which the stream of liberal thought has wended and flowed since issuing from its seventeenth-century headwaters.

Liberals ought also to modify their attitudes and approaches by demonstrating better respect for the nature of theocrats' conceptions of the good and should expect some alterations to their views where they engage with theocrats sincerely and in good faith. At the level of direct interactions with theocrats, liberals should be prepared to learn from their discussions with those parties, instead of simply putting up with what theocrats have to say and then dropping dogmas of their own.[127] For quite apart from the fact that theocrats' beliefs and values are deeply important and meaningful to them, and notwithstanding the respect theocrats deserve by virtue of their being fellow persons, liberals must realize that theocrats' views may contain some truth and certain of their positions could even be worth adopting. After all, theocrats' conceptions of the good have a footing in reasonable views about the existence of otherworldly ends and the value of pursuits in that regard, all of which conscience can reasonably affirm. So liberals should be prepared for mutually transformative discussions and must not assume that their dialogue with theocratic parties will prompt the simple, naked assimilation of their interlocutors.[128] It is difficult to say in advance exactly what kinds of modifications to their views liberals should expect or how interactions between liberals and theocrats will change the landscape of opinion on such divisive issues as abortion, gay marriage, or prayer in public schools. But in adopting the arguments and strategies I have proposed in this book, liberals need not be overly concerned about weakening their rightful commitments or losing their way. For the three principles of conscience shine brightly as fundamental principles of right, and liberals can add those principles to their repertoires, to guide themselves along the path to greater justice, comity, tolerance, and understanding.

As for the matter of the liberal's prerogative to stand back from social and political life, avoiding involvement in daily affairs, that is a weakness of a more conservative strand of liberal theory of the kind developed by Michael Oakeshott.[129] I do not wish to suggest that liberals must forsake themselves, their projects, or their attachments to wade into the fray with theocrats; nor am I contending that government has any right legally to demand greater involvement from liberal citizens in such matters. However, liberals cannot simply leave treatment of serious political and social problems to the hands of others, certainly not with respect to the kinds of religious dilemmas I have pinpointed and discussed. For problems of religious discord now press sharply against the fabric of American society, just as they cut across other countries and regions of the world. Liberals should do what they can to assist in mitigating these problems, taking appropriate stands with respect to government, politics, and policies, spreading the word about liberty of conscience and other politically liberal values. And where liberals are already involved, they might rethink what ideas and policies they promote, how they promote them, and to whom they speak when they are active. Difficult days call for more from liberals, not less, not least because few others can rise to the challenges at hand.

Here one might offer a third objection. One could remark that despite the arguments I have provided, there simply is no way to convince those who stand opposed to philosophy meaningfully to adopt the principles of conscience that I have articulated and defended in these pages. There exist a number of theocrats who "dismiss philosophy as unwarranted," the objector could note; Islamic fundamentalists such as Seyyid Qutb and Hasan al-Banna count as examples.[130] For theocrats with this view, dismissive of philosophy itself, how on earth could one expect to convince them to adopt the three principles of conscience, much less motivate them to behave in ways that observe those principles?

A response to this objection is also available. First, I have offered an argument primarily with respect to theocrats' reasons to affirm liberal institutions, not for their supporting or adopting a philosophical or reflective point of view. The argumentation here is not motivated or expected to turn theocrats into philosophers; rather, it is to prompt them to understand that there are auspicious ways for them to pursue their conceptions of the good more fruitfully than at present, within the limits that reason and their rational commitments require. Second, when one considers the doctrinal complaints of even ardent, antiliberal theocrats, it becomes apparent that they are not as opposed to philosophical argumentation as one might expect. A substantial contingent of Islamic theocrats maintains that the West is in a state of ignorance; they claim that people need enlightenment, and to that extent they not only are not antiphilosophical, necessarily, but may even seek a goal similar to that of many liberal theorists.[131] Hasan al-Banna asks Muslim students to consider the essence of things, for instance, admonishing them not to be deluded by mere appearances. He entreats Muslim students to be "critical, with insight," requesting furthermore that students "encompass with knowledge all of their affairs, and then with an eye of insight, scrutinize it all."[132] None of this seems irreducibly hostile to philosophical thinking, and liberal-minded parties could use these facts to their advantage.

To these considerations one could add that demonstrable changes occur in the philosophical and theological views of theocrats, over time. Louay Safi argues that Qutb rejected violence to overthrow governments; for Qutb, jihad was apparently "[not] a suicide mission."[133] Subsequent strains of Islamist theocrats modified Qutb's ideas in violent, antiliberal directions, it is true, and merely because those theocrats evolved to occupy violent standpoints does not imply that they could easily be moved back to more peaceful positions. Still, two points must be made here. First, there is no reason to think that theocrats can never understand that philosophical thinking of a kind has brought them to where their theological views are today. This fact could be marshaled to help convince them that they may permissibly adopt a more favorable disposition toward abstract thinking, reasoning, and questioning, at least where theocrats may be interested in pondering moral or theological questions.[134] Second, for the less militant and hard-boiled people living in theocratic regions, such as potential new recruits, passive populations, and the great numbers who are largely uninvolved, the strategies and arguments in this book may be used to complement efforts to draw their potential support away from markedly zealous, violent theocratic groups and movements.

As to the question of whether I have provided usable strategies or ideas to motivate theocrats to behave differently from the way they do at present, the answer there, too, is a cautious affirmative. First of all, I have discussed ways in which to prompt theocrats to adopt a friendlier disposition toward liberal institutions. Second, I have noted the importance of liberals infiltrating and involving themselves in ambitious theocratic networks, since those associational systems are strong sources of political mobilization. Third, the case I have made could be joined with other motivational or affective elements that I have not discussed. Martha Nussbaum's contributions on the nature of emotions demonstrate how emotions enjoy substantial cognitive content, so arguments and reasons of the sort I have adduced should help to motivate theocrats to adopt a more agreeable disposition toward liberal institutions and liberty of conscience.[135]

One might retort that the arguments I have furnished will not motivate theocrats because they fail to speak in a detailed way to specifics of particular theocratic doctrines and conceptions of the good. A case to assuage discord between theocrats and liberals will only be helpful where it is embedded in particular religious doctrines, one might claim: grounding the approach in the Bible will be needed for Christian theocrats, locating favorable arguments and passages in the Koran will be required for Muslims, and so on. But the retort misses its mark. For I have given rudiments of arguments suitable for elaboration in the particular languages and idioms of a broad array of religious doctrines. The three principles of liberty of conscience are sententious and concise and can be joined with interpretive treatments of religious doctrines near and far. They may be used in efforts to foster meaningful crosscultural dialogue,[136] furthermore, and the principles may be of interest in the study of comparative religion as well. It is important that political theorists engage in comparative political theory; some scholars, such as Roxanne Euben, are already doing this important work.[137] The arguments I have provided could help light the way for such studies: they identify reasons that theocrats should accept for affirming liberal institutions, something well worth having in hand as the study of comparative political theory progresses.

A fourth objection might focus on whether the case I have made would ask liberals wrongly to stand down from their commitment to protecting women in liberal polities and elsewhere. Women tend to be maltreated under manifestations of patriarchal religious doctrines, the objector may note, and granting semisovereignty to theocratic communities would not assist in the rightful liberal commitment to protecting, empowering, and advancing women's equality.[138] It will not do simply to allow that quasi-sovereign theocratic communities could be matriarchal, either, since in fact most are not. Okin has proposed that granting special rights or structural allowances to groups will result in a differential and bigger impact on women than on men;[139] with this in mind, the objector may contend, quasi sovereignty for theocratic communities would be a recipe for injustice and inequity. Is Okin not correct that in a just world, "all social differentiation among the sexes vanishes"?[140] And would quasi sovereignty for theocratic communities not be undesirable inasmuch as it would institutionalize and protect the unacceptable, even despicable treatment of women in those groups?

In response to this objection, it is first worth considering whether all social differentiation would evanesce in a just society. For the answer is not at all obvious. The supporter of Okin's position needs to have reasons and arguments here, not mere polemics, especially when facing the theocrat's claim that God requires social differentiations of various kinds in the best earthly society. Rhetorical moves cannot elude the fact that theocrats have defensible claims in hand, and principles of liberty of conscience support their aims and efforts to a considerable extent. Second, my aim is decidedly not to justify, recommend, or countenance a political theory that would validate the systematic oppression of women by men. For while it is unfortunately true that women in much of the world "lose out by being women,"[141] I have articulated elements of a liberal theory according to which none shall enjoy arbitrary control over another. My arguments provide reasons why it would be undesirable to live in political society without institutions protecting liberty of conscience, and I have maintained that such a deficiency would be itself downright irrational on religious grounds. I have furthermore identified and discussed mechanisms for ensuring adequate protection of basic human rights, provision of education, and freedom of exit for members of religious communities, with no exception for vulnerable parties in theocratic communities.

The objector may offer a rejoinder here, contending that liberals who adopt the theory articulated in this book will be unable to condemn practices they see as repugnant. The liberal may, for instance, look upon patriarchy as a repulsive state of affairs, but the suggestions from this book seem to ask liberals to use forbearance exactly in cases where they should speak up. Does this not take the teeth out of liberalism, wrongly and without cause?

I have hardly argued that liberals must refrain from condemnation: there are many things liberals will encounter that are worthy of censure and reproach, such as violations of basic rights and liberties, state oppression, racial hatred, misogyny, and enmity of other peoples. If liberals were unable justifiably to condemn anything, liberalism would be a strange doctrine indeed, hardly normative at all. Nor, of course, do I propose that government should curtail citizens' legal rights to condemn oth- ers' ideas; the right to free of speech is not at issue here. The point is rather that where liberals condemn groups, individuals, governments, or ways of life, they should ensure that they do so for the right reasons and on proper grounds. First of all, liberals should only censure other parties where they have adequate reason to think that the condemnation is de- served. This holds for attacks on others' religious doctrines and concep- tions of the good, just as it applies to censure of the people who hold such views. Second, one will need charily to consider the prudential effect of public condemnation. One must be careful to think of how railing against patriarchy may adversely affect vulnerable religious minorities, for ex- ample. Certainly, under existing political conditions, condemnation will not likely yield much by way of salutary effects. Third, liberals' critical ac- tions should be performed in good faith and not be exaggerated because of the apparent oddness of theocrats and theocratic communities.

A fifth and final objection one could raise is that notwithstanding what may have been accomplished in this text, the arguments still have not identified grounds on which to govern theocrats. This is a very seri- ous issue, as I argued at the outset: Does liberal government have any right to govern theocrats dwelling within liberal polities, given their reli- gious objections to that rule? And how does liberty of conscience connect to grounds of governance that liberal polities might enjoy, if at all?

In chapter 2, I argued that there is reason for theocrats to affirm lib- eral institutions and proposed that theocrats are committed rationally to the three principles of liberty of conscience I described. The problem is that neither reason to affirm liberalism nor a rational commitment to principles of conscience provides any obvious grounds for liberal gov- ernment to apply its laws to theocrats. For even if one were to grant that there is reason for theocrats to affirm the principles of conscience I have defended, one could propose that no right to liberty of conscience is im- plied in what I have argued here. After all, neither a reason for someone to do something nor a rational commitment to doing it gives that person a right to do it.[142] Nor does a rational commitment to doing something give oneself or any other party a right to do it, either, regardless of whether that party (an individual, group, or institution, for instance) would promote the good on one's behalf. In addition, even in a case where one could safely say that there was reason for everyone to do something (say, to avoid lying to others, as a rule), that would hardly imply that government could justifiably enforce doing it.

This objection points up a critical problem, but an adequate response is available. First of all, theocrats have gone wrong where they have tried to identify solid grounds for treating others in ways that violate principles of conscience, whether the people in question are members of theocratic communities or not. Not all violations of the three principles of conscience are merely self-regarding actions, after all. More vulnerable members of human communities such as women and children must not be enslaved to religious powers that fail to honor principles of conscience: their liberty of conscience must be protected from those who would foist a strict, illiberal conception of the good on them. The same applies to unbelievers, who must not suffer sanctions under illiberal theocratic structures, and it holds likewise for dissenters, a position that virtually any theocrat could come to occupy if theocratic governance were instituted and enforced. The individual's prima facie right to liberty of conscience is a right that theocrats' religious considerations cannot override unless adequate reason is adduced to do so. It is not logically impossible that theocrats could adduce considerations to override the individual right to liberty of conscience, but it will be very difficult for theocrats to find and adduce such reasons plausibly. This conclusion regarding liberty of conscience should cohere with liberal views broadly and also with codified and widely accepted articulations of individual rights of conscience, such as that featured prominently in the Universal Declaration of Human Rights.[143] None of this implies that liberal governments enjoy a right to govern theocrats dwelling within their borders however they please, of course. Rather, liberal government has a right to govern its theocratic citizens reasonably, respectfully, and conscientiously and would do well not only to be mindful of the methods I have suggested for interacting rewardingly with theocrats but also to develop and include a semisovereign option for theocratic groups satisfying the basic requirements for quasi sovereignty I have described.

Review and Conclusion

THE ULTIMATE APPEAL OF LIBERALISM

IN THIS BOOK, I HAVE WORKED to meet the challenges of theocracy by providing reasons, principles, and explanations to justify liberal principles and institutions that can withstand theocratic challenges. My aim has been to furnish a more complete and powerful response to the problems of theocracy by offering a philosophical solution to the conundrums that theocrats raise for liberalism and by delineating practical applications of the theory for actual implementation.

In chapter 1, I distinguished two types of theocrats, ambitious and retiring, and identified the prudential and moral problems they present for liberalism and liberal institutions. I subsequently pinpointed and discussed a series of moral failures that liberalism has displayed with respect to theocratic dissenters. Liberal governments in liberal democracies have tended to mishandle retiring theocrats badly, as a result prompting violent responses from those groups or from sympathetic third parties. Morally speaking, I proposed, liberalism has failed to provide adequate grounds on which to govern theocratic objectors and stumbled through the reasons and explanations it has offered to justify liberal government's interference in the lives of theocrats. I discussed how these shortcomings contribute to the sense of the illegitimacy of liberal institutions and considered the extent to which such problems might contribute to negative forms of citizen mobilization.

In chapter 2, I ventured to discover reasons for affirming liberal institutions that theocrats should accept. In the course of discussion, I identified and articulated three discrete, cardinal principles of conscience that theocrats can affirm while retaining their reasonable and important commitments. I pointed out that theocrats are rationally committed to those three principles and argued that there is reason for theocrats to affirm the principles as well. I then addressed and forestalled a series of objections to the argument I presented, suggesting that there is cause for both theocrats and liberals to accept the three principles of conscience and reflecting on the potentially broader applicability of the principles I described.

I laid out in chapter 3 elements of a new standard of quasi sovereignty for theocratic communities ensconced in liberal democracies. For retiring theocrats, I argued, a legal structure of that kind would better respect their moral right to religious free exercise. I outlined and considered the details of such a structure, focusing on educational criteria, basic human rights requirements, and the matter of securing members' freedom of exit from theocratic communities. I also differentiated theocratic communities from other communities and groups, discussing reasons for making a quasi-sovereign option available to theocratic communities but not to others. My case considered the prospects of implementing a standard of quasi sovereignty in the United States but proceeded on grounds favorable for extrapolation to other liberal democracies. Providing an option of quasi sovereignty would be to offer a foundation on which to govern retiring theocrats respectfully, I proposed, and so doing would reduce the amount of legal embroilments for theocrats as well.

In chapter 4, I laid out strategies and suggestions for more positive interactions between liberals and ambitious theocrats in the modern world. I argued that liberals should resist temptations to dismiss theocrats as crazy and entreated them instead to engage with theocrats directly in their social networks, respectfully and openly to discuss matters of importance with them, and to provide them with reasons and arguments in favor of liberty of conscience. I noted that this holds auspicious prospects for transforming the attitudes of liberals and theocrats alike; engagement of that kind not only would assist within liberal polities but also holds out hope for increasing comity and understanding around the world.

In the course of building this extended argument, I have considered carefully the four moral failures of liberalism I identified at the outset. My treatment improves on the failings of liberalism and contributes to the stock of liberal argument as well. I noted first that liberalism lacks a well-devised schema for treating theocrats within liberal democracies. I offered advancements here by introducing and defending a schema of quasi sovereignty for theocratic communities: a quasi-sovereign option of the sort I have described could appeal to theocrats on morally appropriate grounds, while at the same time invigorating the liberal commitment to religious free exercise. Semisovereignty would not liberate theocratic communities from the influence of other groups or institutions but could deliver theocratic communities from the excessive entanglements they presently endure, endowing their members with the capacity to build the normative worlds their religious doctrines require. As an important complement to this effort, I provided ideas and stratagems for engaging with ambitious theocrats in their social networks. Implementation of the new proposals I have outlined has the potential to reduce injustices visited on theocratic communities, to mitigate maltreatment in the back-and-forth between theocrats and liberals, and to increase the sense of enfranchisement and legitimacy of liberal institutions among theocrats and liberals alike.

The second moral failure I distinguished was liberalism's absence of proper and identifiable grounds for governing theocrats. I responded to that problem by giving reasons theocrats should, even must, accept for affirming liberal institutions. I introduced three novel, cardinal principles of conscience able to serve in a more adequate, fundamental justification of a liberal order, principles that can be added to the liberal repertoire of argumentation. I did so by accepting as a point of departure theocrats' more reasonable assumptions regarding wayward lives and otherworldly goals, employing arguments and resources from within their conceptions of the good to demonstrate their commitment to principles of conscience. I then provided a new rational solution to the value conflict between liberals and theocrats and in so doing demonstrated that the two respective sets of values are not incommensurable. For the principles of conscience I identified not only appear to be freestanding, delimiting broad parameters of what is and is not permitted; they are also principles that liberals, theocrats, and others can affirm together, outstripping other principles and values.

Importantly, the position I have elaborated does not simply replicate the case that beliefs about the afterlife are fallible or that one could be wrong about the religious doctrine to which one subscribes, since the principles of conscience ground a political argument, identifying political conditions for people's pursuit of the good. Instead of suggesting merely that theocrats could be incorrect about the religious doctrines or conceptions of the good they embrace, I granted that they might be right in thinking that they need strictly to pursue a set of otherworldly ends, and I articulated elements of a political structure suitable to accommodate those goals. But I argued that even if theocrats were correct about the need to pursue otherworldly goals in a strict way, it does not follow that God commands that liberty of conscience ought to play no part in their lives. While I allowed that it could conceivably be true that God disavows freedom of conscience, I noted that theocrats would need to demonstrate that unlikely prospect in order to defeat the three principles of conscience I adduced. A conscientious application of reason and a careful consideration of the demands of rationality lead one to an important and exciting surmise: that God affirms liberty of conscience for humanity.

Third, I proposed that liberals must provide an explanation to justify liberal political institutions' coercion of theocrats in cases where they believe they are permitted or required to do so. That explanation, along with a justification for boundaries of acceptable behavior that liberal polities enforce, can be aided by the three cardinal principles of conscience I identified. I reflected on how liberals might use the principles of conscience to defeat even the most difficult theocratic claims, such as the contention that God commands the faithful to disavow basic human rights, educational criteria for children and youth, or the right to be free to exit from one's theocratic community. This is important because liberals need good reasons to justify the application of laws against theocratic dissenters, and it fits with the liberal's rightful commitment that one must stand down from threats to intervene in the lives of others if no good reason to interfere can be adduced. And liberals and liberal government owe theocratic objectors within liberal polities good reasons for restricting their behavior or otherwise imposing upon them, as a matter of obligation. The arguments I have provided in this book can assist in this respect: they provide a good departure point for reconsidering moral and legal grounds on which to allow or disallow abortion, for assessing more demanding public decency standards, and for rethinking a variety of exemptions and positive accommodations for religious practitioners in liberal societies.

The fourth moral failure of liberalism I noted at the outset was that while the reasons liberals provide for interference in theocrats' lives should be reasons that theocrats should accept, liberals have not yet offered reasons of that kind. I have advanced toward that goal by providing three principles of conscience that are sententious, clear, and directly connected to theocrats' otherworldly concerns and commitments. They are principles theocrats should, even must, accept, but if theocrats do not see the power of these reasons and principles, in the end, that does not mean liberals must tolerate their unacceptable actions within liberal polities. For that matter, while I have argued that liberals and liberal government should rethink the ways in which they handle theocracy and religious extremism at home and abroad, this does not imply that the international effort to eradicate terrorism is misguided. Nor does it mean that liberal states must refrain from taking strong and decisive action against religious extremists who resort to violent means to achieve their ends. The point is that it will generally be better to try to convince or persuade theocrats to turn away from their more illiberal inclinations before leaving it to government to employ coercion against them. Liberals are too quick to think that theocrats are people who cannot be reasoned with, that they cannot be persuaded or influenced to accept liberal principles. Indeed, liberals should try to reach those whose ideas and ways of life do not fit easily with liberal values; liberalism cannot be a doctrine simply for those whose lives are already tamed, whose practices meld quietly with contemporary society. Actually offering theocrats good reasons to support liberty of conscience, in a context of respectful engagement and interactive dialogue, will help to shore up the moral shortcomings of liberalism.

With these considerations in hand, I turn now to a final question: Could liberalism be made more appealing to theocrats? I am hopeful that it could, and if the arguments that I have offered in these pages are sound, there is reason to think that a liberalism of conscience could hold appeal for theocrats. First of all, liberal government appears to be the only sort of government able to meet the institutional criteria required by normative principles of liberty of conscience. Other kinds of government are hostile to religion or fail to provide the resources to protect religious free exercise to the extent that theocrats require. Not all theocrats may be aware of this, but an effort to present them with the case, employing friendlier elements of the various doctrines they affirm, could change that situation. Liberal political philosophers could be of assistance here, working to provide theocrats with reasons for accepting liberalism, following the early attempts of Thomas Hobbes, John Locke, John Stuart Mill, Bernard Bosanquet, and Thomas Hill Green. Reasons to affirm a liberalism of conscience can be communicated broadly, through various institutional and colloquial channels, and to numerous parties and stations both domestically and internationally. The reasons to affirm a liberalism of this kind could be given in an appropriate voice as well: they need not and should not be presented in an insulting, patronizing, or dismissive fashion, so as to articulate as well as possible the importance of liberty of conscience and liberal institutions to theocrats and others alike.

One factor contributing to theocrats' present disaffection with liberal government is the way in which theocrats have found themselves treated under liberal institutions. Liberal government has at times appeared to be partisan, disloyal, imperialistic, and disrespectful of theocrats' values and aspirations. But a political order constructed around the value of liberty of conscience could motivate theocrats and other citizens to develop an understanding of the value of liberal institutions, fostering a deep and lasting attachment to government that protects and honors religious free exercise. An order of that kind could rise above a mere modus vivendi, since in it liberals and theocrats would both be able to affirm the fundamental legitimacy of government on terms acceptable to them. What is more, on the sort of political order toward which I am pointing here, government would not begrudge the protections for religious practice that theocrats could garner. Instead, those defenses would be among the highest, most fundamental protections that government would provide to any of its citizens. In that way, liberal government could prove itself respectful of theocrats and not biased in advocating some narrow set of conceptions of the good. Liberals and liberal government would demonstrate an authentic willingness to provide equitable treatment for a wide variety of religious devotees and a preparedness to take seriously and discuss matters of deep importance to religious practitioners. Government would need to refrain from its historically invasive tendencies with respect to theocratic communities, and theocrats and liberals both would have to modify their existing attitudes and views somewhat, but these do not seem to be outlandish goals by any means.

One might object that this prospective approach can only fail, since theocrats simply will not accept any of the arguments, the reasons, or the policies it embodies. After all, one might say, relations between liberals and theocrats have been notoriously difficult in recent years; as such, the program described here would be impracticable and ultimately unsuccessful. However, even if many of the world's zealous religious devotees were to refuse to accept reasons for them to affirm liberty of conscience and to support liberal institutions, it is surely plausible to believe that some will. Even incremental advances here would be worthwhile, and it is not obvious that a program of the sort I have described would need to be especially costly, troublesome, or time-consuming. Furthermore, it is hard to see how such a program would worsen relations between peoples or do damage to the interests of liberal polities. In addition, the effort to speak anew to theocrats should be important to secular and religious liberals for moral reasons, since theocrats within and outside liberal democracies continue to contend that no sufficient or compelling reason to affirm liberal institutions has yet been given to them. A liberalism of conscience addresses this matter directly.

Nevertheless, even a well-conceived and deftly implemented international effort of the kind I have outlined would not easily harmonize theocratic and liberal values, quell the anger of the most extreme theocrats, or solve all the problems of theocracy. Some theocrats will indeed refuse to accept reasons offered for them to affirm political institutions protecting liberty of conscience; it would be naive to think otherwise. New contingents of extremist religious devotees will continue to issue forth and lash out against liberal institutions and citizens; this, one expects, will remain an unfortunate fact of life in the modern, multicultural world. The point is that many burgeoning theocrats might accept the principles, arguments, and reasons outlined here: peripheral members of theocratic organizations, children and youth, those unimpressed with religious extremists, as well as members of religious faiths maltreated by others, are examples of groups of people that could be receptive to the reasons I have outlined. They might be impressed positively by principles and institutions favoring liberty of conscience, along with a demonstration of liberal government's authentic affirmation of religiosity and the value of religion in people's lives.

It would be unreasonable to expect theocrats and liberals ever to unite around a shared conception of the good; disagreement and dissent over people's values, practices, and ideals are important parts of political life, and free societies will never do away with political and participatory discordance. That there could ever be a politics that excludes none is, similarly, a quixotic dream. But a liberalism of conscience holds the promise of being able to bring theocrats into the fold, to rectify the injustices to which theocrats are subjected, and to assuage centuries of confusion and infelicitous quarrel. A proper theory of government, one relevant to the problems and prospects of modern democratic life, ought to try to accomplish this feat.

Notes

1. A LIBERALISM OF CONSCIENCE

1. John Rawls, *Political Liberalism*, paperback ed. (New York: Columbia University Press, 1996), p. 36.
2. Ibid., p. xxvi.
3. Josephus, *Against Apion*, trans. H. St. J. Thackeray (Cambridge: Harvard University Press, 1976), pp. 355, 359, 363, 367, 389–97.
4. Jean-Jacques Rousseau, *On the Social Contract* (1762), ed. Roger D. Masters, trans. Judith R. Masters (New York: St. Martin's Press, 1978), pp. 124–25.
5. James George Frazer, *The Golden Bough: A Study in Magic and Religion* (New York: Macmillan, 1960), p. 11. See Werner Stark, *The Sociology of Religion*, vol. 1, *Established Religion* (London: Routledge and Kegan Paul, 1966), p. 8; Henri Frankfort, *Kingship and the Gods* (Chicago: University of Chicago Press, 1948).
6. Max Weber, *The Sociology of Religion*, trans. Ephraim Fischoff (1922; reprint, Boston: Beacon, 1964), p. 233; cf. pp. 36, 90, 227. Weber maintains that coercive practice "[posed] no problem" to the ruling class of Islamic polities, since forcible dominion of the faithful over non-believers was seen to be a pleasance to God. According to that view, infidels can be tolerated only "once they have been subjugated" (p. 227). See also G. W. F. Hegel, *The Philosophy of History* (ca. 1831), trans. J. Sibree (New York: Dover, 1956), pp. 111–16, 227, 233.
7. See Robert C. Walton, *Zwingli's Theocracy* (Toronto: University of Toronto Press, 1967).
8. See generally John Fiske, *The Beginnings of Puritan New England; or, The Puritan Theocracy in Its Relations to Civil and Religious Liberty* (Boston: Houghton, Mifflin, 1898). See also John Davenport (possibly John Cotton), *A Discourse About Civil Religion in a New Plantation Whose Design Is Religion* (Cambridge, Mass.: Samuel Green and Marmaduke Johnson, 1663).
9. Rousseau, *On the Social Contract*, p. 124. See similar propositions in Frazer, *The Golden Bough*, pp. 10–12; and in Stark, *The Sociology of Religion*, pp. 7–24.
10. See David L. Webster, "On Theocracies," *American Anthropologist* 78 (1976): 812–28.

11. Herbert Hoover, *The Challenge to Liberty* (New York: Scribner's, 1935), p. 49.
12. Josephus stipulates that "all sovereignty and authority is placed in God," but that authority clearly can be delegated in his view, as he later describes in *Against Apion*. Cf. Seyyid Qutb's fundamentalist Islamic contention: "no sovereignty except God's, no law except from God, and no authority of one man over another, as the authority in all respects belong [*sic*] to God" (*Milestones* [Damascus: Dar Al-Ilm, n.d.], p. 26; cf. pp. 57–58, 60–61, 79, 94–96, 108, 130).
13. H. L. A. Hart, *The Concept of Law* (Oxford: Clarendon, 1961), pp. 123–25.
14. Ibid., p. 123.
15. Weber, *The Sociology of Religion*, p. 227. See also Emile Durkheim, *The Elementary Forms of Religious Life*, trans. Karen E. Fields (1912; reprint, New York: Free, 1995), p. 29ff.
16. Weber, *The Sociology of Religion*, pp. 268, 36. While these Hindu adherents did postulate the existence of God, they did not situate sovereignty in his hands. Even the gods were thought to be subject to what Weber called the "providential power of the harmonious and rational order of the world" (p. 36).
17. Hegel, *The Philosophy of History*, pp. 111–12.
18. See, e.g., Will Kymlicka, *Liberalism, Community, and Culture* (Oxford: Clarendon, 1989), p. 195; idem, *Multicultural Citizenship: A Liberal Theory of Minority Rights* (Oxford: Clarendon, 1995), pp. 40, 165. See also Triloki N. Pandey, "Patterns of Leadership in Western Pueblo Society," in *North American Indian Anthropology*, ed. Raymond J. DeMallie and Alfonso Ortiz (Norman: University of Oklahoma Press, 1994), pp. 328–30.
19. Michael Walzer, *The Revolution of the Saints: A Study in the Origins of Radical Politics* (New York: Atheneum, 1965), p. 57.
20. Common and scholarly use of "theocracy" has had no generally accepted meaning, but one never uses the word to refer to a free and open society or a polity in which the right takes priority over the good; see Rawls, *Political Liberalism*, pp. 173–211. See also Steven D. Smith, "Is a Coherent Theory of Religious Freedom Possible?" *Constitutional Commentary* 15 (1998): 73–86. Smith notes that people are "accustomed to treating 'theocracy' not as a version of, but rather as the antithesis of, 'religious freedom'" (p. 78).
21. For example, the ruling Chinese government denies civil liberties on a nonreligious basis, as does, to a lesser extent, the Québécois government in enforcing French-only laws.
22. See Rawls, *Political Liberalism*, pp. 12–15, 174–76ff. See also Rawls, *The Law of Peoples* (Cambridge: Harvard University Press, 1999), p. 40, noting that peoples of constitutional democracies have no comprehensive doctrine of the good. Theocratic communities could be said to have comprehensive religious doctrines, but it is only the constitutive members of those communities per se who properly hold conceptions of the good. See Rawls, *Political Liberalism*, p. 175. See Josephus, *Against Apion*, pp. 355, 359, 363, 389–97; and cf. Qutb, *Milestones*, referring to Islam as a "comprehensive concept of life and the universe with its own characteristics" (p. 129).

23. Cf. Rawls, *Political Liberalism*, p. 175.

24. Edmund Morgan reminds us that the Puritans endeavored to live a "smooth, honest, civil life" and tried to "force everyone within their power to do likewise" (*The Puritan Family: Religion and Domestic Relations in Seventeenth Century New England* [New York: Harper and Row, 1966], p. 2).

25. Martin Luther King Jr., "Letter from the Birmingham Jail," in *Why We Can't Wait* (New York: New American Library, 1963), p. 70. See also Louis A. DeCaro Jr., *Malcolm and the Cross: The Nation of Islam, Malcolm X, and Christianity* (New York: New York University Press, 1998), chaps. 4, 12.

26. See, e.g., Axel R. Schaefer, "Evangelicalism, Social Reform, and the U.S. Welfare State, 1970–1996," in *Religious and Secular Reform in America: Ideas, Beliefs, and Social Change*, ed. David K. Adams and Cornelis A. van Minnen (New York: New York University Press, 1999), pp. 249–73. Schaefer emphasizes the social and theological diversity of both evangelical and fundamentalist Christians.

27. Michael Sandel, *Democracy's Discontent: America in Search of a Public Philosophy* (Cambridge: Harvard University Press, 1996), p. 3. Cf. Gabriel A. Almond, R. Scott Appleby, and Emmanuel Sivan, *Strong Religion: The Rise of Fundamentalisms Around the World* (Chicago: University of Chicago Press, 2003), pp. 17, 146 passim.

28. See Martha F. Lee, *The Nation of Islam: An American Millenarian Movement* (Syracuse, N.Y.: Syracuse University Press, 1996), chaps. 2, 5, 6.

29. See Duane Murray Oldfield, *The Right and the Righteous: The Christian Right Confronts the Republican Party* (New York: Rowman and Littlefield, 1996), p. 58.

30. Members of the Nation of Islam, for instance, have spoken out strongly against Catholicism and supported a variety of sanctions against Jews; see DeCaro, *Malcolm and the Cross*, pp. 131–32; cf. Lee, *The Nation of Islam*, pp. 80–83, 103–4, 109–12. See also *ADL Fact-Finding Report—The Other Face of Farrakhan: A Hate-Filled Prelude to the Million Man March* (New York: ADL Publications, 1995); Henry Louis Gates Jr., "The Charmer," in *The Farrakhan Factor: African-American Writers on Leadership, Nationhood, and Minister Louis Farrakhan*, ed. Amy Alexander (New York: Grove, 1998), pp. 18–51. The Nation of Islam has published an account of the slave trade that vilifies Jews; it is entitled *The Secret Relationship Between Blacks and Jews, Vol. 1* (Chicago: Historical Research Department, 1991). See Michael Lieb, *Children of Ezekiel* (Durham, N.C.: Duke University Press, 1998), pp. 216–18.

31. Oldfield, *The Right and the Righteous*, p. 60; cf. Ralph Reed, *Active Faith: How Christians Are Changing the Soul of American Politics* (New York: Free, 1996), pp. 192, 273.

32. See Glenn H. Utter and John W. Storey, *The Religious Right* (Santa Barbara, Calif.: ABC-CLIO, 1995), pp. 87–89; see also Oldfield, *The Right and the Righteous*, p. 60; Reed, *Active Faith*, chap. 8.

33. Cf. Sara Diamond, *Not by Politics Alone: The Enduring Influence of the Christian Right* (New York: Guildford, 1998), pp. 76–80.

34. *Yoder v. Wisconsin*, 406 U.S. 205 (1972).

35. *Santa Clara Pueblo v. Martinez*, 436 U.S. 49 (1978).

36. *Reynolds v. United States*, 98 U.S. 145 (1878).

37. *Board of Education of Kiryas Joel School District v. Grumet*, 114 S.Ct. 2481 (1994).

38. See Jaime M. W. Sanders, "Religious Community as a City: The Oregon Constitutional Puzzle of *State of Oregon v. City of Rajneeshpuram*," *Willamette Law Review* 21 (1985): 707–65, at pp. 710, 712–24.

39. Nancy L. Rosenblum, *Membership and Morals: The Personal Uses of Pluralism in America* (Princeton: Princeton University Press, 1998), chap. 4. See also "The Rule of Law in Residential Associations" (note), *Harvard Law Review* 99 (1985): 472–90.

40. For accounts to this effect, see Stephen Macedo, "Liberal Civic Education and Religious Fundamentalism: The Case of God v. John Rawls?" *Ethics* 105 (1995): 468–96. See also Stephen L. Carter, *The Culture of Disbelief: How American Law and Politics Trivialize Religious Devotion* (New York: Basic, 1993); idem, *The Dissent of the Governed: A Meditation on Law, Religion, and Loyalty* (Cambridge: Harvard University Press, 1998); idem, *God's Name in Vain: The Wrongs and Rights of Religion in Politics* (New York: Basic, 2000).

41. See Ron Manuto, "The Life and Death of Rajneeshpuram and the Still Lingering Dilemma of the Religious Clauses of the First Amendment," *Free Speech Yearbook* 30 (1992): 26–39, at pp. 26–27; see also S. Callister, J. Long, and L. Zaitz, "On the Road Again," *The Oregonian*, December 30, 1985, p. 2.

42. See John McLaren and Harold Coward, eds., *Religious Conscience, the State, and the Law* (Albany: SUNY Press, 1999), chap. 8.

43. See *ADL Fact-Finding Report—Armed and Dangerous: Militias Take Aim at the Federal Government* (New York: ADL Publications, 1994). See also Alan M. Schwartz, ed., *Danger: Extremism—The Major Vehicles and Voices on America's Far Right Fringe* (New York: ADL Publications, 1996), pp. 255–61. Whether militia or other militant groups would have attacked the government if the Waco affair had been handled differently is, of course, difficult to determine. It is worth noting, however, that American extremists claim that the Waco incident motivated them against government, and they continue to perform terrorist acts on April 19, the anniversary of the final day of the Waco siege. See " 'No Sympathy' for Dead Children, McVeigh Says," *New York Times*, March 29, 2001; see also Lou Michel and Dan Herbeck, *American Terrorist: Timothy McVeigh and the Oklahoma City Bombing* (New York: Regan, 2001).

44. Militia groups normally are principally concerned with issues other than religious liberty, such as government encroachment on Second Amendment rights, but they are nonetheless excitable over government invasion of religious communities.

45. John Locke, *A Letter Concerning Toleration* (London: Awnsham Churchill, 1689), p. 56.

46. See Paul Abramson, *Political Attitudes in America: Formation and Change* (San Francisco: W. H. Freeman, 1983); Ruy Teixeira, *The Disappearing American Voter* (Washington, D.C.: Brookings, 1992).

47. Geraint Parry, George Moyser, and Neil Day, *Political Participation and Democracy in Britain* (Cambridge: Cambridge University Press, 1992).

48. Sidney Verba, Kay Lehman Schlozman, and Henry E. Brady, *Voice and Equality: Civic Voluntarism in American Politics* (Cambridge: Harvard University Press, 1995). See also Robert D. Putnam, ed., *Democracies in Flux: The Evolution of Social Capital in Contemporary Society* (New York: Oxford University Press, 2002), pp. 405–6, 412–13 passim.

49. See Jack Citrin and Donald Green, "Presidential Leadership and Trust in Government," *British Journal of Political Science* 16 (1986): 431–53. Cf. Christopher J. Eberle, *Religious Conviction in Liberal Politics* (New York: Cambridge University Press, 2002), p. 162.

50. Pippa Norris, "Conclusions: The Growth of Critical Citizens and Its Consequences," in *Critical Citizens: Global Support for Democratic Governance*, ed. Pippa Norris (Oxford: Oxford University Press, 1999), pp. 257–92, at pp. 264–65.

51. See Peter Bachrach and Morton S. Baratz, "Two Faces of Power," *American Political Science Review* 56 (1962): 947–52; idem, "Decisions and Nondecisions: An Analytical Framework," *American Political Science Review* 57 (1963): 632–42. See also Steven Lukes, *Power: A Radical View* (New York: Macmillan, 1974).

52. See Isaiah Berlin, "Two Concepts of Liberty," in *Four Essays on Liberty* (Oxford: Oxford University Press, 1969), pp. 118–72; James Griffin, *Well-Being: Its Meaning, Measure, and Moral Importance* (Oxford: Clarendon, 1986), pp. 31–34, 64–68; Charles Larmore, *The Morals of Modernity* (New York: Cambridge University Press, 1996), pp. 158–63; Steven Lukes, "Making Sense of Moral Conflict," in *Liberalism and the Moral Life*, ed. Nancy L. Rosenblum (Cambridge: Harvard University Press, 1989), pp. 127–42; Alasdair MacIntyre, *After Virtue*, 2d ed. (Notre Dame, Ind.: University of Notre Dame Press, 1984), chap. 6; Bernard Williams, *Moral Luck* (Cambridge: Cambridge University Press, 1977), chap. 5. See also Rawls, *Political Liberalism*, pp. 54–59.

53. Joseph Raz provides the following definition of incommensurability: "Two valuable options are incommensurable if (1) neither is better than the other, and (2) there is (or could be) another option which is better than one but is not better than the other" (*The Morality of Freedom* [Oxford: Clarendon, 1986], p. 325). Cf. Griffin, *Well-Being*, pp. 77–91ff.; see also generally Ruth Chang, ed., *Incommensurability, Incomparability, and Practical Reason* (Cambridge: Harvard University Press, 1997).

54. See John Gray, *Two Faces of Liberalism* (New York: New, 2000); idem, "Where Pluralists and Liberals Part Company," *International Journal of Philosophical Studies* 6 (1998): 17–36; idem, "What Is Dead and What Is Living in Liberalism?" in *Post-liberalism: Studies in Political Thought* (New York: Routledge, 1994), pp. 283–328.

55. 98 U.S. 145 (1878).

56. Ibid., at 161.

57. Ibid., at 164. Cf. *Ng Suey Hi v. Weedin*, 21 F.2d 801 (9th Cir. 1927); *Cleveland v. United States*, 329 U.S. 14 (1946); *The King v. The Superintendent Registrar of Marriages, ex parte Mir-Anwaruddin*, (1917) 1 K.B. 634.

58. *Reynolds*, 98 U.S., at 165.

59. Ibid., at 166, 167–68. Waite added that polygamous communities may also disturb people in neighboring vicinities. See Sarah Barringer Gordon, *The Mormon Question: Polygamy and Constitutional Conflict in Nineteenth-Century America* (Chapel Hill: University of North Carolina Press, 2002), pp. 29–54, discussing putative harms that early American polygamists were said to have inflicted on other members of society. Cf. Martha Nussbaum's contention that there "is nothing in polygamy in the abstract that is oppressive to women, especially if the practice is available to both sexes" (*Women and Human Development: The Capabilities Approach* [New York: Cambridge University Press, 2000], p. 229).

60. *Reynolds*, 98 U.S., at 166. Cf. Laurence Drew Borten, "Sex, Procreation, and the State Interest in Marriage," *Columbia Law Review* 102 (2002): 1089–1128.

61. *Reynolds*, 98 U.S., at 166.

62. Amy Gutmann and Dennis Thompson's conception of deliberative democracy, for example, affirms this view. "At the core of deliberative democracy," they write, "is the idea that citizens and officials must justify any demands for collective action by giving reasons that can be accepted by those who are bound by the action" ("The Moral Foundations of Truth Commissions," in *Truth v. Justice: The Morality of Truth Commissions*, ed. Robert I. Rotberg and Dennis Thompson [Oxford: Princeton University Press, 2000], pp. 22–44, at pp. 35–36). See also generally idem, *Democracy and Disagreement* (Cambridge: Harvard University Press, 1996); idem, *Why Deliberative Democracy?* (Princeton: Princeton University Press, 2004). Cf. Ian Shapiro, *The State of Democratic Theory* (Princeton: Princeton University Press, 2003), pp. 102–3; Ronald Dworkin, *Freedom's Law: The Moral Reading of the American Constitution* (Cambridge: Harvard University Press, 1996), pp. 7–15, 25–34 passim; Jeremy Waldron, "Judicial Review and the Conditions of Democracy," *Journal of Political Philosophy* 6, no. 4 (1998): 335–55; George Klosko, *Democratic Procedures and Political Consensus* (New York: Oxford University Press, 2000), esp. chaps. 2–4.

63. Consider, e.g., John Stuart Mill's remarks on this issue: "[The] burthen of proof is supposed to be with those who are against liberty; who contend for any restriction or prohibition . . . [the] *a priori* assumption is in favour of freedom" (*On Liberty and Other Essays*, ed. John Gray [Oxford: Oxford University Press, 1991 (1859)], p. 472). See also Gerald F. Gaus, *Value and Justification: The Foundations of Liberal Theory* (Cambridge: Cambridge University Press, 1990), chap. 8; and idem, *Justificatory Liberalism* (New York: Oxford University Press, 1996), chap. 17.

64. See T. M. Scanlon, *What We Owe to Each Other* (Cambridge: Harvard University Press, 2001), pp. 191–206, 210–23ff. A reason or principle that someone cannot reasonably reject could be one that a person must accept, but it could also be a reason or principle toward which one is neutral.

65. Rawls, *Political Liberalism*, p. 143. Cf. Gutmann and Thompson, "The Moral Foundations of Truth Commissions," pp. 37–38: "The very activity of providing an account that other citizens can be expected to understand as reasonable (even if not right) indicates the willingness of citizens to acknowledge one another's membership in a common democratic enterprise." Cf. also Eberle, *Religious Conviction in Liberal Politics*, pp. 11–14 passim.

66. See John Skorupski, "Irrealist Cognitivism," *Ratio* 12 (1999): 436–59, at pp. 440, 446–47.

67. See Amy Gutmann, *Democratic Education* (Princeton: Princeton University Press, 1987); idem, "Civic Education and Social Diversity," *Ethics* 105 (1995): 557–79; idem, "Challenges of Multiculturalism in Democratic Education," in *Public Education in a Multicultural Society: Policy, Theory, Critique*, ed. Robert K. Fullinwinder (New York: Cambridge University Press, 1996), pp. 156–79; Meira Levinson, *The Demands of Liberal Education* (New York: Oxford University Press, 1999); Stephen Macedo, *Liberal Virtues: Citizenship, Virtue, and Community in Liberal Constitutionalism* (Oxford: Clarendon, 1990); idem, "Liberal Civic Education and Religious Fundamentalism"; idem, *Diversity and Distrust: Civic Education in a Multicultural Democracy* (Cambridge: Harvard University Press, 2000); Rob Reich, *Bridging Liberalism and Multiculturalism in American Education* (Chicago: University of Chicago Press, 2002).

68. See generally Levinson, *The Demands of Liberal Education*, and Reich, *Bridging Liberalism and Multiculturalism*.

69. Susan Moller Okin, " 'Mistresses of Their Own Destiny': Group Rights, Gender, and Realistic Rights of Exit," *Ethics* 112 (2002): 205–30, at p. 206. See also idem, "Is Multiculturalism Bad for Women?" *Boston Review* 22 (1997): 25–28; idem, "Feminism and Multiculturalism: Some Tensions," *Ethics* 108 (1998): 661–84. Ayelet Shachar has argued similar points in recent years; see her *Multicultural Jurisdictions: Cultural Differences and Women's Rights* (New York: Cambridge University Press, 2001). See also idem, "Group Identity and Women's Rights in Family Law: The Perils of Multicultural Accommodation," *Journal of Political Philosophy* 6 (1998): 285–305; Mary Becker, "The Politics of Women's Wrongs and the Bill of 'Rights': A Bicentennial Perspective," *University of Chicago Law Review* 59 (1992): 453–517.

70. Okin, " 'Mistresses of Their Own Destiny,' " p. 216.

71. Ibid., p. 229.

72. For arguments in favor of interventions for the sake of citizenship, see Eamonn Callan, *Creating Citizens: Political Education and Liberal Democracy* (New York: Clarendon, 1997). See also Macedo, *Liberal Virtues*.

73. Cf. Rawls, *Political Liberalism*, pp. 386–90.

74. Ronald Dworkin, *Life's Dominion: An Argument About Abortion, Euthanasia, and Individual Freedom* (New York: Vintage, 1994), pp. 162–68 passim. Dworkin proposes that "the right to procreative autonomy, from which a right of choice about abortion flows, is well grounded in the First Amendment" (p. 166).

75. See ibid., pp. 157–59, 162–68, 172–76.

76. See Christopher L. Eisgruber, "The Constitutional Value of Assimilation," *Columbia Law Review* 96 (1996): 87–103, at pp. 90–91, 99–103 passim. See also idem, "Political Unity and the Powers of Government," *UCLA Law Review* 41 (1994): 1297–1336; and idem, *Constitutional Self-Government* (Cambridge: Harvard University Press, 2001).

77. See Rawls, *Political Liberalism*, pp. 136–37, 216–17, 393–94, 428–30. See also Samuel Freeman, "Public Reason and Political Justifications," *Fordham Law Review* 72 (2004): 2021–72, at pp. 2045–53.

78. Rawls, *Political Liberalism*, pp. 15–22, 49–50, 54–58.

79. Ibid., pp. 178–83, 187–90.

80. See generally Stuart Hampshire, *Justice Is Conflict* (Princeton: Princeton University Press, 2000).

81. Included here could be economic incentives for theocrats internationally, since many (but by no means all) theocratic polities are not only impoverished but arguably are also resentful of liberal-democratic wealth.

82. Rawls distinguishes between public reason and secular reason, understanding the latter as "reasoning in terms of comprehensive nonreligious doctrines" ("The Idea of Public Reason Revisited," in *Collected Papers*, ed. Samuel Freeman [Cambridge: Harvard University Press, 1999], pp. 573–615, at p. 583; cf. pp. 587–88). Theocrats could object even to public reasons so construed if those reasons were not shown to be consistent with or overdetermined by commands of God.

83. See Thomas Hobbes, *Leviathan* (1651), ed. Richard Tuck (New York: Cambridge University Press, 1996), parts 3, 4; idem, *Considerations Upon the Reputation, Loyalty, Manners, & Religions, of Thomas Hobbes of Malmesbury* (1662; reprint, London: William Crooke, 1680); idem, *Behemoth: The History of the Causes of the Civil Wars of England* (1679), ed. William Molesworth (New York: Burt Franklin, 1963). See also Locke's *Letter;* and see idem, *The Reasonableness of Christianity: As Delivered in the Scriptures* (1695), ed. and intro. John C. Higgins-Biddle (Oxford: Clarendon, 1999).

84. Jeff Spinner-Halev, *Surviving Diversity: Religion and Democratic Citizenship* (Baltimore: Johns Hopkins University Press, 2000), p. 213; see also pp. 142–65, 201–19 passim. Cf. Michael W. McConnell, "Old Liberalism, New Liberalism, and People of Faith," in *Christian Perspectives on Legal Thought*, ed. Michael W. McConnell, Robert F. Cochran Jr., and Angela C. Carmella (New Haven: Yale University Press, 2001), pp. 5–24, at pp. 5, 17–24. Cf. also "Wagering on Religious Liberty" (note), *Harvard Law Review* 116

(2003): 946–68, providing the refreshing argument that the liberal state should "take religion seriously on its own terms" (p. 950).

85. See Robert Audi, "The Separation of Church and State and the Obligations of Citizenship," *Philosophy and Public Affairs* 18 (1989): 259–96; idem, "Liberal Democracy and the Place of Religion in Politics," in Robert Audi and Nicholas Wolterstorff, *Religion in the Public Square: The Place of Religious Convictions in Public Debate* (London: Rowman and Littlefield, 1997), pp. 1–66 passim; and idem, *Religious Commitment and Secular Reason* (Cambridge: Cambridge University Press, 2000). See also William A. Galston, "Two Concepts of Liberalism," *Ethics* 105 (1995): 516–34; idem, *Liberal Pluralism: The Implications of Value Pluralism for Political Theory and Practice* (New York: Cambridge University Press, 2002), pp. 40–42. For further sensitive treatments of these matters, see Kent Greenawalt, *Private Consciences and Public Reasons* (Oxford: Oxford University Press, 1995); idem, "Five Questions about Religion Judges Are Afraid to Ask," in *Obligations of Citizenship and Demands of Faith: Religious Accommodation in Pluralist Democracies*, ed. Nancy L. Rosenblum (Princeton: Princeton University Press, 2000), pp. 196–244. See also Charles Larmore, *Patterns of Moral Complexity* (New York: Cambridge University Press, 1987), chap. 6; idem, *The Morals of Modernity*, pp. 30–35, 41–44, 46, 167–69; Nussbaum, *Women and Human Development*, chap. 5; and J. Judd Owen, *Religion and the Demise of Liberal Rationalism: The Foundational Crisis of the Separation of Church and State* (Chicago: University of Chicago Press, 2001), pp. 165–66 passim.

86. See, e.g., Stanley Fish, "Mission Impossible," in *The Trouble With Principle* (Cambridge: Harvard University Press, 1999), pp. 162–86; William Connolly, "Secularism, Partisanship, and the Ambiguities of Justice," in *Political Theory and Partisan Politics*, ed. E. Portis, A. Gundersen, and R. Shively (Albany: SUNY Press, 2000), pp. 149–72. Cf. generally Richard Rorty, *Contingency, Irony, and Solidarity* (New York: Cambridge University Press, 1989).

87. See Audi, *Religious Commitment and Secular Reason*, pp. 47–48, 175. For theocrats living in modern democracies, the reasons to affirm liberalism may take a slightly different form than they do for theocrats dwelling in other kinds of polities.

2. LIBERALISM AND THE LIBERTY OF CONSCIENCE

1. See Edward J. Bond, *Reason and Value* (Cambridge: Cambridge University Press, 1983), chap. 2; cf. Bernard Williams's distinction between "internal" and "external" reasons, in his "Internal and External Reasons," in *Rational Action: Studies in Philosophy and Social Science*, ed. R. Harrison (Cambridge: Cambridge University Press, 1979), pp. 17–28.

2. I assume that there may be weight to David Hume's concern regarding the putative impuissance of reason to motivate persons; see Hume's *A Treatise*

of Human Nature (1739), ed. L. A. Selby-Bigge (Oxford: Clarendon, 1888), 2d ed., ed. P. H. Nidditch (1978), pp. 415–18, 457–61, 468–70; see also James Dreier, "Humean Doubts and the Practical Justification of Morality," in *Ethics and Practical Reason*, ed. G. Cullity and B. Gaut (Oxford: Oxford University Press, 1997), pp. 81–99.

3. See John Rawls, *Political Liberalism*, paperback ed. (New York: Columbia University Press, 1996), pp. 54–59.

4. Cf. Richard Swinburne's arguments for God's existence, in his *The Existence of God*, 2d ed. (Oxford: Clarendon, 2004). Cf. also Alvin Plantinga, "Reason and Belief in God," in *Faith and Rationality: Reason and Belief in God*, ed. Alvin Plantinga and Nicholas Wolterstorff (Notre Dame, Ind.: University of Notre Dame Press, 1983), pp. 16–93; idem, *Warranted Christian Belief* (New York: Oxford University Press, 2000). See J. L. Mackie, *The Miracle of Theism: Arguments For and Against the Existence of God* (New York: Oxford University Press, 1982); and William Lane Craig and Walter Sinnott-Armstrong, *God? A Debate Between a Christian and an Atheist* (New York: Oxford University Press, 2004).

5. See Rawls, *Political Liberalism*, pp. 24, 35–40, 58–66. Cf. Joseph Raz's distinction between reasonable persons and views, in his "Disagreement in Politics," *American Journal of Jurisprudence* 43 (1998): 25–52, at pp. 33–34ff. See also Samuel Freeman, "Public Reason and Political Justifications," *Fordham Law Review* 72 (2004): 2021–72, at pp. 2045–53ff.

6. Rawls, *Political Liberalism*, pp. 60–62. This point holds whether or not God exists. Cf. Jürgen Habermas's attempt to distinguish between philosophical and religious discourse, in his "Transcendence from Within, Transcendence in the World," in *Religion and Rationality: Essays on Reason, God, and Modernity*, ed. E. Mendieta (Cambridge, Mass.: MIT Press, 2002), pp. 67–94.

7. I take affirmation to be an expression of deep appeal such that, with respect to political theories, ideologies, or institutional arrangements, one affirms them where one believes in their fundamental legitimacy. Cf. A. John Simmons, "Associative Political Obligations," *Ethics* 106, no. 2 (1996): 247–73; idem, "Justification and Legitimacy," *Ethics* 109, no. 4 (1999): 739–71.

8. The United States government allowed the Mormons to run an Indian Placement Service for several years, through which Indian children were removed from their communities and placed in Mormon homes for schooling. See Robert Gottlieb and Peter Wiley, *America's Saints: The Rise of Mormon Power* (New York: Putnam's, 1984), pp. 157–58; see also J. Herschell Barnhill, "Civil Rights in Utah: The Mormon Way," *Journal of the West* 25, no. 4 (1986): 24. Cf. the treatment of Aboriginal children of mixed descent who were taken from their families for the purposes of receiving Christian education in white foster homes; see Chandran Kukathas, "The Life of Brian; or, Now for Something Completely Difference-Blind," in *Multiculturalism Reconsidered: Culture and Equality and Its Critics*, ed. Paul Kelly (Malden, Mass.: Polity, 2002), pp. 184–203, at pp. 198, 202–3.

9. R. M. Hare, *Freedom and Reason* (Oxford: Clarendon, 1963), pp. 22–25, 30, 71.

10. Aristotle, *Politics*, ed. and trans. Ernest Barker (New York: Oxford University Press, 1962), 1278a. Mechanics, slaves, and freemen do not qualify as citizens of Aristotle's state because they are unable to participate in the good life of citizens and cannot achieve their excellence; see ibid., 1277b–1278a.

11. The response of the Amish to assaults by civil authority on their way of life "has been to sell their farms and to remove to jurisdictions, here or abroad, wherein hopefully they will be allowed peaceably to follow the will of God" ("Brief for Respondent at 26, Yoder (No. 70–110)," cited in Robert Cover, "The Supreme Court, 1982 Term—Foreword: *Nomos* and Narrative," *Harvard Law Review* 97 [1983]: 4–68, at pp. 28–29). Cf. the Tash Hasidim in Quebec, who are largely indifferent to the polity in which they reside so long as they are "left alone"; see Jan Feldman, *Lubavitchers as Citizens: A Paradox of Liberal Democracy* (Ithaca, N.Y.: Cornell University Press, 2003), p. 73.

12. Thomas Cartwright and the English Puritans are a good example of a suspect group, perceived as threatening by Elizabeth I; see A. F. Scott Pearson, *Church and State: Political Aspects of Sixteenth-Century Puritanism* (Cambridge: Cambridge University Press, 1928), pp. 61–63ff.

13. See, e.g., Harold O. J. Brown, *Heresies: The Image of Christ in the Mirror of Heresy and Orthodoxy from the Apostles to the Present* (Garden City, N.J.: Doubleday, 1984); Larry D. Eldridge, *A Distant Heritage: The Growth of Free Speech in Early America* (New York: New York University Press, 1994), p. 95ff.; Walter Nigg, *The Heretics*, ed. and trans. R. Winston and C. Winston (New York: Knopf, 1962); Walter L. Wakefield and Austin P. Evans, ed. and trans., *Heresies of the High Middle Ages* (New York: Columbia University Press, 1991).

14. Herod's murderous rule over Jerusalem is an example of ascension of this kind.

15. I borrow this phrase from Edmund Burke; see *A Vindication of Natural Society* (1757), ed. Frank N. Pagano (Indianapolis: Liberty Fund, 1982), pp. 44–45. Cf. Manasses at the Temple of Jerusalem; Junius Brutus proposes that once "King Manasses had polluted the Temple at Jerusalem . . . God not only taxed Manasses, but all the people also" (*A Defence of Liberty Against Tyrants* [*Vindiciae Contra Tyrannos*] [1689], ed. H. J. Laski [Gloucester: Peter Smith, 1963], p. 95).

16. See Seyyid Qutb, *Milestones* (Damascus: Dar Al-Ilm, n.d.), pp. 84, 93. Qutb maintains that "one should accept the *Shari'ah* [Divine Law] without any question and reject all other laws in any shape or form. This is Islam. There is no other meaning of Islam" (p. 36).

17. T. M. Scanlon, "The Difficulty of Tolerance," in *The Difficulty of Tolerance: Essays in Political Philosophy* (New York: Cambridge University Press, 2002), pp. 187–201, at p. 193.

18. Rawls, *Political Liberalism*, p. 36; see also pp. 24, 37, 58–66.

19. Cf. Charles Larmore, *Patterns of Moral Complexity* (New York: Cambridge University Press, 1987), pp. 74–77 passim.

20. Robert Audi proposes that an argument can be religious or theological by dint of its "essentially religious content," if, for instance, it expresses a divine command. Arguments also may be evidentially religious where their premises, conclusions, or warrant cannot be known "apart from reliance on religious considerations" such as "scripture or revelation or clerical authority." In addition, religious arguments can be motivationally religious if an "essential part" of their design is to "accomplish a religious purpose"; this concerns the matter of the presentation of arguments rather than their internal structure or content. See Robert Audi, *Religious Commitment and Secular Reason* (Cambridge: Cambridge University Press, 2000), pp. 70, 71, 73. In the idiom of natural theology, the following argument will not rely in any relevant way on scripture, revelation, or clerical authority.

21. Rawls, *Political Liberalism*, pp. 36–38, 58–62. Cf. Jeffrey Stout, *The Flight From Authority: Religion, Modernity, and the Quest for Autonomy* (Notre Dame, Ind.: University of Notre Dame Press, 1981); idem, *Democracy and Tradition* (Princeton: Princeton University Press, 2004).

22. John Locke, *A Letter Concerning Toleration* (London: Awnsham Churchill, 1689), pp. 9–10.

23. Consider Qutb's comments acknowledging that people can "change [their] beliefs, concepts and attitudes toward life" and that "the capacity exists in human nature to change completely from one way of life to another; and this is much easier for it than many partial changes" (*Milestones*, pp. 95, 136).

24. See Michael W. McConnell, "Old Liberalism, New Liberalism, and People of Faith," in *Christian Perspectives on Legal Thought*, ed. M. W. McConnell, R. F. Cochran, Jr., and A. G. Carmella (New Haven: Yale University Press, 2001), pp. 13–15, 17.

25. John Rawls, *A Theory of Justice* (Cambridge: Harvard University Press, 1971), sec. 33, p. 206. "Justice as fairness," Rawls writes, "provides . . . strong arguments for an equal liberty of conscience" (ibid., sec. 34, p. 211).

26. Ibid., sec. 33, p. 207; cf. idem, *Political Liberalism*, p. 311ff.

27. Rawls, *A Theory of Justice*, sec. 33, p. 207. One might respond to Rawls's point by suggesting that theocrats are rightly prepared to gamble with their temporal well-being for the sake of much more valuable otherworldly ends. The theocrat's risks, however, are not only temporal but also spiritual: he may be led down a road to spiritual ruination if forced by authorities (even his own) to adhere to religious practices that God disavows.

28. Rawls, *Political Liberalism*, p. 311.

29. Ibid., pp. 312–13; cf. pp. 19, 73–74, 104. Rawls states that parties in the original position should affirm a principle of justice "[guaranteeing] equal liberty of conscience," so long as the larger conception of justice to which the principle belongs "is a workable conception" (ibid., p. 311).

30. Ibid., pp. 312–13.
31. Ibid., p. 314.
32. Ibid., pp. 313–14.
33. Williams made this remark in *The Bloudy Tenet of Persecution, for Cause of Conscience* (1644); see Edwin S. Gaustad, *Liberty of Conscience: Roger Williams in America* (Grand Rapids, Mich.: Eerdmans, 1991), p. 70.
34. See Charles E. Curran, *Directions in Fundamental Moral Theology* (Notre Dame, Ind.: University of Notre Dame Press, 1985), p. 216; see also C. H. Pierce, *Conscience in the New Testament* (London: SCM, 1955), pp. 13–53; and Eric D'Arcy, *Conscience and Its Right to Freedom* (New York: Sheed and Ward, 1961), p. 5.
35. *Summa Theologica*, I q. 79 a. 12, 13. See John Finnis, *Aquinas: Moral, Political, and Legal Theory* (Oxford: Oxford University Press, 1998), p. 123; cf. D'Arcy, *Conscience and Its Right to Freedom*, pp. 87–141 passim.
36. On these features, see, respectively, Gaustad, *Liberty of Conscience*, p. 71; and Locke, *A Letter Concerning Toleration*, p. 8.
37. Cf. Chandran Kukathas, *The Liberal Archipelago: A Theory of Diversity and Freedom* (New York: Oxford University Press, 2003), noting how particular attachments of conscience can overcome self-interest (p. 48); see also pp. 52–53, 56.
38. Cf. Hobbes's argument in chap. 12 of *Leviathan*, noting the perils of those who claim religious knowledge but who are insincere and distinguishing others who are simply selfish, seeking riches or dignity from putative religion. See Hobbes, *Leviathan* (1651), ed. Richard Tuck (New York: Cambridge University Press, 1996).
39. Rawls, *Political Liberalism*, pp. 13, 175–76.
40. That is to say, the principle may remain particular to members of a specific religious community; see R. M. Hare, *The Language of Morals* (Oxford: Clarendon, 1952), pp. 177–79. A rational commitment to any of the principles of rejection, affirmation, or distinction does not itself require one to hold that the principles must be universalized across all communities and peoples.
41. See Karl Marx, "On the Jewish Question," in *The Marx-Engels Reader* (1843), ed. Robert C. Tucker (New York: Norton, 1972), p. 29. Cf. Michael Walzer, *On Toleration* (New Haven: Yale University Press, 1997): "Militant atheism made the communist regimes of Eastern Europe as intolerant as any other orthodoxy would have done—and politically weak as a result: they were unable to incorporate large numbers of their own citizens" (p. 77).
42. It does not prohibit or preclude the possibility of communal life, however, which Hutterites and other theocrats endorse.
43. Cf. Kukathas, *The Liberal Archipelago*, proposing that the good society will be "one in which none would be required to live in groups or in associations (under terms) they reject" (p. 93). See Martha Nussbaum, *Women and Human Development: The Capabilities Approach* (New York: Cambridge

University Press, 2000), reflecting that, in the particular context of India, disestablishment "would constitute a statement that Muslims were not fully equal citizens, absent a time of mutual respect and civil harmony, which may not come about in the foreseeable future" (p. 211).

44. See John Locke, *Second Treatise of Government* (1690), ed. C. B. Macpherson (Indianapolis: Hackett, 1980), sec. 12.

45. See Donald B. Kraybill, *The Riddle of Amish Culture*, rev. ed. (Baltimore: Johns Hopkins University Press, 2001), pp. 184–87. The Amish refer to this period as *rumspringa*, or the "running around" time, which begins at age sixteen. Kraybill reports that Amish youth return to their communities to join the church at a rate greater than 90 percent (p. 186).

46. See Charles Kurzman, "Critics Within: Islamic Scholars' Protests Against the Islamic State in Iran," in *An Islamic Reformation?* ed. Michaelle Browers and Charles Kurzman (New York: Lexington, 2004), pp. 79–100.

47. Qutb, *Milestones*, p. 56.

48. Kukathas, *The Liberal Archipelago*, pp. 4–5. Kukathas contends that "[in] a free society . . . only the freedom to associate is fundamental" (p. 5).

49. Ibid., pp. 15, 23, 25, 30, 39, 42, 74–75, 119, 131, 143.

50. Ibid., pp. 74–75, cf. p. 76 n. 2.

51. Ibid., p. 41, cf. p. 64.

52. Ibid., pp. 50–55, 113.

53. Ibid., p. 55. The emphasis is in the original.

54. Ibid., p. 25.

55. Ibid., p. 47.

56. Ibid., pp. 49, 55, 70–71, 74, 113.

57. Ibid., p. 113.

58. Ibid., p. 115.

59. Ibid.

60. Ibid., p. 116, cf. p. 115.

61. Consider the following statement in particular: "[If] liberty of conscience is taken to be of fundamental importance, then it demands not only that dissenters be respected but also that those who wish to remain loyal to their traditions or practices equally be respected" (ibid., p. 137). Cf. Rawls, *A Theory of Justice*, pp. 206–7; idem, *Political Liberalism*, p. 311.

62. See James Bohman, "Public Reason and Cultural Pluralism: Political Liberalism and the Problem of Moral Conflict," *Political Theory* 23, no. 2 (1995): 253–79, at p. 263.

63. See Stanley Fish, "Liberalism Doesn't Exist," *Duke Law Journal* 1987 (1987): 997–1001; idem, *The Trouble with Principle* (Cambridge: Harvard University Press, 1999), pp. 162–86, 242–50ff. Cf. Richard Rorty, *Contingency, Irony, and Solidarity* (New York: Cambridge University Press, 1989).

64. Charles Larmore, *The Morals of Modernity* (New York: Cambridge University Press, 1996), p. 128.

65. Ibid., p. 128. The forms of life people adopt can be truly valuable, according to Larmore's readings of Kant and Mill, "only if [they] understand them

as ones [they] choose, or would choose, from a position of critical detachment, in something like an experimental spirit" (ibid.).

66. Ibid., p. 131.

67. Ibid.

68. Cf. Alasdair MacIntyre, *Three Rival Versions of Moral Inquiry* (Notre Dame, Ind.: University of Notre Dame Press, 1990).

69. See Ahmad S. Moussalli, *Radical Islamic Fundamentalism: The Ideological and Political Discourse of Sayyid Qutb* (Beirut: American University of Beirut, 1992), pp. 167, 217–18. See also Qutb, *Milestones*, p. 30.

70. See James Bohman, "Citizenship and Norms of Publicity: Wide Public Reason in Cosmopolitan Societies," *Political Theory* 27, no. 2 (1999): 176–202, at p. 177. See also Steven D. Smith, *Foreordained Failure: The Quest for a Constitutional Principle of Religious Freedom* (New York: Oxford University Press, 1995), pp. 96–97 passim.

71. Larmore, *The Morals of Modernity*, p. 123; see also idem, "Public Reason," in *The Cambridge Companion to Rawls*, ed. Samuel Freeman (New York: Cambridge University Press, 2003), pp. 368–93. William Galston proposes that value pluralists can coherently affirm basic liberal principles; see his *Liberal Pluralism: The Implications of Value Pluralism for Political Theory and Practice* (New York: Cambridge University Press, 2002), pp. 30–31, 34–35 passim.

72. Cf. Christopher J. Eberle, *Religious Conviction in Liberal Politics* (New York: Cambridge University Press, 2002), pp. 204–7, 228–31, arguing against the prospects of basic liberal principles enjoying such broad appeal.

73. Larmore, "Public Reason," pp. 377–79 passim.

74. Locke, *A Letter Concerning Toleration*, p. 7.

75. Ibid., p. 8.

76. Ibid.

77. Ibid., pp. 7–8.

78. Cf. Locke's discussion of forms and rites of worship as distinct from articles of faith and religious doctrines; see ibid., p. 28.

79. Jonas Proast, *The Argument of the Letter concerning Toleration, Briefly Consider'd and Anser'd* (Oxford: George West and Henry Clements, 1690), pp. 4, 5.

80. Ibid., p. 7.

81. Ibid., pp. 8–11.

82. Ibid., pp. 11, 12–14, 16–19, 23. Cf. Richard Vernon, *The Career of Toleration: John Locke, Jonas Proast, and After* (Montreal: McGill-Queen's University Press, 1997), p. 18.

83. Proast, *The Argument of the Letter concerning Toleration*, p. 26.

84. Jeremy Waldron, "Locke: Toleration and the Rationality of Persecution," in *John Locke: A Letter Concerning Toleration in Focus*, ed. John Horton and Susan Mendus (New York: Routledge, 1991), pp. 98–124, at p. 119.

85. This point is distinct from John Stuart Mill's suggestions regarding the need to familiarize oneself with other relevant arguments and positions in

order truly to know one's own or on the various benefits of freely and fully discussing other people's opinions and views. See generally his *On Liberty and Other Essays* (1859), ed. John Gray (Oxford: Oxford University Press, 1991).

86. Charles Taylor, "What's Wrong with Negative Liberty," in *Philosophy and the Human Sciences: Philosophical Papers, Vol. 2* (New York: Cambridge University Press, 1985), pp. 211–29, at pp. 213, 218–19.

87. Ibid., pp. 223, 227. Charles Manson and Andreas Baader are good examples of people who labored under visions fraught with hidden, false appreciations, on Taylor's reckoning; they suffered from senses of purpose "shot through with confusion and error" (see pp. 227, 228). Cf. Kukathas, *The Liberal Archipelago*, pp. 47–48, 52–57, 113–16.

88. This point is also distinct from Taylor's notion that while an agent cannot be the final authority on his own freedom, others may not be in a better position "to understand his real purposes," either ("What's Wrong with Negative Liberty," p. 216). Cf. Jeff Spinner-Halev, *Surviving Diversity*, pp. 60–61, providing an analogous argument concerning the value of cultures placing "enabling constraints" on people's lives. Cf. also Joseph Raz, *Ethics in the Public Domain: Essays in the Morality of Law and Politics* (New York: Oxford University Press, 1994), pp. 160–63.

89. To this, one could add that what looks like fear or superstition on the part of theocrats (for example, an unwillingness to associate with outsiders) may be freely chosen and adopted through such experiences as voluntary return to religious communities. See Feldman, *Lubavitchers as Citizens*, pp. 7, 136; cf. pp. 116, 118, 151ff.

90. Louay Safi, *Tensions and Transitions in the Muslim World* (Lanham, Md.: University Press of America, 2003), p. 80. Qutb declares: "Our first step will be to raise ourselves above the [ignorant] society and all its values and concepts. We will not change our own values and concepts either more or less to make a bargain with this [ignorant] society. Never! We and it are on different roads, and if we take even one step in its company, we will lose our goal entirely and lose our way as well" (*Milestones*, p. 21).

91. Safi, *Tensions and Transitions in the Muslim World*, p. 80. Safi notes that Qutb apparently opposed using violence in the pursuit of martyrdom. Cf. Qutb's proposition that the act of "striving through fighting" includes the need of physical power; see *Milestones*, pp. 61–62, 72–73, 79–80, 141, 149–52.

92. Eberle, *Religious Conviction in Liberal Politics*, p. 183.

93. For example, a person could hold unpopular political views that she thinks are important to air publicly and also believe that all controversial political opinions should be voiced. But it would remain possible for her still not to believe in a broad principle of freedom of speech, even though her commitments may compel her rationally to reach that conclusion.

94. Cf. Robert Nozick, *The Nature of Rationality* (Princeton: Princeton University Press, 1993), pp. 133–81; Christine M. Korsgaard, "The Normativity of

Instrumental Reason," in *Ethics and Practical Reason*, ed. G. Cullity and B. Gaus (New York: Oxford University Press, 1997); Christine M. Korsgaard, G. A. Cohen, Raymond Geuss, Thomas Nagel, and Bernard Williams, *The Sources of Normativity*, ed. Onora O'Neill (New York: Cambridge University Press, 1996).

95. Consider the example of the man who spontaneously forms the erroneous belief that his house is on fire. Provided that he cares about his house and does not want it to burn, he would be irrational if he took no corrective plan of action (for example, calling the fire brigade and racing home to assist). Rationality requires that the man follow some such plan of action, given his belief that his house is in flames, even though there would be no reason for him to perform the actions that he does since his house is safe and secure.

96. Cf. Larmore, *The Morals of Modernity*, pp. 370–71.

97. Nussbaum, *Women and Human Development*, p. 189. Nussbaum notes there that such an account of religious functioning would "leave out many of the ways in which people search for the good by subordinating themselves to authority or hierarchy, or by aligning themselves with the purposes of a corporate body."

3. HOW SHOULD LIBERAL DEMOCRACIES
TREAT THEOCRATIC COMMUNITIES?

1. Cf. John Rawls, *Political Liberalism*, paperback ed. (New York: Columbia University Press, 1996), pp. 12–15, 174–76ff. Cf. also idem, *The Law of Peoples* (Cambridge: Harvard University Press, 1999), p. 40, noting that peoples of constitutional democracies have no comprehensive doctrine of the good.

2. Rawls, *Political Liberalism*, p. 175.

3. Cf. ibid., pp. 13, 175.

4. Mary Ann Glendon and Raul F. Yanes, "Structural Free Exercise," *Michigan Law Review* 90 (1991): 477–550, at pp. 536–37. This conception of a theocratic community is distinct from Avishai Margalit's understanding of "encompassing groups," since these are generally anonymous groups in which the members do not "know each other personally"; see *The Decent Society* (Cambridge: Harvard University Press, 1996), p. 140; see also pp. 137–43, 173–81, 277–79. See also Avishai Margalit and Joseph Raz, "National Self-Determination," *Journal of Philosophy* 87 (1990): 439–61; Chandran Kukathas, *The Liberal Archipelago: A Theory of Diversity and Freedom* (New York: Oxford University Press, 2003), pp. 165–75.

5. Triloki N. Pandey, "Patterns of Leadership in Western Pueblo Society," in *North American Indian Anthropology*, ed. Raymond J. DeMallie and Alfonso Ortiz (Norman: University of Oklahoma Press, 1994), pp. 328–30.

6. Peter M. Whiteley, *Deliberate Acts: Changing Hopi Culture Through the Oriabi Spirit* (Tucson: University of Arizona Press, 1988), pp. 210–13, 227–31.

7. John A. Hostetler, *Amish Society*, 3d ed. (Baltimore: Johns Hopkins University Press, 1980), pp. 84–86.

8. Ibid., p. 111.

9. *Board of Education of Kiryas Joel Village School District v. Grumet*, 114 S.Ct. 2481, 2485 (1994).

10. Robert Gottlieb and Peter Wiley, *America's Saints: The Rise of Mormon Power* (New York: Putnam's, 1984), pp. 227–28, 230–31.

11. "Complaint for Declaratory Relief," *State of Oregon v. City of Rajneeshpuram*, docket no. 84–359 FR, p. 16; see Janice L. Sperow, "Rajneeshpuram: Religion Incorporated," *Hastings Law Journal* 30 (1985): 917–68, at p. 932 n. 130.

12. Sperow, "Rajneeshpuram," pp. 935–36; see generally Lewis F. Carter, *Charisma and Control in Rajneeshpuram: The Role of Shared Values in the Creation of a Community* (New York: Cambridge University Press, 1990).

13. See Ron Manuto, "The Life and Death of Rajneeshpuram and the Still Lingering Dilemma of the Religion Clauses of the First Amendment," *Free Speech Yearbook* 30 (1992): 26–39, at pp. 26–27.

14. *Yoder v. Wisconsin*, 406 U.S. 205 (1972).

15. *Santa Clara Pueblo v. Martinez*, 436 U.S. 49 (1978).

16. *Reynolds v. United States*, 98 U.S. 145 (1878).

17. *Grumet*, 114 S.Ct. 2481.

18. See Jaime M. W. Sanders, "Religious Community as a City: The Oregon Constitutional Puzzle of *State of Oregon v. City of Rajneeshpuram*," *Willamette Law Review* 21 (1985): 707–65, at pp. 710, 712–24.

19. See Nancy L. Rosenblum, *Membership and Morals: The Personal Uses of Pluralism in America* (Princeton: Princeton University Press, 1998), chap. 3.

20. See Lucas A. Swaine, "Principled Separation: Liberal Governance and Religious Free Exercise," *Journal of Church and State* 38 (1996): 595–619.

21. See Joshua Cohen, "Moral Pluralism and Political Consensus," in *The Idea of Democracy*, ed. D. Copp, J. Hampton, and J. Roemer (New York: Cambridge University Press, 1989), pp. 270–91; see also Rawls, *Political Liberalism*, pp. 35–40; idem, *The Law of Peoples*, pp. 11–12, 15–16, 124ff.

22. See James Madison, "Memorial and Remonstrance," in *The Papers of James Madison* (1785; reprint, Chicago: University of Chicago Press, 1962), 8:298–300; cf. also Thomas Jefferson, "A Bill for Establishing Religious Freedom," in *The Founders' Constitution* (1779), vol. 5, ed. P. Kurland and R. Lerner (Chicago: University of Chicago Press, 1987), p. 77.

23. See *Grumet*, 114 S.Ct., at 2489; see also *Lemon v. Kurtzman*, 403 U.S. 602 (1971).

24. Williams's idea of a "wall of separation" between church and state is discussed in Swaine, "Principled Separation," pp. 597–98; see also Mark DeWolfe Howe, *The Garden and the Wilderness: Religion and Government in American Constitutional History* (Chicago: University of Chicago Press, 1965), p. 6.

25. Cf. Douglas Laycock's characterization of formal neutrality, a standard that prohibits religious groups and associations from being singled out for

harsh treatment but is satisfied where they are treated as any other group; see his "Summary and Synthesis: The Crisis in Religious Liberty," *George Washington Law Review* 60 (1992): 843–56, at p. 848; see also Abner S. Greene, "The Political Balance of the Religion Clauses," *Yale Law Journal* 102 (1993): 1611–44.

26. On religious holidays, see *Sherbert v. Verner*, 374 U.S. 398 (1963); on religious symbols in the military, see *Goldman v. Weinberger*, 475 U.S. 503 (1986); and on due process, see Nancy Rosenblum, "The Moral Uses of Pluralism: Freedom of Association and Liberal Virtue Illustrated with Cases on Religious Exemption and Accommodation," University Center for Human Values Working Papers No. 3 (Princeton University, Princeton, N.J., 1993), p. 15.

27. On this point, see Lawrence Friedman, *Total Justice* (New York: Russell Sage Foundation, 1985).

28. Paul Lansing and Maureen Feldman, "The Ethics of Accommodating Employees' Religious Needs in the Workplace," *Labor Law Journal* 48 (1997): 371–80, at p. 377.

29. See Laycock, "Summary and Synthesis," p. 846ff.; see also Michael McConnell, "Accommodation of Religion: An Update and a Response to the Critics," *George Washington Law Review* 60 (1992): 685–742.

30. That is, accommodation claims based on establishment arguments are rare.

31. Rosenblum, "The Moral Uses of Pluralism," p. 15.

32. Michael McConnell and Richard Posner, "An Economic Approach to Issues of Religious Freedom," *University of Chicago Law Review* 56 (1989): 1–60, at pp. 35–37. See also Michael McConnell, "Believers as Equal Citizens," in *Obligations of Citizenship and Demands of Faith: Religious Accommodation in Pluralist Democracies*, ed. Nancy L. Rosenblum (Princeton: Princeton University Press, 2000), pp. 90–110.

33. *Sherbert*, 374 U.S., at 404; but cf. *Goldman*, 475 U.S. 503 (1986), permitting the United States Air Force to punish an orthodox Jewish rabbi for refusing to remove his yarmulke indoors. See Swaine, "Principled Separation," pp. 613–14.

34. Will Kymlicka, *Multicultural Citizenship: A Liberal Theory of Minority Rights* (Oxford: Clarendon, 1995), p. 31.

35. Ibid., p. 177.

36. McConnell, "Accommodation of Religion," p. 687.

37. Kymlicka, *Multicultural Citizenship*, p. 177.

38. Cf. Nancy L. Rosenblum, "Introduction: Pluralism, Integralism, and Political Theories of Religious Accommodation," in *Obligations of Citizenship and Demands of Faith: Religious Accommodation in Pluralist Democracies*, ed. Nancy L. Rosenblum (Princeton: Princeton University Press, 2000), pp. 3–31.

39. Cf. Thomas Hobbes, *Leviathan* (1651), ed. Richard Tuck (New York: Cambridge University Press, 1996), chap. 21.

40. Laycock, "Summary and Synthesis," p. 854.

41. See, e.g., *Employment Division, Dept. of Human Resources of Oregon v. Smith*, 494 U.S. 872 (1990), where a concern of that kind was raised. See also *People v. Woody*, 61 Cal. 2d 716, 394 P.2d 813, 40 Cal. Reptr. 69 (1964).

42. On genealogical structure, see *Martinez*, 436 U.S. 49 (1978); on polygamous family structures, see *Reynolds*, 98 U.S. 145 (1878), and Sarah Barringer Gordon, *The Mormon Question: Polygamy and Constitutional Conflict in Nineteenth-Century America* (Chapel Hill: University of North Carolina Press, 2002); on a single religious leader, see *Grumet*, 114 S.Ct. 2481 (1994).

43. *Yoder*, for example, was the culmination of more than fifty years of serious conflict between the Amish and state governments; for a historical account, see Albert N. Keim, *Compulsory Education and the Amish: The Right Not to Be Modern* (Boston: Beacon, 1975), pp. 1–15. Statutes and court rules increasingly require litigants and their lawyers to enter into a variety of settlement processes as well, with penalties for noncompliance. See Judith Resnik, "Trial as Error, Jurisdiction as Injury: Transforming the Meaning of Article III," *Harvard Law Review* 113 (2000): 924–1037, at pp. 926–28.

44. Michael McConnell, "Free Exercise Revisionism and the *Smith* Decision," *University of Chicago Law Review* 57 (1990): 1109–53, at p. 1110. See also John Wybraniec and Roger Finke, "Religious Regulation and the Courts: The Judiciary's Changing Role in Protecting Minority Religions from Majoritarian Rule," *Journal for the Scientific Study of Religion* 40, no. 3 (2001): 427–44. Wybraniec and Finke find that minority religious groups with "high [levels] of separation, antagonism, [and] distinctiveness" are more likely not only to be embroiled in court cases but to lose them as well (p. 441). As they put it, religious minorities "are the first to benefit when religious regulations are lifted, and the first to be stifled when regulations are allowed" (ibid.).

45. Jerold S. Auerbach, *Justice Without Law? Resolving Disputes Without Lawyers* (New York: Oxford University Press, 1983), pp. 4–16.

46. On filing lawsuits, see Donald B. Kraybill, *The Riddle of Amish Culture*, rev. ed. (Baltimore: Johns Hopkins University Press, 2001), pp. 115, 265, 272. On defending against lawsuits, cf. *Yoder v. Helmuth* (Wayne County case no. 35747, Common Pleas Court, Ohio, 1947), where leaders of an Amish community refused to defend their practice of shunning in court; and see Perry Sekus, "Dispute Resolution Among the Old Order Amish," *Ohio State Journal on Dispute Resolution* 4 (1989): 315–25. On appealing decisions, see John A. Hostetler, "The Amish and the Law: A Religious Minority and Its Legal Encounters," *Washington and Lee Law Review* 41 (1984): 33–47, at pp. 44–45.

47. Hostetler, "The Amish and the Law," p. 46. Hostetler quotes an Amish man who expresses the idea clearly: "The trouble with a lawsuit is that if you lose you lose, and if you win, you lose too."

48. The Amish consider worldly government to be evil, since under it some parties hold coercive power over others; see Sekus, "Dispute Resolution,"

pp. 315–318ff. The Satmar Hasidim, in contrast to the Amish and other theocrats, have fewer objections to litigating in secular courts; see Jerome Mintz, *Hasidic People: A Place in the New World* (Cambridge: Harvard University Press, 1992), pp. 189–97.

49. On this point, see generally McConnell, "Free Exercise Revisionism." See also J. Morris Clark, "Guidelines for the Free Exercise Clause," *Harvard Law Review* 83 (1969): 327–65, at pp. 327–29, 336–38 passim.

50. According to Robert Cover, the Garrisonians believed that they were obligated to withdraw from participation in public life in order to forswear the sin of slavery; see "The Supreme Court 1982, Term—Foreword: *Nomos and Narrative*," *Harvard Law Review* 97 (1983): 4–68, at pp. 35–40.

51. See Steven Runciman, *The Byzantine Theocracy* (Cambridge: Cambridge University Press, 1977), p. 119.

52. St. Alypius the Paphylagonian is reported to have "stood on a column for fifty-three years" until "paralysis forced him to lie down" (ibid., p. 118).

53. This is apart from the matter of whether relief ought to be given to such individuals. Cf. Clark, "Guidelines for the Free Exercise Clause," pp. 358–59.

54. 406 U.S. 205 (1972).

55. Brief for Respondent at 21, *Yoder* (No. 70–110); quotation cited in Cover, "*Nomos* and Narrative," p. 29.

56. *Mueller v. Allen*, 463 U.S. 388 (1983).

57. *Bowen v. Kendrick*, 487 U.S. 589 (1988).

58. *Yoder*, 406 U.S. 205, 211, 222, 224 (1972); on the Amish as law abiding, see *Yoder*, 406 U.S. 205, 213, 222 (1972).

59. It also violates the First Amendment of the United States Constitution; see generally Swaine, "Principled Separation."

60. Full accommodation may ask nonmembers to implicate themselves in such practices by requiring subsidies for theocratic communities.

61. Manuto, "The Life and Death of Rajneeshpuram," p. 27; see also S. Callister, J. Long, and L. Zaitz, "On the Road Again," *The Oregonian*, December 30, 1985, p. 2.

62. Isaiah Berlin, *The Crooked Timber of Humanity: Chapters in the History of Ideas* (New York: Knopf, 1991), p. 12.

63. Fikret Adanir, "Religious Communities and Ethnic Groups Under Imperial Sway: Ottoman and Habsburg Lands in Comparison" (unpublished paper, 2001). See Hercules Millas, "Non-Muslim Minorities in the History of Republican Turkey: The Greek Case," in *The Ottomans and the Balkans: A Discussion of Historiography*, ed. S. Faroqhi and F. Adanir (Boston: Brill, 2002); cf. Kymlicka, *Multicultural Citizenship*, pp. 158–58; and idem, "Two Models of Pluralism and Tolerance," in *Toleration: An Elusive Virtue*, ed. David Heyd (Princeton: Princeton University Press, 1996), pp. 83–87.

64. *Cherokee Nation v. Georgia*, 30 U.S. (5 Pet.) 1 (1831).

65. Ibid., 1, 17.

66. *Johnson & Graham' Lessee v. McIntosh*, 21 U.S. (8 Wheat.) 543 (1823); *Cherokee Nation*, 30 U.S. (5 Pet.) 1 (1831); and *Worcester v. Georgia*, 31 U.S.

(6 Pet.) 515 (1832). See Alex Tallchief Skibine, review of *Braid of Feathers: Pluralism, Legitimacy, Sovereignty, and the Importance of Tribal Court Jurisprudence*, by Frank Pommersheim, *Columbia Law Review* 96 (1996): 557–88, at p. 561.

67. Act of March 3, 1871, chap. 120, sec. 1, 16 Stat. 566, codified at 25 U.S.C., sec. 71 (1994).

68. Charles F. Wilkinson, *The Impact of Indian History on the Teaching of American History*, Occasional Papers in Curriculum Series of the Newbury Library, D'Arcy McNickle Center for the History of the American Indian, no. 2 (1984), p. 116, quoted in Judith Resnik, "Dependent Sovereigns: Indian Tribes, States, and the Federal Courts," *University of Chicago Law Review* 56 (1989): 671–759, at p. 696.

69. See Charles F. Wilkinson, "Civil Liberties Guarantees when Indian Tribes Act as Majority Societies: The Case of the Winnebago Retrocession," *Creighton Law Review* 21 (1988): 773–99, at pp. 773, 774–75.

70. Resnik, "Dependent Sovereigns," p. 694; on the inability of individuals to make Bill of Rights claims against their tribes, see *Talton v. Mayes*, 163 U.S. 376, 384 (1896); and *Martinez*, 436 U.S. 49, 56 (1978); on federal decisions, see *Tee-Hit-Ton Indians v. United States*, 348 U.S. 272, 288 (1955), according to which case Indian land was decided not to hold the status of property belonging to Indians and does not properly receive protection under the Fifth Amendment, unless Congress clearly states that the land belongs to Indians. See also *United States v. Sioux Nation of Indians*, 448 U.S. 371, 415 n. 29 (1980), remarking that the taking of an aboriginal land title is not subject to Fifth Amendment compensation.

71. 25 U.S.C., secs. 1301–1303; see Resnik, "Dependent Sovereigns," pp. 694 n. 103, 727.

72. Tribes, but not individual Indians, cannot be sued without their consent; the doctrine of tribal immunity has protected them from serious financial losses. The U.S. Supreme Court has encouraged Congress to evaluate afresh the doctrine of tribal sovereign immunity (see *Kiowa Tribe v. Manufacturing Technologies, Inc.*, 118 S.Ct. 1700, 1705 [1998]). Interestingly, the Court has also now decided that where individual claimants attempt to sue states under federal regulatory guidelines, in state or federal courts, a common-law defense of sovereign immunity may be claimed by states (see *Hans v. Louisiana*, 134 U.S. 1, 14–15 [1890]; *Seminole Tribe v. Florida*, 517 U.S. 44, 72–73 [1996]; *Alden v. Maine*, 119 S.Ct. 2240, 2246 [1999]). See also Carlos Manuel Vázquez, "Sovereign Immunity, Due Process, and the *Alden* Trilogy," *Yale Law Journal* 109 (2000): 1927–81; Lauren Ouziel, "Waiving States' Sovereign Immunity from Suit in Their Own Courts: Purchased Waiver and the Clear Statement Rule," *Columbia Law Review* 99 (1999): 1584–1607, at pp. 1584–85, 1591–94.

73. L. Scott Gould, "The Consent Paradigm: Tribal Sovereignty at the Millennium," *Columbia Law Review* 96 (1996): 809–902, at p. 810. The doctrine of inherent sovereignty holds that, in the words of Felix Cohen, "the most

basic principle of all Indian law . . . is the principle that those powers which are lawfully vested in an Indian tribe are not, in general, delegated powers granted by express acts of Congress" (*Felix S. Cohen's Handbook of Federal Indian Law* [Charlottesville: Bobbs-Merrill, 1982], p. 122). See also *Three Affiliated tribes v. Wold Eng'g,* 476 U.S. 877, 891 (1986).

74. Skibine, review of *Braid of Feathers,* p. 560.

75. Philip P. Frickey, "Adjudication and Its Discontents: Coherence and Conciliation in Indian Law," *Harvard Law Review* 110 (1997): 1754–84, at p. 1754.

76. Resnik, "Dependent Sovereigns," p. 696. See also generally Milner S. Ball, "Constitution, Court, Indian Tribes," *American Bar Foundation Research Journal* (1987): 1–140; Russel Lawrence Barsh and James Youngblood Henderson, *The Road: Indian Tribes and Political Liberty* (Berkeley: University of California Press, 1980); and Robert A. Williams Jr., "The Algebra of Federal Indian Law: The Hard Trail of Decolonizing and Americanizing the White Man's Indian Jurisprudence," *Wisconsin Law Review* (1986): 219–99, at pp. 219ff.

77. *Cherokee Nation,* 30 U.S. (5 Pet.) at 1, 17.

78. *McIntosh,* 21 U.S. (8 Wheat.), at 560–61.

79. Compare Aristotle's discussion of natural slavery in *Politics,* ed. and trans. Ernest Barker (New York: Oxford University Press, 1962), book 1, chaps. 4–7. Aristotle says of natural slaves that they may apprehend reasoning in others but lack it themselves (1254b); mutatis mutandis, this characterizes a particularly inept understanding of the nature of Indian quasi sovereignty, whereby the tribe's legislative autonomy is believed to require constant guidance from liberal government.

80. Some Indian villages qualify as theocratic communities, however, such as certain of the New Mexican Pueblos.

81. There exist two references to Indians on apportionment and one in the Indian commerce clause as well. Wilkinson argues that reference to Indians can be found in three additional places: Congress's war-making powers (U.S. Const. art. I, 8, clause 11), treaties standing as supreme law (U.S. Const. art. VI, 2), and on presidential treaty-making powers (U.S. Const. art. II, 2, clause 2; Wilkinson, "Civil Liberties Guarantees," pp. 774–75). See U.S. Const. amend. XIV, 2; see also Resnik, "Dependent Sovereigns," p. 691ff. No Aboriginal and treaty right is explicitly recognized by the Canadian Constitution, but it seems to be recognized by the language of Schedule B to the *Canada Act 1982* (U.K.), 1982, clause 11 (also known as the *Constitution Act, 1982*).

82. Cf. Mark D. Rosen, "Our Nonuniform Constitution: Geographical Variations of Constitutional Requirements in the Aid of Community," *Texas Law Review* 77 (1999): 1129–94. This precondition does not require quasi-sovereign groups to be rural isolationists. Theocratic communities living in separable enclaves, such as the Tash Hasidim who dwell in Broisbriand, Quebec, could also qualify for quasi sovereignty. See generally William

Shaffir, "Separation from the Mainstream in Canada: The Hassidic Community of Tash," in *The Jews in Canada*, ed. Robert J. Bryn, William Shaffir, and Morton Weinfeld (Toronto: Oxford University Press, 1993), pp.
126–41. See also Jan Feldman, *Lubavitchers as Citizens: A Paradox of Liberal
Democracy* (Ithaca, N.Y.: Cornell University Press, 2003), pp. 72–74.

83. On this point, see William A. Galston, "Two Concepts of Liberalism,"
Ethics 105 (1995): 516–34, at pp. 533–34.

84. See Kukathas, *The Liberal Archipelago*, chap. 3 passim. Cf. Susan Moller
Okin, " 'Mistresses of Their Own Destiny': Group Rights, Gender, and Realistic Rights of Exit," *Ethics* 112 (2002): 205–30; Ayelet Shachar, "On Citizenship and Multicultural Vulnerability," *Political Theory* 28, no. 1 (2000):
64–89; idem, *Multicultural Jurisdictions: Cultural Differences and Women's
Rights* (New York: Cambridge University Press, 2001).

85. Rawls delineates more demanding criteria for decent societies and peoples, as well as for decent hierarchical societies, as he calls them; see *The
Law of Peoples*, pp. 3–5, 59–88. See also generally Henry Shue, *Basic Rights:
Subsistence, Affluence, and U.S. Foreign Policy* (Princeton: Princeton University Press, 1980); cf. Martha Nussbaum, *Women and Human Development: The Capabilities Approach* (New York: Cambridge University Press,
2000), pp. 186, 192, 230–35.

86. William Galston, *Liberal Purposes: The Implications of Value Pluralism for
Political Theory and Practice* (New York: Cambridge University Press,
2002), p. 23; cf. pp. 41, 128. Galston adds that similar practices clearly impeding normal development of children, including infant skull binding
and malnourishment, should be disallowed in a liberal polity (pp. 23–24).

87. G. W. F. Hegel suggests that the refusal to educate a young person rele-
gates the child to slavery with respect to his family or community, which
is, as he calls it, "gangrene of the ethical order at the tenderest point of its
innermost life." See *Hegel's Philosophy of Right* (1821), trans. T. M. Knox
(New York: Oxford University Press, 1967), p. 118; see also Hegel, *The Philosophy of History* (1831), trans. J. Sibree (New York: Dover, 1956), pp.
283–89. The ability of government to regulate action affecting children
generally should be greater than its ability to regulate action affecting
adults alone; cf. Clark, "Guidelines for the Free Exercise Clause," p. 363;
Prince v. Massachusetts, 321 U.S. 158 (1944); *Ginsberg v. New York*, 390 U.S.
629 (1968). Cf. also Eamonn Callan, *Creating Citizens: Political Education
and Liberal Democracy* (New York: Oxford University Press, 1997), pp.
152–61, discussing problems of what he calls the "Ethically Servile Child."

88. See generally Amy Gutmann, *Democratic Education* (Princeton: Princeton
University Press, 1987); idem, "Civic Education and Social Diversity,"
Ethics 105 (1995): 557–79; idem, "Challenges of Multiculturalism in Education," in *Public Education in a Multicultural Society: Policy, Theory, Critique*, ed. Robert Fullinwinder (Cambridge: Cambridge University Press,
1996), pp. 156–79; Stephen Macedo, *Liberal Virtues: Citizenship, Virtue,
and Community in Liberal Constitutionalism* (Oxford: Clarendon, 1990);

idem, "Liberal Civic Education and Religious Fundamentalism: The Case of God v. John Rawls?" *Ethics* 105 (1995): 468–96; idem, *Diversity and Distrust: Civic Education in a Multicultural Democracy* (Cambridge: Harvard University Press, 2000). See also Meira Levinson, *The Demands of Liberal Education* (New York: Oxford University Press, 1999); Rob Reich, *Bridging Liberalism and Multiculturalism in American Education* (Chicago: University of Chicago Press, 2002).

89. See Jeff Spinner-Halev, *Surviving Diversity: Religion and Democratic Citizenship* (Baltimore: Johns Hopkins University Press, 2000), pp. 110, 123–28.

90. Cf. Callan, *Creating Citizens*, discussing "adequate" and "reasonable" development of people's moral powers (pp. 148–49). See Rawls, *Political Liberalism*, pp. 18–20, 81, 202–3, 332, 420. Cf. Joseph Raz, *The Morality of Freedom* (Oxford: Clarendon, 1986), pp. 369–99 passim.

91. Callan, *Creating Citizens*, p. 132. Cf. Rawls, *Political Liberalism*, p. 199; Galston, *Liberal Pluralism*, pp. 93–109; cf. also *Peirce v. Society of Sisters*, 268 U.S. 510 (1925).

92. Spinner-Halev, *Surviving Diversity*, p. 89. Cf. T. M. Scanlon, "The Difficulty of Tolerance," in *The Difficulty of Tolerance: Essays in Political Philosophy* (New York: Cambridge University Press, 2002), pp. 187–201. Scanlon argues that the goods at stake at the level of political society, "such as the right to vote, to hold office, and to participate in the public forum, do not lose their meaning if they are extended to people with whom we disagree about the kind of society we would like to have, or even to those who reject its basic tenets" (pp. 194–95). Cf. also generally Sidney Verba, Kay Lehman Schlozman, and Henry E. Brady, *Voice and Equality: Civic Voluntarism in American Politics* (Cambridge: Harvard University Press, 1995).

93. Spinner-Halev, *Surviving Diversity*, p. 71. Cf. Reich, *Bridging Liberalism*, discussing the differences between teaching "of" religion and teaching "about" religion (pp. 198–99ff.). Educational measures of this kind would help to satisfy the Hohfeldian concern that conscience deserves respect insofar as it respects its own duty to be informed; see Wesley N. Hohfeld, *Fundamental Legal Conceptions as Applied in Judicial Reasoning, and Other Legal Essays*, ed. Walter W. Cook (New Haven, Yale University Press, 1919).

94. Callan, *Creating Citizens*, p. 149.

95. Ibid., p. 133. Reich contends that "minimalist autonomy requires that a child be able to examine his own political values and beliefs, and those of others, with a critical and sympathetic eye" (*Bridging Liberalism*, p. 162; see also pp. 113–41, 161–62, 197–98 passim). Cf. Levinson, *The Demands of Liberal Education*, pp. 58–61.

96. Callan, *Creating Citizens*, p. 148. Cf. generally Macedo, *Liberal Virtues*.

97. Callan, *Creating Citizens*, pp. 152–53.

98. Ibid., p. 133.

99. Consider, for instance, the substantial proportion of Lubavitcher women who are *ba'alot teshuva*, or "voluntary returnees to Judaism" (Feldman, *Lubavitchers as Citizens*, pp. 7, 136). Those individuals may appear to be

ethically servile, but they have chosen their community membership often with fairly broad knowledge, critical abilities, and some experience of other ways of life.

100. Callan, *Creating Citizens*, pp. 134, 153.

101. For scholarly debate demonstrating this point, see Stephen Macedo and Yael Tamir, eds., *NOMOS XLIII: Moral and Political Education* (New York: New York University Press, 2002), part 1 (pp. 23–189).

102. Inadequate schools in theocratic communities could face disestablishment, for example, as part of a set of incentives for meeting basic educational criteria that a quasi-sovereign framework could employ; see Aaron Saiger, "Disestablishing Local School Districts as a Remedy for Educational Inadequacy," *University of Chicago Law Review* 99 (1999): 1830–70, at pp. 1853ff. See also Shachar, "On Citizenship and Multicultural Vulnerability," for a discussion of problems related to delegating "full jurisdictional powers" to theocratic communities and similar groups (pp. 79–81 passim). Cf. Kukathas, *The Liberal Archipelago*, pp. 136, 140, 142–47; and Brian Barry, *Culture and Equality: An Egalitarian Critique of Multiculturalism* (Cambridge: Harvard University Press, 2001), pp. 141–45.

103. On conditions of membership, cf. *Martinez*, 436 U.S. 49 (1978); on regulation regarding property, cf. the Canadian case of *Hofer v. Hofer et al.* 13 DLR (3d) (1970). In that case, two Hutterites were expelled from their community as apostates and subsequently demanded their share of the community's assets. Members of Hutterite colonies hold all property in common, and Hutterite representatives argued that the colony's religious life would be severely damaged by state interference in their communal practices. The Canadian Supreme Court rightly accepted the colony's claim; a well-formed schema for quasi sovereignty would give theocratic communities more robust autonomy on property issues, largely allowing them to decide such matters for themselves. Spinner-Halev suggests that communities such as these, with only communal property, might each set up a modest "exit fund" for departing members (*Surviving Diversity*, p. 77). See Kymlicka, *Multicultural Citizenship*, pp. 160–63; and Shachar, *Multicultural Jurisdictions*, p. 109. See also John A. Hostetler, *Communitarian Societies* (New York: Holt, Rinehart and Winston, 1974), pp. 34–46 passim.

104. For an innovative approach to creating community-based courts for "insular communities," see Mark D. Rosen, "The Radical Possibility of Limited Community-Based Interpretation of the Constitution," *William and Mary Law Review* 43 (2002): 927–1010.

105. Some theocratic communities have no wish to incarcerate offenders or to mete out corporal punishment, instead preferring to use alternative methods such as intervention, shunning, or excommunication in handling wayward theocrats; the Old Order Amish are an example. See generally Hostetler, *Amish Society*; see also Kymlicka, *Multicultural Citizenship*, chap. 8. Cf. Larry D. Eldridge, *A Distant Heritage: The Growth of Free Speech in Early America* (New York: New York University Press, 1994), chap. 5.

106. See Carol Weisbrod, *Family, Church and State*, Legal History Program Working Paper no. 2 (University of Wisconsin, Institute for Legal Studies, Madison, 1985), pp. 9, 20.

107. Congress passed the Major Crimes Act in 1885, conferring jurisdiction over Indians for certain felony crimes; it is now amended and codified at 18 U.S.C., sec. 1153 (1982). An act of this kind would be appropriate for members of semisovereign theocratic communities as well. Clarity on jurisdiction, punishment, and sentencing for felony crimes in theocratic communities would help to secure fair and reliable treatment for felony offenses; I leave it open as to whether jurisdictional power to adjudicate on felony crimes might be delegated to state authorities.

108. See *Montana v. United States*, 450 U.S. 544, 564 (1981).

109. 397 U.S. 664, 666–67 (1970).

110. See McConnell and Posner, "An Economic Approach to Issues of Religious Freedom," pp. 46–47.

111. See Rosenblum, *Membership and Morals*, pp. 349–63.

112. See Madison, "Memorial and Remonstrance," pp. 298–300.

113. See Swaine, "Principled Separation," pp. 600–610ff.

114. Ibid., pp. 600–05 passim. This is a point with which Veit Bader openly disagrees: see his "Taking Religious Pluralism Seriously: Arguing for an Institutional Turn. Introduction," *Ethical Theory and Moral Practice* 6, no. 1 (2003): 3–22; and "Religious Pluralism: Secularism or Priority for Democracy?" *Political Theory* 27, no. 5 (1999): 597–633. See also idem, "Religious Diversity and Democratic Institutional Pluralism," *Political Theory* 31, no. 2 (2003): 265–94, at pp. 282–84 passim.

115. Gould, "The Consent Paradigm," p. 811.

116. Skibine, review of *Braid of Feathers*, p. 559.

117. See *Indian Self-Determination and Education Assistance Act of 1975*, Pub. L. no. 93–638, 88 Stat. 2203, codified as amended at 5 U.S.C., secs. 3371, 3372; 25 U.S.C., sec. 450; 42 U.S.C., sec. 20046, 4762 (1994). The act describes Congress's "commitment to the maintenance of the Federal Government's unique and continuing relationship with, and responsibility to, individual Indian tribes and to the Indian people through the establishment of a meaningful Indian self-determination policy" (25 U.S.C., sec. 450a[b] [1994]). See Gould, "The Consent Paradigm" p. 812ff.

118. I do not suggest that a civil rights act was inappropriate for Indians, however, since that may have been warranted because of their status as a national minority group; see Kymlicka, *Multicultural Citizenship*, esp. chaps. 2, 5, 8.

119. Gould, "The Consent Paradigm," p. 815; see *South Dakota v. Bourland*, 113 S.Ct. 2309 (1993).

120. See Mark D. Rosen, "The Outer Limits of Community Self-Governance in Residential Associations, Municipalities, and Indian Country: A Liberal Theory," *Virginia Law Review* 84 (1998): 1053–1144; idem, "Our Nonuniform Constitution"; idem, "The Radical Possibility."

121. On the states' role, cf. Richard C. Schragger, "The Role of the Local in the Doctrine and Discourse of Religious Liberty," *Harvard Law Review* 117 (2004): 1810–92; Mark D. Rosen, "Extraterritoriality and Political Heterogeneity in American Federalism," *University of Pennsylvania Law Review* 150 (2002): 855–972. Rosen identifies grounds for "allowing rich political heterogeneity among states" (p. 863), providing a possible political basis on which different states might support quasi sovereignty for theocratic communities.

122. Cf. Amy Gutmann, "Religion and State in the United States: A Defense of Two-Way Protection," in *Obligations of Citizenship and Demands of Faith: Religious Accommodation in Pluralist Democracies*, ed. Nancy L. Rosenblum (Princeton: Princeton University Press, 2000), pp. 127–64, at pp. 149–53.

123. Bader, "Religious Diversity and Democratic Institutional Pluralism," p. 279.

124. Cf. Christopher L. Eisgruber, "The Constitutional Value of Assimilation," *Columbia Law Review* 96 (1996): 87–103; idem, "Political Unity and the Powers of Government," *UCLA Law Review* 41 (1994): 1297–1336; and idem, *Constitutional Self-Government* (Cambridge: Harvard University Press, 2001). Cf. Kukathas, *The Liberal Archipelago*, pp. 7, 20, 22, 160, 166–210; James S. Liebman and Brandon L. Garrett, "Madisonian Equal Protection," *Columbia Law Review* 104 (2004): 837–974, at pp. 844–84, 950–74 passim.

125. Statutes similar to the First Amendment in other liberal democracies could serve as a basis for semisovereignty in those polities. See John Witte Jr., *Religion and the American Constitutional Experiment*, 2d ed. (Boulder, Colo.: Westview, 2005), pp. 233–46. Witte discusses the prospects of international norms of religious liberty serving to develop "a more integrated American constitutional law of religious liberty" (p. 235).

126. See Lucas A. Swaine, "Blameless, Constructive, and Political Anger," *Journal for the Theory of Social Behavior* 25 (1996): 257–74.

127. Rawls, *Political Liberalism*, pp. 191–94ff.

128. Ibid., p. 197.

129. Ibid., pp. 199–200.

130. Ibid., p. 197; see Berlin, *The Crooked Timber of Humanity*, pp. 11–19.

131. Existing standards also fail to promote personal autonomy for members of theocratic communities in that those standards simply damage the fabric of the communities in which theocrats live, doing little to help members choose their conceptions of the good. See Spinner-Halev, *Surviving Diversity*, pp. 57–85.

132. Sovereign immunity from off-community lawsuits could be provided as a benefit to theocratic communities, under an "infant government" rationale of sorts, since theocratic communities will not likely be affluent and may be devastated by lawsuit. Cf. Caleb Nelson, "Sovereign Immunity as a Doctrine of Personal Jurisdiction," *Harvard Law Review* 115 (2002): 1559–1654.

133. This kind of community would also include the town whose members wish for religious reasons to forbid the sale or consumption of alcohol within town limits but who are unremarkable in other respects. Cf. McConnell, "Believers as Equal Citizens," p. 95.

134. See Kent Greenawalt, "Freedom of Association and Religious Association," in *Freedom of Association*, ed. Amy Gutmann (Princeton: Princeton University Press, 1998), pp. 109–44, at pp. 124–26. See also *Thomas v. Review Board*, 450 U.S. 707, 713 (1981).

135. See Greenawalt, "Freedom of Association," pp. 115–20, 125.

136. This basis for disallowing noncomprehensive religious communities from acquiring quasi sovereignty serves to mitigate the problem of "runaway precedents" described by Gutmann; see "Religion and State in the United States," pp. 149–53.

137. Greenawalt, "Freedom of Association," p. 125. Greenawalt's example includes the stipulation that the community members are mostly "atheists or agnostics," which I exclude here for the sake of the argument at hand. Cf. *Africa v. Commonwealth*, 662 F.2d 1025 (3d Cir. 1981).

138. Thoreauvian transcendentalism comes close to being religious at points. One notes Thoreau's telling remark, in his journal entry of September 7, 1851, that his profession was "always to be on the alert to find God in nature." If Thoreauvians were to find God there, identifying otherworldly powers and undertaking practices of worship in their respect, that would qualify them as religious; short of that, they remain nonreligious. See *The Journal of Henry D. Thoreau* (14 vols. bound as 2), vols. 1–7 (1837–October 1855), ed. Bradford Torrey and Francis H. Allen (New York: Dover 1962), p. 262. Cf. Thoreau, "Life Without Principle," in *Thoreau: Political Writings*, ed. Nancy L. Rosenblum (New York: Cambridge University Press, 1996), pp. 103–21, at pp. 112–13. See also Kent Greenawalt, "Five Questions about Religion Judges Are Afraid to Ask," in *Obligations of Citizenship and Demands of Faith: Religious Accommodation in Pluralist Democracies*, ed. Nancy L. Rosenblum (Princeton: Princeton University Press, 2000), pp. 196–244, at pp. 206–24, arguing for a flexible, analogical approach to understanding religion.

139. Nussbaum, *Women and Human Development*, pp. 206–7; see also Spinner-Halev, *Surviving Diversity*, p. 212. Cf. McConnell's contention: "The essential problem is that religious believers have an allegiance to an authority outside the commonwealth" ("Believers as Equal Citizens," p. 91).

140. Galston, *Liberal Pluralism*, p. 45.

141. Groups such as Icarians and Owenites could be included here. The Icarians' communist community, in Nauvoo, Illinois, endured from 1849 to 1860. The Owenites' utopian settlement at "New Harmony," in Indiana, was even more ephemeral; both the Icarians and Owenites watched their communities collapse because of internal conflict. See Etienne Cabet, *Travels in Icaria*, trans. Leslie J. Roberts (New York: Syracuse University Press, 2003); John Fletcher Clews Harrison, *Robert Owen and the Owenites*

in Britain and America: The Quest for the New Moral World (London: Routledge and Kegan Paul, 1969); and Robert Owen, *A New View of Society* (New York: E. Bliss and E. White, 1825).

142. These points place further weight against the notion that allowing a quasi-sovereign option in a liberal democratic order would lead to "runaway precedents" for nonreligious communities. See Gutmann, "Religion and State in the United States," pp. 149–53. See also Nancy L. Rosenblum, "Pluralism and Democratic Education: Stopping Short by Stopping with Schools," in *NOMOS XLIII: Moral and Political Education*, ed Macedo and Tamir, pp. 147–69. Galston notes that accommodations for the Amish have not led to "an escalation of faith-based demands" for public education accommodation (*Liberal Pluralism*, p. 121).

143. See Greenawalt, "Five Questions about Religion," pp. 200–206. See also Bader, "Religious Diversity and Democratic Institutional Pluralism," p. 276.

144. Rosen, "The Outer Limits of Community Self-Governance," p. 1089.

145. Ibid., pp. 1089–1106, 1125–44 passim.

146. See Greenawalt, "Freedom of Association," pp. 125–27.

147. Cf. McConnell, "Accommodation of Religion," p. 687. McConnell adds a criterion of "unequal treatment" that must be met before government takes action, but it is unclear why that element is necessary, especially if the obstacle placed by government can be removed without great cost.

4. INSPIRING PUBLIC REASON

1. See John Rawls, "The Idea of Public Reason Revisited," in *The Law of Peoples* (Cambridge: Harvard University Press, 1999), pp. 133, 137.

2. See Robert Audi, *Religious Commitment and Secular Reason* (New York: Cambridge University Press, 2000); James Bohman, "Public Reason and Cultural Pluralism: Political Liberalism and the Problem of Moral Conflict," *Political Theory* 23, no. 2 (1995): 253–79; idem, *Public Deliberation: Pluralism, Complexity, and Democracy* (Cambridge, Mass.: MIT Press, 1996); idem, "Citizenship and Norms of Publicity: Wide Public Reason in Cosmopolitan Societies," *Political Theory* 27, no. 2 (1999): 176–202, at pp. 186–87; Kent Greenawalt, *Private Consciences and Public Reasons* (New York: Oxford University Press, 1995); Amy Gutmann and Dennis Thompson, *Democracy and Disagreement* (Cambridge: Harvard University Press, 1996), pp. 55–65 passim; John Rawls, *Political Liberalism*, paperback ed. (New York: Columbia University Press, 1996), pp. 212–54; Rawls, "The Idea of Public Reason Revisited," pp. 129–80; Paul J. Weithman, *Religion and the Obligations of Citizenship* (New York: Cambridge University Press, 2002), pp. 65, 138; Nicholas Wolterstorff, "The Role of Religion in Political Issues," in Robert Audi and Nicholas Wolterstorff, *Religion in the Public Square* (London: Rowman and Littlefield, 1997). Cf. Jeff Spinner-Halev, *Surviving Diversity: Religion and Democratic Citizenship* (Baltimore: Johns

Hopkins University Press, 2000), pp. 142–65, providing an interesting assessment of public reason and religious argumentation.

3. See Rawls, *Political Liberalism*, pp. 54–58, 178–89, 223–30, 393–95; Audi, *Religious Commitment and Secular Reason*, pp. 84–86, 92–93; Weithman, *Religion and the Obligations of Citizenship*, pp. 135ff., 142, 208–17.

4. See Bohman, "Citizenship and Norms of Publicity," p. 178.

5. See Rawls, *Political Liberalism*, pp. 217, 218, 226, 243. See also Wolterstorff, "The Role of Religion in Political Issues," pp. 96ff.

6. The justification is also logically prior to particular decisions or disputes on policy matters, since theocrats may object to the very idea of voting on such issues, as part of a rejection of liberalism and liberal institutions more broadly. Cf. generally Christopher J. Eberle, *Religious Conviction in Liberal Politics* (New York: Cambridge University Press, 2002).

7. Cf. Eberle, *Religious Conviction in Liberal Politics*, pp. 11–14, 75, 104–5, 227–29 passim.

8. James T. Richardson, "Minority Religions and the Context of Violence: A Conflict/Interactionist Perspective," *Terrorism and Political Violence* 13, no. 1 (2001): 103–33, at p. 122. See Martin E. Marty, *Pilgrims in Their Own Land: 500 Years of Religion in America* (Boston: Little, Brown, 1984), discussing one hundred new American religious sects. See also Martin E. Marty and R. Scott Appleby, eds., *Accounting for Fundamentalisms: The Dynamic Character of Movements* (Chicago: University of Chicago Press, 1994).

9. David Tucker, "What Is New About the New Terrorism and How Dangerous Is It?" *Terrorism and Political Violence* 13, no. 3 (2001): 1–14, at p. 8.

10. Ami Pedahzur, William Eubank, and Leonard Weinberg, "The War on Terrorism and the Decline of Terrorist Group Formation: A Research Note," *Terrorism and Political Violence* 14, no. 3 (2002): 141–47. See also Leonard Weinberg and Ami Pedahzur, eds., *Religious Fundamentalism and Political Extremism* (Portland, Ore.: Frank Cass Publishers, 2004), chap. 5, esp. pp. 83–86.

11. Pedahzur, Eubank, and Weinberg, "The War on Terrorism," p. 146.

12. Ibid. See Bruce Hoffman, *Inside Terrorism* (New York: Columbia University Press, 1998), pp. 86–129.

13. Tucker, "What Is New About the New Terrorism," p. 4.

14. Jonathan Fox, "Do Religious Institutions Support Violence or the Status Quo?" *Studies in Conflict and Terrorism* 22 (1999): 119–39. Cf. Gabriel A. Almond, R. Scott Appleby, and Emmanuel Sivan, *Strong Religion: The Rise of Fundamentalisms Around the World* (Chicago: University of Chicago Press, 2003), p. 235ff. The authors write: "Fundamentalist violence, per se, is a response to government oppression and/or to the growth or empowerment of social groups deemed threatening to fundamentalist interests" (p. 235).

15. Jean-François Mayer, "Cults, Violence and Religious Terrorism: An International Perspective," *Studies in Conflict and Terrorism* 24 (2001): 361–76.

See also Richardson, "Minority Religions and the Context of Violence," pp. 110–12, 114–15, 123.

16. Mayer, "Cults, Violence and Religious Terrorism, pp. 366–67 passim. See Ian Reader, *A Poisonous Cocktail? Aum Shinrikyo's Path to Violence* (Copenhagen: NIAS Publications, 1996).

17. Mayer, "Cults, Violence and Religious Terrorism," pp. 362, 367–69.

18. See Catherine Wessinger, *How the Millennium Comes Violently: From Jonestown to Heaven's Gate* (New York: Seven Bridges, 2000); Susan Juster, *Doomsayers: Anglo-American Prophecy in the Age of Revelation* (Philadelphia: University of Pennsylvania Press, 2003), chap. 4. Cf. Almond, Appleby, and Sivan, *Strong Religion*, pp. 90–115.

19. Tucker, "What Is New About the New Terrorism," p. 8. The Old Order Amish are a counterexample to this view: the Ordnung forbids them from conforming to mainstream practices and requires that they remain apart from contemporary social and political life, but their doctrine and communities have evolved such that Amish persons pose no threat of violence to nonmembers.

20. Cf. Rawls, *Political Liberalism*, p. 144; cf. also pp. 170, 199.

21. See, e.g., Brian Barry, *Culture and Equality: An Egalitarian Critique of Multiculturalism* (Cambridge: Harvard University Press, 2001), chap. 5 passim; Richard Arneson and Ian Shapiro, "Democratic Autonomy and Religious Freedom: A Critique of *Wisconsin v. Yoder*," in *NOMOS XXXVIII: Political Order*, ed. Ian Shapiro and Russell Hardin (New York: New York University Press, 1996), pp. 365–411; Ian Shapiro, *The State of Democratic Theory* (Princeton: Princeton University Press, 2003), pp. 4, 36–48, 102–3; George Kateb, "Can Cultures Be Judged? Two Defenses of Cultural Pluralism in Isaiah Berlin's Work," *Social Research* 99, no. 4 (1999): 1009–38; and Richard Rorty, *Objectivity, Relativism, and Truth: Philosophical Papers, Vol. 1* (Cambridge: Cambridge University Press, 1991), p. 188. Cf. Richard Rorty, "Religion in the Public Square: A Reconsideration," *Journal of Religious Ethics* 31, no. 1 (2003): 141–49; Susan Moller Okin, " 'Mistresses of Their Own Destiny': Group Rights, Gender, and Realistic Rights of Exit," *Ethics* 112 (2002): 205–30; and idem, "Is Multiculturalism Bad for Women?" *Boston Review* 22 (1997): 25–28.

22. Richardson, "Minority Religions and the Context of Violence," p. 117; see Christopher G. Ellison and John P. Bartkowski, " 'Babies Were Being Beaten': Exploring Child Abuse Accusations at Ranch Apocalypse," in *Armageddon in Waco: Critical Perspectives on the Branch Davidian Conflict*, ed. Stuart Wright (Chicago: University of Chicago Press, 1995), pp. 111–49.

23. Richardson, "Minority Religions and the Context of Violence," p. 105. See also Michael Barkun's chapter "Religious Violence and the Myth of Fundamentalism," in Weinberg and Pedahzur, *Religious Fundamentalism and Political Extremism* (chap. 3, pp. 55–70). Martha Nussbaum supplies the following odd attribution in her otherwise sensitive treatment of religion: "We may and do . . . judge that any cult or so-called religion that diverges

too far from the shared moral understanding that is embodied in the core of the political conception does not deserve the honorific name of religion" (*Women and Human Development: The Capabilities Approach* [New York: Cambridge University Press, 2000], p. 190).

24. Richardson, "Minority Religions and the Context of Violence," pp. 122–23. Cf. Reader, *A Poisonous Cocktail?* pp. 37–53, 90–92. Cf. also Mark Juergensmeyer, *Terror in the Mind of God: The Global Rise of Religious Violence*, rev. ed. (Berkeley: University of California Press, 2001), p. 124, discussing the performative strength of violent actions with respect to audiences that witness them.

25. John Wybraniec and Roger Finke, "Religious Regulation and the Courts: The Judiciary's Changing Role in Protecting Minority Religions from Majoritarian Rule," *Journal for the Scientific Study of Religion* 40, no. 3 (2001): 427–44, at p. 430.

26. Ibid., p. 431. Wybraniec and Finke note that Jehovah's Witnesses continue to face outright persecution in various European countries, despite the fact that in several nations they are the second largest religious group (p. 442 n. 7).

27. Mayer, "Cults, Violence and Religious Terrorism," pp. 366–67.

28. See Mark R. Mullins, "Aum Shinrikyo as an Apocalyptic Movement," in *Millennium, Messiahs, and Mayhem: Contemporary Apocalyptic Movements*, ed. Thomas Robbins and Susan J. Palmer (New York: Routledge, 1997), pp. 313–24.

29. See Massimo Introvigne, "The Magic of Death: The Suicides of the Solar Temple," in *Millennialism, Persecution, and Violence: Historical Cases*, ed. Catherine Wessinger (Syracuse, N.Y.: Syracuse University Press, 2000), pp. 138–57, at p. 157. See Richardson, "Minority Religions and the Context of Violence," pp. 113–15.

30. See Okin, "Is Multiculturalism Bad for Women?"; Okin, "'Mistresses of Their Own Destiny.'"

31. J. Gordon Melton and Robert L. Moore, *The Cult Experience: Responding to the New Religious Pluralism* (New York: Pilgrim, 1982), pp. 17–18.

32. See Mullins, "Aum Shinrikyo as an Apocalyptic Movement," pp. 319–20. See also Susumu Shimazono, "In the Wake of Aum: The Formation and Transformation of a Universe of Belief," *Japanese Journal of Religious Studies* 22 (1995): 381–415.

33. Mayer, "Cults, Violence and Religious Terrorism," pp. 368–70ff.

34. Richardson, "Minority Religions and the Context of Violence," pp. 107–8.

35. Ibid., p. 108.

36. See Will Kymlicka, *Multicultural Citizenship: A Liberal Theory of Minority Rights* (Oxford: Clarendon, 1995), p. 168. Kymlicka refers to violations of basic human rights in national minority groups, some of which, such as the Pueblo Indians, live in theocratic communities.

37. Clyde Wilcox, Joseph Ferrara, John O'Donnell, Mary Bendyna, Shawn Geehan, and Rod Taylor, "Public Attitudes Toward Church-State Issues:

Elite-Mass Differences," *Journal of Church and State* 34, no. 2 (1992): 259–77.

38. Ibid., pp. 264, 268. Cf. generally John Zaller, *The Nature and Origin of Mass Opinion* (New York: Cambridge University Press, 1992). On the causal efficacy of changing beliefs in order to change attitudes, see Anna A. Romero, Christopher R. Agnew, and Chester A. Insko, "The Cognitive Mediation Hypothesis Revisited: An Empirical Response to Methodological and Theoretical Criticism," *Personality and Social Psychology Bulletin* 22 (1996): 651–65; and Ley A. Killeya and Blair T. Johnson, "Experimental Induction of Biased Systematic Processing: The Directed Thought Technique," *Personality and Social Psychology Bulletin* 24 (1998): 17–33.

39. David C. Leege and Lyman A. Kellstedt, *Rediscovering the Religious Factor in American Politics* (Armonk, N.Y.: M. E. Sharpe, 1993), p. 194.

40. John C. Ortberg Jr., Richard L. Gorsuch, and Grace J. Kim, "Changing Attitude and Moral Obligation: Their Independent Effects on Behavior," *Journal for the Scientific Study of Religion* 40, no. 3 (2001): 489–96.

41. Ibid.; cf. also Richard L. Gorsuch, "Attitudes, Interests, Sentiments, and Moral Obligations," in *Functional Psychological Testing*, ed. R. C. Johnson and R. B. Cattell (Larchmont, N.Y.: Brunner/Mazel, 1986).

42. Ortberg, Gorsuch, and Kim, "Changing Attitude and Moral Obligation," p. 490; see Richard L. Gorsuch and John C. Ortberg Jr., "Moral Obligations and Attitudes: Their Relation to Behavioral Intentions," *Journal of Personality and Social Psychology* 44 (1983): 1025–28.

43. Ortberg, Gorsuch, and Kim, "Changing Attitude and Moral Obligation," p. 494. The authors confirm that religious values can underlie moral obligations (ibid.).

44. Ibid., p. 491.

45. Ibid., p. 494. Ortberg, Gorsuch, and Kim determine that moral obligations "added to predicting over and above both attitude and social norms" (ibid.).

46. Ibid., p. 495. Cf. George Klosko, *Democratic Procedures and Liberal Consensus* (New York: Oxford University Press, 2000), discussing "antidemocratic attitudes" stemming from fundamentalism (pp. 97–104).

47. Gorsuch and Ortberg, "Moral Obligations and Attitudes," p. 491. See also Wendy Wood, "Attitude Change: Persuasion and Social Influence," *Annual Review of Psychology* 51 (2000): 539–70, at pp. 546–47, discussing current research in cognitive dissonance and its relation to attitude change. Cf. the alternative intuitionist model proposed in Jonathan Haidt, "The Emotional Dog and Its Rational Tail: A Social Intuitionist Approach to Moral Judgment," *Psychological Review* 108, no. 4 (2001): 814–34. I acknowledge and discuss the importance of social networks and embeddedness below.

48. See Robert R. Huckfeldt and John D. Sprague, "Networks in Context: The Social Flow of Political Information," *American Political Science Review* 81 (1987): 1197–1216; idem, "Discussant Effects on Vote Choice: Intimacy,

Structure and Interdependence," *Journal of Politics* 53 (1991): 122–158; idem, *Citizens, Politics, and Social Communication: Information and Influence in an Election Campaign* (New York: Cambridge University Press, 1995); Ronald Lake and Robert Huckfeldt, "Social Networks, Social Capital, and Political Participation," *Political Psychology* 19 (1998): 567–84; Alan S. Zuckerman, Laurence A. Kotler-Berkowitz, and Lucas A. Swaine, "Anchoring Political Preferences: The Structural Bases of Stable Electoral Decisions and Political Attitudes in Britain," *European Journal of Political Research* 33 (1998): 285–321; and Richard J. Timpone, "Ties that Bind: Measurement, Demographics, and Social Connectedness," *Political Behavior* 20 (1991): 53–77.

49. James C. Cavendish, Michael R. Welch, and David C. Leege, "Social Network Theory and Predictors of Religiosity for Black and White Catholics: Evidence of a 'Black Sacred Cosmos'?" *Journal for the Scientific Study of Religion* 37, no. 3 (1998): 397–410, at p. 405. See also Ted G. Jelen, "Political Christianity: A Contextual Analysis," *American Journal of Political Science* 36 (1992): 692–714; David C. Leege, "The Parish as Community," *Notre Dame Study of Catholic Parish Life* 10 (1987): 1–14; Kevin M. Murphy and Andrei Shleifer, "Persuasion in Politics," *American Economic Review* 94, no. 2 (2004): 435–39; Kenneth D. Wald, Dennis E. Owen, and Samuel S. Hill Jr., "Churches as Political Communities," *American Political Science Review* 82 (1988): 531–48; Michael R. Welch, "Religious Participation and Commitment Among Catholic Parishioners: The Relative Importance of Individual, Contextual, and Institutional Factors," in *Church and Denominational Growth*, ed. David A. Roozen and C. Kirk Hadaway (Nashville, Tenn.: Abingdon, 1993), pp. 324–35; and Kenneth D. Wald, Dennis E. Owen, and Samuel S. Hill Jr., "Political Cohesion in Churches," *Journal of Politics* 52, no. 1. (February 1990): 197–215.

50. Cavendish, Welch, and Leege, "Social Network Theory," p. 405.

51. Kenneth D. Wald, *Religion and Politics in the United States*, 4th ed. (Lanham, Md.: Rowman and Littlefield, 2003), pp. 35–36.

52. Peer Scheepers and Frans van der Slik, "Religion and Attitudes on Moral Issues: Effects of Individual, Spouse, and Parental Characteristics," *Journal for the Scientific Study of Religion* 37, no. 4 (1998): 678–91, at p. 688. This study was conducted in the Netherlands, but the authors surmise that the effects of primary circles will be even stronger in less secular societies, such as the USA (p. 689).

53. Kevin W. Welch, "An Interpersonal Influence Model of Traditional Religious Commitment," *Sociological Quarterly* 22 (1981): 81–92. See also Michael R. Welch and John Baltzell, "Geographic Mobility, Social Integration, and Church Attendance," *Journal for the Scientific Study of Religion* 23 (1984): 75–91; cf. Cavendish, Welch, and Leege, "Social Network Theory," p. 398.

54. Wald introduced the idea of "infiltration" to denote instances where religious groups "seek to place one of [their] members in office" (*Religion and*

Politics in the United States, p. 126). There is reason to think that a similar process could work for liberals, where they place themselves in some sector of ambitious theocrats' social networks.

55. See Audi, *Religious Commitment and Secular Reason*, pp. 157, 165–66, 175. See also Rawls, describing how the duty of civility "involves a willingness to listen to others" (*Political Liberalism*, p. 217).

56. See Nussbaum, noting how it is "rash and usually counterproductive to approach religious people with a set of apparently external moral demands, telling them that these norms are better than the norms of their religion" (*Women and Human Development*, p. 178).

57. Formal symbolic or financial endorsement of religious organizations by government is another matter, of course, and government should not take that course of action. See Lucas A. Swaine, "Principled Separation: Liberal Governance and Religious Free Exercise," *Journal of Church and State* 38, no. 3 (1996): 595–619.

58. See, e.g., Nadia Abu-Zahra, "Islamic History, Islamic Identity, and the Reform of Islamic Law: The Thought of Husayn Ahmad Amin," in *Islam and Modernity: Muslim Intellectuals Respond*, ed. John Cooper, Ronald L. Nettler, and Mohamed Mahmoud (New York: I. B. Tauris, 1998), pp. 82–104; Azzam S. Tamimi, *Rachid Ghannouchi: A Democrat Within Islamism* (New York: Oxford University Press, 2001); Abdullahi Ahmad An-Na'im, *Toward an Islamic Reformation: Civil Liberties, Human Rights, and International Law* (Syracuse, N.Y.: Syracuse University Press, 1990); and Nasr Abu Zaid and Esther R. Nelson, *Voice of an Exile: Reflections on Islam* (Westport, Conn.: Praeger, 2004). See also Chibli Mallat, *The Renewal of Islamic Law: Muhammad Baqer as-Sadr, Najaf, and the Shi'i International* (New York: Cambridge University Press, 1993); and Mehran Tamadonfar, "Islam, Law, and Political Control in Contemporary Iran," *Journal for the Scientific Study of Religion* 40, no. 2 (2001): 205–20.

59. Liberals should not attempt to infiltrate retiring theocratic communities, since so doing risks damaging or destroying the *nomoi* of those groups. Instead, liberals will need conscientiously to limit themselves to informal and occasional interactions with group members and countenance only limited engagement between liberal government and leaders of retiring communities.

60. These opportunities will presumably be enhanced by the transformation of stable, long-term social networks into more flexible, "loose connections," as Robert Wuthnow describes them; see his "United States: Bridging the Privileged and the Marginalized?" in *Democracies in Flux: The Evolution of Social Capital in Contemporary Society*, ed. Robert D. Putnam (New York: Oxford University Press, 2002), pp. 59–102; see also Robert D. Putnam, conclusion to *Democracies in Flux*, pp. 393–416, at 402–4. Cf. Spinner-Halev, *Surviving Diversity*, pp. 149–56.

61. See Lee Sigelman, Clyde Wilcox, and Emmett H. Buell Jr., "An Unchanging Minority: Popular Support for the Moral Majority, 1980 and 1984," *Social Science Quarterly* 68 (1987): 876–84.

62. Ibid., p. 249. Wald notes that the Christian Right has only been an occasional force in elections, even though its groups have "affected national policies" (*Religion and Politics in the United States*, p. 241).

63. See generally Nancy L. Rosenblum, *Membership and Morals: The Personal Uses of Pluralism in America* (Princeton: Princeton University Press, 1998). Bohman supports a need for group formation to remain "open, pluralistic, and dynamic" ("Public Reason and Cultural Pluralism," p. 273), maintaining that religious conflict over standards of justification "demands a 'wide view' of public reason" ("Citizenship and Norms of Publicity," p. 192).

64. Wald, *Religion and Politics in the United States*, pp. 246–92, esp. p. 250.

65. In a survey of registered American voters holding evangelical theological convictions, conducted in 1983, more than 25 percent did not recognize Jerry Falwell or the Moral Majority; see Stuart Rothenberg and Frank Newport, *The Evangelical Voter* (Washington, D.C.: Free Congress Research and Education Foundation, 1984), pp. 100, 140. Cf. Christian Smith, *Christian America? What Evangelicals Really Want* (Berkeley: University of California Press, 2000), esp. chap. 2.

66. Wald, *Religion and Politics in the United States*, p. 304.

67. Ibid., pp. 262–63.

68. Sam Reimer and Jerry Z. Park, "Tolerant (In)civility? A Longitudinal Analysis of White Conservative Protestants' Willingness to Grant Civil Liberties," *Journal for the Scientific Study of Religion* 40, no. 4 (2001): 735–45, at p. 741. Cf. Alan Wolfe, *One Nation, After All* (New York: Viking, 1998), chaps. 2, 3.

69. Wald, *Religion and Politics in the United States*, pp. 158–59.

70. Ibid., p. 279.

71. See Stephen Macedo, "Transformative Constitutionalism and the Case of Religion: Defending the Moderate Hegemony of Liberalism," *Political Theory* 26, no. 1 (1998): 56–80.

72. Weithman, *Religion and the Obligations of Citizenship*, pp. 65, 138.

73. Paul A. Djupe and J. Tobin Grant, "Religious Institutions and Political Participation in America," *Journal for the Scientific Study of Religion* 40, no. 2 (2001): 303–14, at pp. 303, 309, 311.

74. Ibid., p. 310. Djupe and Grant find that churches can "recruit members to participate in politics" (p. 311), but that is very different from the suggestion that criticism of new participants' reasons for participating will prompt their political disengagement. Liberals' disseminating and discussing principles of conscience could, of course, encourage the political involvement of religious practitioners.

75. Cavendish, Welch, and Leege, "Social Network Theory," pp. 401, 403–4.

76. Lake and Huckfeldt, "Social Networks, Social Capital, and Political Participation," pp. 581–82; cf. Richard E. Petty, Duane T. Wegener, and Leandre R. Fabrigar, "Attitudes and Attitude Change," *Annual Review of Psychology* 48 (1997): 609–47; Wood, "Attitude Change," pp. 539–70.

77. Cf. Weithman, *Religion and the Obligations of Citizenship*, pp. 65, 138; Audi, *Religious Commitment and Secular Reason*, pp. 169, 180, 206.

78. Leege et al., *Rediscovering the Religious Factor*, p. 89.

79. Ibid., pp. 88–90, 94–95.

80. Benton Johnson and Richard H. White, "Protestantism, Political Preference, and the Nature of Religious Influence," *Review of Religious Research* 9 (1967): 28–35.

81. Wald, *Religion and Politics in the United States*, pp. 196–97; see also idem, "Evangelical Politics and Status Issues," *Journal for the Scientific Study of Religion* 28 (1989): 1–16.

82. Wald, *Religion and Politics in the United States*, pp. 96–97.

83. Reimer and Park, "Tolerant (In)civility?" pp. 741, 743. See also James L. Guth, "The Politics of the Christian Right," in John C. Green, James L. Guth, Corwin E. Smidt, and Lyman A. Kellstedt, *Religion and the Culture Wars: Dispatches from the Front* (Lanham, Md.: Rowman and Littlefield, 1996); Mark A. Shibley, *Resurgent Evangelicalism in the United States: Mapping Cultural Change Since 1970* (Columbia, S.C.: University of South Carolina Press, 1996).

84. Reimer and Park, "Tolerant (In)civility?" p. 743. See also Christian S. Smith, *American Evangelicalism: Embattled and Thriving* (Chicago: University of Chicago Press, 1998); Clyde Wilcox, Ted G. Jelen, and Sharon Linzey, "Rethinking the Reasonableness of the Religious Right," *Review of Religious Research* 36 (1995): 263–76; and Arthur Miller, Patricia Gurin, and Gerald Gurin, "Group Consciousness and Political Participation," *American Journal of Political Science* 25 (1981): 494–511. Some scholars have gone so far as to argue that support for the Christian Right has been motivated by hatred of outgroups; see Ted G. Jelen, *The Political Mobilization of Religious Belief* (New York: Praeger, 1991). Cf. Kai Erikson, *Wayward Puritans: A Study in the Sociology of Deviance* (New York: Wiley, 1966), pp. 3–29, discussing the idea of "boundary maintenance"; and S. Alexander Haslam, Craig McGarty, and John C. Turner, "Salient Group Memberships and Persuasion: The Role of Social Identity in the Validation of Beliefs," in *What's Social About Social Cognition? Research on Socially Shared Cognition in Small Groups*, ed. Judith L. Nye and Aaron M. Brower (Thousand Oaks, Calif.: Sage, 1996), pp. 29–56.

85. Richard Rose and Derek Urwin, "Social Cohesion, Political Parties, and Strains in Regimes," *Comparative Political Studies* 2 (1969): 7–67.

86. See Djupe and Grant, outlining various ways in which religious institutions promote political participation by members ("Religious Institutions," pp. 303–4).

87. See Leege et al., *Rediscovering the Religious Factor*, p. 135ff.

88. Ibid., pp. 131, 132, 135.

89. See Clyde Wilcox, "The Fundamentalist Voter: Politicized Religious Identity and Political Attitudes and Behavior," *Review of Religious Research* 31, no. 1 (1989): 54–67, at p. 55. Wilcox discusses differences between fundamentalists and evangelicals at pp. 56–58.

90. Leege et al., *Rediscovering the Religious Factor*, p. 74. Wald distinguishes between fundamentalists and evangelicals at pp. 227–30 of *Religion and Politics in the United States*. Cf. Ahmad S. Moussalli, *Radical Islamic Fundamentalism: The Ideological and Political Discourse of Sayyid Qutb* (Beirut: American University of Beirut, 1992), describing features of Islamic fundamentalism at pp. 213–30. Cf. also Almond, Appleby, and Sivan, *Strong Religion*, pp. 17, 90–115 passim; Klosko, *Democratic Procedures and Political Consensus*, pp. 105–11ff.; Smith et al., *American Evangelicalism*, pp. 233–47; Weinberg and Pedahzur, *Religious Fundamentalism*.

91. This would be better than simply attempting to rely on changes to laws in liberal polities; as Wald has noted, the incidence of morning prayer readings in U.S. public schools remains significant despite the existence of laws disallowing the practice. See Wald, *Religion and Politics in the United States*, pp. 103–4. Sound principles of separation of church and state prohibit morning prayers in public schools; see generally Swaine, "Principled Separation."

92. See Stanley Fish, "Mission Impossible," in *The Trouble with Principle* (Cambridge: Harvard University Press, 1999), pp. 162–86.

93. Clyde Wilcox and Ted Jelen, "Evangelicals and Political Tolerance," *American Politics Quarterly* 18 (1990): 25–46; see Wald, *Religion and Politics in the United States*, pp. 313–14. Cf. also Vyacheslav Karpov, "Tolerance in the United States and Poland," *Journal for the Scientific Study of Religion* 41, no. 2 (2002): 267–88.

94. See Robert Wuthnow, "Religious Commitment and Conservatism: In Search of an Elusive Relationship," in *Religion in Sociological Perspective*, ed. Charles Y. Glock (Belmont, Calif.: Wadsworth, 1973), pp. 117–32. In fairness, psychological experimentation shows that religious commitment certainly does not automatically motivate resistance to tyranny; see Wald, *Religion and Politics in the United States*, pp. 300–305ff. Cf. Klosko, *Democratic Procedures and Liberal Consensus*, chaps. 3, 4 passim.

95. Djupe and Grant, "Religious Institutions," p. 311. For an extended analysis of political activities and opinions of U.S. clergy, see Paul A. Djupe and Christopher P. Gilbert, *The Prophetic Pulpit: Clergy, Churches, and Communities in American Politics* (Lanham, Md.: Rowman and Littlefield, 2003). See also James L. Guth, John C. Green, Corwin E. Smidt, Lyman A. Kellstedt, and Margaret M. Poloma, *The Bully Pulpit: The Politics of Protestant Clergy* (Lawrence, Kans.: University Press of Kansas, 1997); Wood, "Attitude Change," p. 541; Sharon R. Lundgren and Radmila Prislin, "Motivated Cognitive Processing and Attitude Change," *Personality and Social Psychology Bulletin* 24 (1998): 715–26.

96. Leege et al., *Rediscovering the Religious Factor*, p. 248.

97. Mark D. Brewer, Rogan Kersh, and R. Eric Petersen, "Assessing Conventional Wisdom About Religion and Politics: A Preliminary View from the Pews," *Journal for the Scientific Study of Religion* 42, no. 1 (2003): 125–36, at p. 134.

98. Leege et al., *Rediscovering the Religious Factor*, p. 87; Wald, Owen, and Hill, "Churches as Political Communities"; Wald, Owen, and Hill, "Political Cohesion in Churches."

99. Wald, *Religion and Politics in the United States*, pp. 220–21.

100. Ibid., pp. 254–57. See also John Courtney Murray, *We Hold These Truths: Catholic Reflections on the American Proposition* (New York: Image, 1964).

101. See Andrew M. Greely, *American Catholics Since the Council: An Unauthorized Report* (Chicago: Thomas More, 1985). See also Wald, *Religion and Politics in the United States*, pp. 255–56.

102. See Wilcox, Jelen, and Linzey, "Rethinking the Reasonableness of the Religious Right," pp. 263, 264–65 passim. Cf. Nathan Adler's ascription of an irrational, frenetic, "antinomian personality" to members of New Age and other religious groups; see *The Underground Stream: New Life Styles and the Antinomian Personality* (New York: Harper and Row, 1972).

103. Wilcox, Jelen, and Linzey, "Rethinking the Reasonableness of the Religious Right," p. 267.

104. Ibid., p. 269.

105. Ibid., pp. 270–72.

106. Ibid., p. 271.

107. Ibid., p. 272. This could provide recommendatory support for the thesis that similar ambitious groups will, for organizational reasons, relegate members with authoritarian tendencies and feelings of inadequacy to the periphery.

108. Cf. Gerald F. Gaus, *Value and Justification: The Foundations of Liberal Theory* (New York: Cambridge University Press, 1990), pp. 319–29, 480–81, passim. Cf. also Rawls, *Political Liberalism*, pp. 310–14; Eberle, *Religious Conviction in Liberal Politics*, pp. 146, 200.

109. See Audi and Wolterstoff, *Religion in the Public Square*, p. 105; cf. Weithman, *Religion and the Obligations of Citizenship*, pp. 152ff., 159.

110. See Bohman, "Public Reason and Cultural Pluralism," pp. 265, 268ff.; Bohman, "Citizenship and Norms of Publicity," pp. 183–87.

111. Cf. Bohman, "Public Reason and Cultural Pluralism," p. 257; Bohman, "Citizenship and Norms of Publicity," pp. 176–77ff.

112. See Wald, *Religion and Politics in the United States*, pp. 44–47.

113. If civil religion were merely a "code subscribed to, in varying degrees, by all religions in the nation," then perhaps this would count. But that is too lax to count as a civil religion in any meaningful sense; see Wald, *Religion and Politics in the United States*, p. 56. See also Michael Walzer, *On Toleration* (New Haven: Yale University Press, 1997), pp. 76–80.

114. Wald, *Religion and Politics in the United States*, pp. 56, 58, 62–3. Cf. Robert N. Bellah, *The Broken Covenant: American Civil Religion in Time of Trial*, 2d ed. (Chicago: University of Chicago Press, 1992); Robert N. Bellah and Phillip E. Hammond, *Varieties of Civil Religion* (San Francisco: Harper and Row, 1980); Robert N. Bellah and Charles Y. Glock, eds., *The New Religious Consciousness* (Berkeley: University of California Press, 1976).

115. See Wald, *Religion and Politics in the United States*, pp. 182–83ff.; see also Milton Rokeach, "Religious Values and Social Compassion," *Review of Religious Research* 11 (1969): 24–39. Cf. Michael Walzer, *The Revolution of the Saints: A Study in the Origins of Radical Politics* (New York: Atheneum, 1965), pp. 56–57ff.

116. Lawrence Foster, "Cults in Conflict: New Religious Movements and the Mainstream Religious Tradition in America," in *Uncivil Religion: Interreligious Hostility in America*, ed. Robert N. Bellah and Frederick E. Greenspahn (New York: Crossroad, 1987), pp. 185–204, esp. pp. 193ff.

117. Cf. Weithman, *Religion and the Obligations of Citizenship*, pp. 9, 132.

118. See Wald, *Religion and Politics in the United States*, p. 43. See also Roger Finke and Rodney Stark, *The Churching of America: 1776–1990* (New Brunswick, N.J.: Rutgers University Press, 1992). Cf. David S. Lovejoy, *Religious Enthusiasm in the New World: Heresy to Revolution* (Cambridge: Harvard University Press, 1985), chaps. 9–11. Following a distinction of Shaftesbury's, Lovejoy, pp. 225–30, describes a kind of "noble enthusiasm" that is fitting here.

119. Wald, *Religion and Politics in the United States*, pp. 76–78, 79–83.

120. Ibid., pp. 269, 273–75.

121. See Audi, *Religious Commitment and Secular Reason*, pp. 165–66, 175.

122. Liberal government will need to work to ensure that its allied countries respect religion, endeavoring to promote a fair and evenhanded treatment of religious groups and peoples around the world, so as to avoid charges of favoritism or partisanship with existing allies.

123. The United States' new Office of Global Communications, an institution similar to the now defunct United States Information Agency, could be of service here as well, but first it would have to work to secure greater credibility with foreign nations and peoples.

124. See Audi and Wolterstoff, *Religion in the Public Square*, p. 105; cf. Weithman, *Religion and the Obligations of Citizenship*, pp. 152–55, 159; Nancy L. Rosenblum, "Pluralism, Integralism, and Political Theories of Religious Accommodation," in *Obligations of Citizenship and Demands of Faith: Religious Accommodation in Pluralist Democracies*, ed. Nancy L. Rosenblum (Princeton: Princeton University Press, 2000), pp. 3–31, at pp. 15–21. See also Michael J. Sandel, *Liberalism and the Limits of Justice* (New York: Cambridge University Press, 1982); idem, "Freedom of Conscience or Freedom of Choice?" in *Articles of Faith, Articles of Peace*, ed. James Davison Hunter and Os Guinness (Washington, D.C.: Brookings Institution, 1990), pp. 74–93. Cf. Charles Larmore, *The Morals of Modernity* (New York: Cambridge University Press, 1996), pp. 129–31; and John Tomasi, *Liberalism Beyond Justice: Citizens, Society, and the Boundaries of Political Theory* (Princeton: Princeton University Press, 2001), chap. 2.

125. See Charles Larmore, "Public Reason," in *The Cambridge Companion to Rawls*, ed. Samuel Freeman (New York: Cambridge University Press, 2003), pp. 368–93, at pp. 371–75 passim.

126. Cf. Gerald Gaus's arguments regarding the need for public justification to supply "what are reasons from the other's perspective"; see his *Value and Justification*, pp. 321–22, 466–60, 476–83 passim. As Gaus puts it, "[it] will do no good to provide another with considerations that are reasons from your perspective but not from his. Our concern with justification derives from the presupposition that the other, if fully rational, would have good reason to act on the principle" (p. 321).

127. Cf. T. M. Scanlon's notion of "the spirit of toleration," which he describes as being "in part . . . a spirit of accommodation, a desire to find a system of rights that others . . . could also be asked to accept" ("The Difficulty of Tolerance," in *The Difficulty of Tolerance: Essays in Political Philosophy* [New York: Cambridge University Press, 2002], pp. 187–201, at p. 198).

128. Cf. Larmore, "Public Reason," pp. 382–83, 386–87.

129. See generally Michael Oakeshott, *On Human Conduct* (Oxford: Clarendon, 1975); idem, "On Being Conservative," in *Rationalism in Politics and Other Essays* (Indianapolis: Liberty Fund, 1991); idem, *The Politics of Faith and the Politics of Scepticism*, ed. Timothy Fuller (New Haven: Yale University Press, 1996). See also Lucas Swaine, "Political Theory and the Conduct of Faith: Oakeshott on Religion in Public Life," *Contemporary Political Theory* 4, no. 1 (2005): 63–82.

130. Moussalli, *Radical Islamic Fundamentalism*, p. 221. See ibid., pp. 222–25; Seyyid Qutb, *Milestones* (Damascus: Dar Al-Ilm, n.d.), pp. 109–16 passim; Hasan al-Banna, *Letter to a Muslim Student* (London: Islamic Foundation, 1995), pp. 20–27. Cf. Hamid Algar, *Wahhabism: A Critical Essay* (Oneonta, N.Y.: Islamic Publications International, 2002). Cf. also Leszek Kolakowski, *God Owes Us Nothing: A Brief Remark on Pascal's Religion and on the Spirit of Jansenism* (Chicago: University of Chicago Press, 1995), pp. 81–82ff., 121–22 passim.

131. See Qutb, *Milestones*, pp. 10–12, 19–22, 46–48, 79–84, 96–98, 129–40. Qutb's disposition with regard to philosophical thinking is only partly favorable; see pp. 17–18, 40–41, 54, 109–16, 138–39. See also Moussalli, *Radical Islamic Fundamentalism*, p. 211.

132. Al-Banna, *Letter to a Muslim Student*, pp. 24, 26. Al-Banna directs Muslim students to be positive, to avoid insulting others' beliefs, and to work instead to elucidate the innate goodness of people (pp. 26–27).

133. Moussalli, *Radical Islamic Fundamentalism*, pp. 205, 227–28; Louay Safi, *Tensions and Transitions in the Muslim World* (Lanham, Md.: University Press of America, 2003), pp. 80–82. Cf. Qutb, *Milestones*, articulating what seems to be a significantly less pacifistic political view, at pp. 61–62, 72–73, 79–80, 141, 149–52. Cf. also Roxanne Euben, "Killing (for) Politics: Jihad, Martyrdom, and Political Action," *Political Theory* 30, no. 1 (2002): 4–35; Abdulaziz H. Al-Fahad, "From Exclusivism to Accommodation: Doctrinal and Legal Evolution of Wahhabism," *New York University Law Review* 79 (2004): 485–519.

134. Cf. Albert Hourani, *Arabic Thought in the Liberal Age, 1798–1939* (New York: Cambridge University Press, 1983), pp. 126–27ff., describing Islamic reformers' attempts to overturn conservative views of acceptable interpretation of the Koran.

135. See Martha C. Nussbaum, *The Therapy of Desire: Theory and Practice in Hellenistic Ethics* (Princeton: Princeton University Press, 1994); idem, *Poetic Justice: The Literary Imagination in Public Life* (Boston: Beacon, 1995), chap. 3; idem, *Upheavals of Thought: The Intelligence of Emotions* (New York: Cambridge University Press, 2001).

136. See Safi, *Tensions and Transitions*, pp. 146–51.

137. See Roxanne Euben, *Enemy in the Mirror: Islamic Fundamentalism and the Limits of Modern Rationalism* (Princeton: Princeton University Press, 1999); idem, "Killing (for) Politics." Cf. Thomas Pangle, *Political Philosophy and the God of Abraham* (Baltimore: Johns Hopkins University Press, 2003).

138. See generally Nussbaum, *Women and Human Development*.

139. See Susan Okin, *Justice, Gender, and the Family* (New York: Basic, 1989), pp. 171–72; idem, "Is Multiculturalism Bad for Women?"; idem, "Feminism and Multiculturalism: Some Tensions," *Ethics* 108 (1998): 661–84; and idem, "'Mistresses of Their Own Destiny.'" See also Ayelet Shachar, *Multicultural Jurisdictions: Cultural Differences and Women's Rights* (New York: Cambridge University Press, 2001). Cf. Jan Feldman, *Lubavitchers as Citizens: A Paradox of Liberal Democracy* (Ithaca, N.Y.: Cornell University Press, 2003), pp. 136, 139.

140. Okin, *Justice, Gender, and the Family*, p. 172.

141. Nussbaum, *Women and Human Development*, p. 298.

142. Certainly, no right is implied in either case: a person may have a reason to steal from another, but that gives him no right to do it.

143. See the Universal Declaration of Human Rights (General Assembly resolution 217 A [III], December 10, 1948), article 18. See also the preamble, article 1; and the International Covenant on Civil and Political Rights (General Assembly resolution 2200A [XXI], December 16, 1966), article 9.

Index

abortion issue, 22, 138, 172n. 64
abstract beliefs, 141
accommodation, xviii, 71, 79; failures of,
81–87; full, 87–90; semisovereignty
compared with, 102–4. *See also*
exemptions
affirmation, 174n. 7
affirmation, principle of, xvii, 49, 50, 52,
130, 148
Afghanistan, 4, 36, 38
Against Apion (Josephus), 2
Almond, Gabriel A., 195n. 14
ambitious theocrats, 9–10, 157; approaches
to, 133–35; public realm and, 10–12, 16,
25, 122, 136–37; social networks, 136–37.
See also extremist religious groups;
theocrats
American founders, 145
Amish, Old Order, 8, 9, 34, 175n. 11; educational laws and, 86, 87; liberty of conscience and, 56, 178n. 45; litigation, 85,
184nn. 43, 46, 47, 184–85n. 48; Ordnung, 74, 85, 196n. 18; as pacifistic, 13,
31; punishment and, 10, 184n. 86,
190n. 105; Supreme Court cases, 11, 86,
87, 184n. 43
Anabaptists, 3
anticult movement, 129
Anti-Defamation League of B'nai
B'rith, 14
antiestablishment arguments, 75–78
appeal, 30
Appleby, R. Scott, 195n. 14
Aquinas, Thomas, 47
*Argument of the Letter concerning Toleration,
Briefly Consider'd and Answer'd, The*
(Proast), 62–63
Aristotle, 34, 175n. 10, 187n. 79
assimilation, 22
associational liberty, 118

atrocity tales, 128–29
attitudes, 134–35; identity and, 140; modification of liberal, 149–50; modification
of theocratic, 151–52; social networks
and, 135–40, 198n. 47, 199n. 52
Audi, Robert, 26, 176n. 20
Aum Shinrikyo, 128, 130, 132
authoritarian polities, 7, 35, 52
autonomy, 189n. 95, 189–90n. 99; personal, 112–13, 143–44, 192n. 31

Bader, Veit, 108
Banna, Hasan al-, 151, 152, 206n. 132
beliefs: modification of, 61–63; rational
commitment and, 68–69, 180n. 93,
181n. 95. *See also* attitudes; otherworldly
values
benefits of liberal government, 33–34
Berlin, Isaiah, 89, 111
Bill of Rights, 92
Bohman, James, 143
Branch Davidians, 14, 128, 168n. 43

Callan, Eamonn, 96, 97, 98
Calvin, Johannes, 3
Catholic pastoral letters, 142
Catholics, 3, 138, 141
Cavendish, James, 139
Challenge of Peace, The, 142
Cherokee Nation v. Georgia, 92, 93
Christian Coalition, 138
Christian Right, xiii, 9, 133, 137–38, 201n.
62. *See also* Protestant evangelicals
Church of Jesus Christ of Latter-day
Saints, 9, 12, 18, 61, 74, 174n. 8
Church of the Lamb of God, 130–31
citizens, perceptions of legitimacy, xiv–xv,
14–15, 22, 27, 157
civil liberties groups, 136
civil religion, 144, 204n. 113

(CONTINUED FROM FRONT FLAP)

By doing so, liberal societies will rein-vigorate their own traditions, while also assuaging religious conflict. In addition to philosophical arguments, Swaine pro-poses a new legal standard that offers theocratic communities quasi sovereign-ty within liberal democracies.

Theocrats also have much to gain from embracing liberalism and the principle of liberty of conscience. Swaine argues that liberalism can be made more appealing to the values and concerns of theocrats if the liberal commitment to freedom of conscience is clarified and modified and if liberals take a fresh approach to con-ceptualizing and promulgating liberal principles, institutions, and laws.

LUCAS SWAINE is assistant professor of government at Dartmouth College. His work has been published in numer-ous journals, including *Ethics, Journal of Political Philosophy,* and *Contemporary Po-litical Theory.*